Regional Government Competition

This monograph provides a coherent and systematic explanation of China's regional economic development from the perspective of regional government competition. It gives an almost unknown exposition of the mechanisms of China's regional economic development, with numerous supporting cases drawn from China and elsewhere. This book is an invaluable resource for anyone interested in learning more about the development and transformation of China's regional economy from both the Chinese and global perspectives.

Chen Yunxian is Professor, Economist and Deputy Governor of Guangdong Province, China.

Gu Wenjing is Professor at Guangdong University of Finance and Economics, China.

Routledge Studies in the Modern World Economy

For more information about this series, please visit www.routledge.com/
Routledge-Studies-in-the-Modern-World-Economy/book-series/SE0432

Regional Government Competition

Chen Yunxian and Gu Wenjing

Routledge
Taylor & Francis Group
LONDON AND NEW YORK

First published in English 2019
by Routledge
2 Park Square, Milton Park, Abingdon, Oxon OX14 4RN

and by Routledge
605 Third Avenue, New York, NY 10017

First issued in paperback 2020

Routledge is an imprint of the Taylor & Francis Group, an informa business

Translated and updated by Yong Heming, Peng Jing, Chen Dinggang and Chen Zimin

This book is published with financial support from Chinese Fund for the Humanities and Social Sciences

Published in Chinese 2017 by Peking University Press

British Library Cataloguing-in-Publication Data
A catalogue record for this book is available from the British Library

Library of Congress Cataloging-in-Publication Data
Names: Chen, Yunxian, author. | Gu, Wenjing, 1970– author.
Title: Regional government competition / by Chen Yunxian
    and Gu Wenjing.
Description: Abingdon, Oxon ; New York, NY : Routledge, 2019. |
    Series: Routledge studies in the modern world economy |
    "Published in Chinese 2017 by Peking University Press"—
    Title verso. | Includes bibliographical references and index.
Identifiers: LCCN 2018042706 | ISBN 9781138320895 (hardback) |
    ISBN 9780429453014 (ebook)
Subjects: LCSH: Regional economics—China. | Economic
    development—China. | China—Economic conditions.
Classification: LCC HC427.95 .C43349 2019 | DDC 338.951—dc23
LC record available at https://lccn.loc.gov/2018042706

ISBN 13: 978-0-367-50440-3 (pbk)
ISBN 13: 978-1-138-32089-5 (hbk)
ISBN 13: 978-0-429-45301-4 (ebk)

Typeset in Galliard
by Apex CoVantage, LLC

Contents

Figures

Tables

Foreword

Region is a relative concept. Globally speaking, a country is a region; for a country, an area is a region. Regions share commonalities, similarities and generalities, but are also characterized by their individuality, particularity and diversity. Regional government is a government organization which administers affairs within its own jurisdiction, with a relatively fixed area, a relatively concentrated population and institutional governance. Regional government has the attributes of publicity and coerciveness.

The external possibility of regional government competition

The publicity of regional management is mainly reflected in ensuring regional public spending and maintaining regional markets and social stability by means of taxation, industry and commerce, public security and monitoring and supervision, and in ensuring its openness, fairness and impartiality through administrative legislation and justice. The coercive power of regional administration is embodied not only in the three super-economy coercive forces of legislation, justice and administration, but also in the economic coercion derived from its financial rights and rights to administer its affairs. Superficially, regional government manages economic development, urban construction and social livelihood, but in essence, its administration is reflected in its effective allocation of tangible and intangible resources of various categories, existing and potential, within its jurisdiction.

Social welfare resources correspond to people's livelihood and are categorized into "non-operational resources" in market economy. The guideline policies for the management and allocation of such resources can be generalized as "social guarantee, general underpinning, fair play, and effective promotion". Industrial resources correspond to economic development and are referred to as "operational resources" in market economy. The guideline policies for the management and allocation of such resources can generalized as "planning, guidance; support and regulation; supervision and administration".

City resources correspond to urban construction and fall into "quasi-operational resources" in a market economy, covering public services systems that ensure smooth regional economic and social activities as well as the "hard" and "soft" infrastructure that provides public services for regional production and people's lives, for example, public facilities, transportation, telecommunications, power and water supply, landscaping, environmental protection, project development, education, science, culture, health, sports, journalism, publishing, radio and television. They are so called because their development and management can be implemented either by government, in which case they are public and non-operational in nature, or through market channels, in which case they become a commodity and operational. The choice of whether they are conducted by government or through market mechanisms depends on a range of factors, such as regional revenues and expenditure, market demand and public acceptability.

The practices of regional administration in the world and the successful experience of China's reform and opening up show that regional government will, partly or wholly, resort to market mechanisms in its allocation, development and management of quasi-operational resources under the fundamental principles of "general underpinning, fair play, effective promotion" of social welfare services and public product provision. This aims to prevent the idleness and waste of urban resources and eliminate problems of urban resource depletion, low-quality operations and disorderly urban management owing to investment without earnings, construction without operation and focusing on public welfare while overlooking effectiveness. In the transformation from "quasi-operational resources" to "operational resources", the determination of the nature of the entities of resource allocation – that is, the nature of the ownership and its governance structure, whether solely foreign-owned enterprises, joint ventures, cooperatives, joint-stock companies or private or state-owned businesses – must be in line with market rules, and its resource allocation and capital operations must be conducted through market competition, whether BOT, PPP, bonds or stocks. From the onset, the mode of "government promotion, social participation and market operation" opens up external possibilities of inter-regional government competition.

The intrinsic necessity of regional government competition

Two serious drawbacks reside in western market economics. On the one hand, government, market and society are considered independent, and government has been excluded from the market; on the other hand, government is deemed to have a single function of public administration and is deprived of a competitive function in economic development and urban construction.

Regional government's basic policy of "general underpinning, fair play and effective promotion" of non-operational resources and the regulation, supervision and management policies for operational resources make it the centralized agent of both the region and the central government. These also enable it to promote social stability through basic social guarantees and public services and to regulate regional economy through pricing, taxation, interest rates, exchange rates and legal means. In practice, regional government achieves its publicity and coercive power by utilizing public revenues and expenditure and increasing taxes and other sources of revenue to provide budget arrangements for government administration, national defense and security, culture and education, science, health and utilities, etc. This is accomplished by providing social consumption expenses in the industrial, transportation, commercial and agricultural sectors; by providing fiscal investment expenditure in government investments, which comprise infrastructure, scientific R&D and policy-oriented financial investment in industries that need urgent development; and by providing transfer expenditure, mainly composed of social security and various fiscal subsidies. By so doing, regional government plays the "quasi-state" and "quasi-macro" roles.

Regional government's participation in the allocation of and competition for quasi-operational resources and its planning, guidance and support for operational resources make it the centralized agent of a non-government entity in the region, and enable it to compete with other regions through innovation in institution, management and technology. Under such circumstances, regional government possesses management rights as its jurisdictional power, which allows it to allocate resources so as to maximize regional benefits, mainly through investment attraction, development, investment and operation and management of regional projects. Although this role of regional government differs from enterprises in objectives, development modes, regulatory factors and evaluation criteria, the competitive mechanism becomes the driving force for regional governments as the same agent of resource allocation as of enterprises within certain areas; their rules of behavior must meet the requirements of market mechanisms. Regional government then plays the "quasi-enterprise" and "quasi-micro" roles.

Regional government's "dual role" and the competitiveness stemming from it in practice remedy the drawbacks of traditional market economic theories. According to modern market economics, not only are enterprises the entity of market competition but regional governments as well. The operating mechanisms of regional government explain the inherent inevitability of regional competition.

The relations and differences between regional government competition and business competition

Enterprises generally compete for the allocation of industrial resources, and regional governments mainly compete for the allocation of city resources. Relative independence and complementarities exist between enterprises and regional governments, but they differ as follows:

First, differences in fields of competition. Enterprises are micro-economic entities. They mainly compete for commodity markets and focus on industrial resources allocation. Market equilibrium theory, which takes manufacturers as its main subject, occupies a dominant position in western classical economics. Enterprises regard the pursuit of profit maximization as a precondition and assume the competitive forms of supply, demand, market equilibrium prices, perfect market competition, monopolistic competition, oligopolistic market, different market structures and competitive strategies, etc. Enterprise competition is the precondition and basis for regional government competition.

Regional government is the subject of mezzo-economics. Competition between regional governments focuses on factor markets and city resources allocation. Factor markets include land, capital, labor forces, property rights, and hardware and software markets such information engineering. Regional government improves its competitiveness through the quantity, quality, structure and layout of urban resources. Regional government can also make policies and initiatives to regulate the allocation of regional factors and to attract and influence the direction of factor flow outside the region, so as to optimize the allocation of resources and eventually enhance regional competitiveness. Factor market competition affects enterprise commodity market competition.

Second, differences in means of competition. Enterprises seek to maximize profits mainly by increasing labor productivity – to effectively influence costs, prices, supply and demand and scale – and by optimizing the allocation of corporate resources to promote their cost minimization. Regional government makes every effort to increase total factor productivity as its chief means of sustainable growth. After simple dilatation through competing for tangible factors, such as land, projects and capital, the bottleneck of diminishing capital profits makes extensive economic growth difficult to continue. When nothing more can be added to regional input of all tangible factors, regional government will have to depend on the investment, increase and improvement of intangible factors such as technological advancement (with innovation as the core), resource allocation optimization and structural adjustment as well as institution, organization, legislation, environment, etc. as the new driving forces of regional economy development and urban construction.

Third, differences in paths of competition. Enterprises are investment growth-oriented. The continuous improvement of business performance comes from the constant input of production factors, including capital, labor, land, technology, entrepreneurship and so on. The initial strategy for businesses investment is mainly extensive expansion of quantity, followed by the quality-enhancing stage and then the stage of business management. In all these stages, sustained and effective inputs become critical. Regional government is efficiency growth-riented. In light of the experiences of regional economies in the world, their economic growth path starts from the factor-driven stage (also known as the resource allocation stage) to the investment-driven stage (also known as the efficiency improvement stage) and then to the innovation-driven stage (also called the sustainable growth stage). Regional government makes efforts to optimize the combination of tangible and intangible factors, with efficiency improvement as the focus of its growth.

Fourth, differences in orientations of competition. Enterprises regard demand-side expansion as their orientation. Business competition starts from market demand, demand quantities, demand structure, corporate strategies and tactics. The ability to adapt to market requirements becomes essential to their survival and success. Regional government regards supply-side optimization as its orientation. Regional government's determined direction for economic development, urban construction and facilitation of people's livelihood is to promote supply-side structural reforms by effectively allocating the supply of land, capital, projects, technology, work forces and other tangible resources; by effectively regulating the supply of prices, taxation, interest rates, exchange rates, law and other intangible resources; and through innovation in institution, organization and technology.

And, finally, differences in modes of competition. Enterprises adopt the ERP (enterprise resources planning) mode to exercise effective and integrated management of materials, finance, information and customer resources and to achieve inter-regional, inter-sector and inter-industrial coordination and effective allocation in terms of logistics and personnel, financial and information flow. Guided by market demands, enterprises will strive for effective integration of resources, adjustment of functions, improvement of production efficiency and eventual enhancement of competitiveness. Regional government, however, may establish the DRP (district resources planning) mode to effectively allocate resources such as land, population, finance, environment, technology and policies, design layouts and make appropriate arrangements according to regional planning and strategies. Equipped with systematic management notions and approaches, regional government employs layout design and planning as the basis to make judgment upon market changes, deploy regional resources, enhance regional competitiveness, realize the best regional TFP and achieve sustainable economic and social development in the region.

The representation of regional government competition

The relations and differences in competition between regional governments and enterprises reveal that competition between regional governments and that between enterprises are two systems of competition on different levels of the modern market economy. They are mutually independent but related, constituting the double entities of competition of the modern market economy. Competition between enterprises is the basis of competition in the market economy and leads to competition between regional governments. Regional governments compete for the optimization of resources allocation via systems, policies, projects and environment. It is a different kind of competition, above the level of enterprise competition, which in turn influences, supports and promotes enterprise competitiveness. Enterprise competition takes place only across enterprises. Regional government can only act as a planner and guide of industrial development; an assistant and regulator of commodity production; and a supervisor and manager of market order. It has no right to exercise direct intervention in micro-level enterprise operations. Regional government competition takes place only across regional governments. It follows the rules of market economy and competes in terms of projects, policies and public affairs in relation to regional resource allocation, economic development, urban construction and people's livelihoods.

Project competition

There are three main categories of projects: national key projects, social investment projects and foreign investment projects. The first category includes special national key projects; major projects for national science and technology programs; major infrastructure projects for national science and technology programs; and major state-financed construction and industrial projects. The second category includes projects in high-tech industries, newly emerging industries, equipment manufacturing, raw materials, finance, logistics and other services. The third category includes projects concerning intelligent manufacturing, cloud computing and big data, networking, intelligent urban construction and so on.

Regional governments compete for projects in order to directly acquire capital, talents and industry; effectively solve regional financing, land acquisition and other issues through legitimate project policies and rational public services; guide, through project implementation, regional land development and urban infrastructure construction; increase investment; promote industrial development; optimize the allocation of resources; enhance policy capabilities; and facilitate the sustainable development of regional economy and community. Consequently, project competition becomes one of the key issues for regional government work that leads the direction of regional development. Awareness of the importance of projects, development, efficiency, advantages, conditions, policies and risks becomes an essential requirement for regional government in market competition.

Competition of industrial chain development

Generally speaking, each region has its own industrial foundation with its own characteristics, which are in most cases contingent upon natural resource endowments in the region. The crux of the matter lies in how to maintain and optimize regional internal resources endowments and how to synergize and obtain high-end resources from outside the region. The key is optimization of industrial structure and effective development of industrial chains, and the breaking point is developing towards high-end industries, forming industrial agglomeration and leading industrial clustering.

Regional government competition for industrial chain development unfolds mainly in two aspects. The first is concerned with factors of production. Low-end or primary factors of production cannot form a stable and long-lasting competitive edge. Only by introducing, investing in and developing high-end and high-level factors of production – such as industrial technology, modern information technology, network resources, transport facilities and professional personnel, research and development think tanks, etc. – can powerful and competitive industries be built up. The second is concerned with industrial clustering and industrial underpinnings. Regional competitiveness reveals that effective industrial clustering, employing the existing regional industrial base as the leading force, can reduce business transaction costs and improve enterprise profitability. The industrial smile curve makes manifest that the most valuable areas are located at both ends of the value chain – R&D and market. As a result, an important route for regional government to follow in achieving sustainable development is to cultivate competitive industries, develop industrial chains and introduce "targeted" investment according to the structural requirements of the industry.

Competition for talents, science and technology

The primary issue in competition for talents and science and technology is the recognition of the doctrines that human resources are primary resources and that science and technology are primary productive forces. The most fundamental task is to improve local personnel training systems and increase regional investment in personnel training and technological innovation, and the greatest essence resides in creating conditions for talent attraction, introduction, training and employment. The competitiveness of science and technology talents is measured by regional science and technology human resources indexes; the number of people engaged in scientific and technological activities per ten thousand people; the number of scientists and engineers per ten thousand people; the total number of scientific and technological activities per ten thousand people; the number of students in colleges and universities per ten thousand people; annual investment in science and technology talent training index per ten thousand people; total operating expenses of science and technology activities; the percentage of GDP for science and technology expenditure; per capita research funding; the percentage of local fiscal expenditure for financial allocations to local science and technology; per capita government expenditure on education; total local fiscal expenditure on education; number of full-time college teachers; and other indicators. Regional government makes efforts to improve and enhance related indicators so as to reinforce the overall competitiveness of talent in science and technology.

Fiscal and financial competition

Regional fiscal competition covers fiscal revenue and expenditure competition. Fiscal revenue is mainly achieved through the pursuit of economic growth and the accrual of taxes. Apart from social consumption and transfer expenditure, competition is chiefly realized through government investment, such as investment in infrastructure, science and technology R&D, investment of fiscal policy funds in industries that need urgent development and other fiscal investment expenditure. Fiscal investment expenditure is an important force for driving economic growth. The overall size of fiscal revenues and expenditure is limited; regional government must actively build various platforms for investment and financing – as well as mobilize and attract regional, national and international financial institutions, funds, personnel, information and other financial resources to the greatest possible extent – in order to benefit regional economic development, urban construction, social and livelihood services. Preferential policies and measures adopted by regional governments drive each other into competition for fiscal spending and monetary absorption.

Infrastructure competition

Infrastructure competition takes place in the construction of both infrastructure hardware and smart city software. The former includes transportation platforms of highways, ports and aviation; energy supply platforms of electricity, gas and others; information platforms of cable and networks; and science and technology, industrial, entrepreneurial and creative parks. The latter includes intelligent city-building platforms of big data, cloud computing and the Internet of things. Infrastructure systems, which can be rated as advanced, adaptive and backward, underpin economic and social development in the region. The moderately advanced infrastructure supply in a region will provide optimal services for urban structure, facility size and spatial layout in market competition so that enterprise costs are reduced, production efficiency enhanced and industrial development facilitated. Whether regional infrastructure is complete directly brings forth differences in regional economy and affects its future.

Competition in environmental systems

In addition to infrastructure, environmental systems here mainly cover the construction of ecological environment, humanistic environment, policy environment, social credit systems and the like. Regional government competition entails environments for development, including the harmony between investment development and ecological protection; the matching between investment attraction and policy services; the agreement between pursuit of wealth and social returns; and the mutual support between legal supervision and social credit. Favorable environment systems are the recipe for success in investment solicitation, project construction and sustainable development; this has been proven by successful experience in China and overseas.

Competition in policy systems

This involves policies implemented by regional government on both foreign and regional levels and is also true between countries. Policies are public products that are non-exclusive and imitative. Therefore, good competitive policy systems must be (1) realistic, i.e. in line with reality and the requirements for socioeconomic development; (2) advanced, in the sense that they are foresighted and innovative; (3) workable, in the sense that they are clear, targeted and enforceable; (4) organized, in the sense that specialized agencies and people perform duties and put them into operation; and (5) effective, which means that there are inspection, monitoring, assessment and evaluation mechanisms, including the involvement of third parties playing their role so as to achieve policy objectives effectively. Whether policy systems are sound or not has great impact upon regional competition.

Competition in management efficiency

Regional government management efficiency is an overall indication of administrative activities, speed, quality and efficiency; this covers macro-efficiency, micro-efficiency, organizational efficiency and individual efficiency. In terms of administrative compliance, regional government bodies should follow the norms of legality, interest and quality, and in terms of administrative efficiency, they should follow the norms of quantity, time, speed and budgeting. Competition in management efficiency is in nature competition of organizational systems, government obligations, service awareness, work skills and technological platforms. Developed regions have been practicing, without precedent, the paralleled and integrated service modes.

Regional government competition is embodied in the above-mentioned eight types and is in essence reflected in their policies regarding the allocation of regional resources towards operational resources, so as to enhance enterprise vitalities, and towards non-operational resources, so as to create favorable environments; these are, in their ways, rules and supporting policies to be employed to manage quasi-operational resources, so as to achieve sustainable growth in the region. In a nutshell, regional government competition is basically reflected in competition in the optimization of resource allocation.

Government Foresighted Leading (GFL) as the core of regional competition

Competition entails innovation, and innovation is competitiveness. Continuous innovation is sustained competitiveness. Regional innovation is the core of regional government competition. Innovation in notion, institution, organization, administration and technology is indispensable in regional government competition. GFL becomes essential to regional competition and development.

First, notional foresighted leading is the actual competitiveness in the factor-driven stage of economic growth, which has been amply demonstrated throughout the world. In this very stage, economic growth is chiefly achieved through the expansion of production input, like land, labor and other natural resources; there is a focus on competition for resources and in prices, which are prone to such problems as excessive exploitation of production factors, lower production efficiency, technological backwardness, resource depletion, brain drain and social conflicts. Consequently, development notions, direction and modes in this stage become decisive. Advanced notions tend to determine the modes and trends of regional development. Regional government's innovative notions – e.g. the overall command of regional factors, strategic positioning, development paths, modes and layout and a driving force for development – become the focus of regional competition. Therefore, for the facilitation of stable, coordinated regional development, it is of primary significance to follow foresighted leading notions of "coordination", "green" and "openness" in the factor-driven stage.

Second, organizational foresighted leading plays a key role in competition in the investment-driven stage, in which period expanding investment, and intensifying its stimulation to economic growth, is the primary means of regional competition. Driven by investment multiplier effects, investment can enormously expedite economic growth; this has been demonstrated in the Keynesian theory of effective demand. Investment is of great significance for increasing effective demand and boosting GDP. Especially during economic downturns, government can increase investment to reverse the trend of economic downturn and drag economy out. However, problems like quick ups and downs in economy and the lagging-behind of technology and innovation may ensue after single short-term stimulus of investment as a result of "investment hunger" and "investment dependence". Under such circumstances, innovation in organizational administration becomes crucial. That requires the intensification of investment management standards; rapid organizational responsive capabilities; closer relations to market and enterprise services; network and matrix structuring; and streamlined administration so as to achieve greater efficiency and flexibility and improve investment effectiveness. Organizational foresighted leading is crucial to stable and orderly economic development and inter-regional competition in the investment-driven stage.

Third, technological and institutional foresighted leading is the key to scoring success in regional competition in the innovation-driven stage. Innovation has the most explosive driving force for economic development and pushes the socio-economy to transform from quantity- to quality-type, reflecting overall breakthroughs in socio-economic performance and in optimized social allocation. At this stage, technological innovation is the core of all driving forces, and institutional innovation is the fundamental guarantee for continuous technological innovation. Technological innovation gives birth to new formats, new products, new industries and new models. Institutional innovation protects and promotes the integrated innovative development of science and technology, finance and industry, which combine to stimulate innovation-driven sustainability. Technological and institutional foresighted leading become an important means of regional competition at this stage.

Finally, overall foresighted leading is the inevitable choice for competition in the wealth-driven stage. Under the assumption that regional economic development in the world follows the sequence of factor-driven, investment-driven, innovation-driven and wealth-driven stages, then the wealth-driven stage of economic growth requires not only innovation in notions, technology, organizations and institutions but also overall foresighted leading, so as to achieve and guarantee the sustained advantages of regional competition. This stage is characterized by the full play of individual creativity; comprehensive balance between work and life; rapid development of tertiary industries; growing awareness of the importance of resources environments; and continuously emerging models of economic and individual development. Therefore, the flexible, quick and diverse development of regional economy in the wealth-driven stage requires the coordination of institutions, policies and measures to match the pulse of the wealth-driven times, orient the values of the wealth-driven stage and maintain the sustainability and vitality of the economy. Overall continuous innovation and foresighted leading – in the whole process and over the full range of factors – are the inevitable options for regional competition at this stage.

The dual nature of regional government as "quasi-state" ("quasi-macro") and "quasi-enterprise" ("quasi-micro") constitutes a pattern of competition of "double entities" between regional governments and between enterprises by means of the mechanisms of market economy and an optimal combination of "effective government" and "effective market" in modern market economy. The organic integration of "effective government" and "effective market" is the mature market economy in the real sense.

Preface

Economic globalization and regional economic development are of great significance in the twenty-first century. Regional economic competition and integration around the globe, in particular, have facilitated economic globalization and, eventually, promoted the prosperity and development of the global economy.

Theoretical studies in regional economy have, over the past decade or so, attracted increasing attention from economists. Dr. Chen Yunxian's research has been devoted exclusively to this area, focusing on the regional government that lies behind regional economic development. He has published *Foresighted Leading – Theoretical Thinking and Practice of China's Regional Economic Development* (Springer, Germany, 2013), *Government Foresighted Leading – Theory and Practice of the World's Regional Economic Development* (Routledge, Oxford, 2017), *Mezzoeconomics – Innovations and Developments in Theoretical Configuration of Economics*(American Academic Press, 2018) and *Regional Government Competition* (Routledge, Oxford, 2019), for which publication is well underway.

This monograph takes the classification of resources as the starting point for the analysis of regional government competition. Regional resources may be classified into operational, non-operational and quasi-operational types on the basis of the three major functions of regional government, i.e. economic development, urban construction and social wellbeing. In the light of such an analysis, resources that correspond to economic development in market economy fall into the operational type, i.e. industrial resources, and enterprises are the major economic entities for this type. Resources that correspond to social wellbeing fall into the non-operational type in market economy; this covers social welfare and public products and its major economic entities are regional governments. Resources that correspond to urban construction fall into the quasi-operational type in market economy, i.e. urban resources, and its major economic entities can be both enterprises and government. Regional urban resources are chiefly employed for public services that provide guarantees for the normal operation of social and economic activities in a region or a country, as well as for all the necessary facilities for public services, so as to underpin social production and residential livelihood. The quasi-operational type is so called because these resources lie in the "borderline areas" in economics, which traditionally falls into the "overlapping zone" between government and market and can be undertaken by either enterprises or government in order to achieve the purpose of serving social wellbeing.

Based on the classificatory analysis of three types of resources and their allocating power, market and government can be divided into weak, semi-strong and strong types. Viewed from the perspective of resource allocation, weak effective government chiefly regulates the allocation of non-operational resources, semi-strong effective government both non-operational and operational resources and strong effective government quasi-operational resources in addition to the other two types. The optimal resource allocation can be realized through functional complementation of government, enterprises and market mechanisms, in which case government can be considered effective.

It follows that regional governments compete mainly in the allocation and regulation of quasi-operational resources. Regional government exercises macro-level regulation in the "quasi-state" role and participates in regional market competition in the "quasi-enterprise" role. Whether regional government can exert foresighted leadership in the allocation and regulation of quasi-operational resources is determined by the innovative capabilities of regional government; these are represented by its policy-making and concrete measures for notional, institutional, organizational and technological innovation.

Regional government's focuses on notional, institutional, organizational and technological innovation may vary in different stages of economic development, matching respectively with factor-driven, investment-driven, innovation-driven and wealth-driven stages. Regional government's major competitive force in the innovation-driven stage is the effective integration of institutional and technological innovation; overall innovation will become the key force for regional government to expedite economic growth in the wealth-driven stage.

The "double-strong mechanism" of strong market and strong government, which involves regional government ameliorating and perfecting the allocating modes for three types of resources, is a representative model in the modern market economy. The combination of the three modes of market developing itself from weak to strong and the three modes of government allocating resources from weak to strong generates nine different models. The emergence of the "double-strong mechanism" of strong effective market and strong effective government marks the start of the modern market economy's maturity and represents the most advanced stage of market economic development. Mature market economy results from the effective integration and operation of effective government and effective market.

This monograph concludes with the notion of "establishing the new engine for global economic development". The mature market system that comprises effective government and effective market requires the role to be promoted and given full play in order for enterprises to compete in the allocation of industrial resources, and for government to compete in the allocation of urban resources with a view to establishing new engines for global investment, innovation and governance that integrate tangible and intangible factors worldwide. The new engine for global investment embodies promoting supply-side structural reform, strengthening infrastructural investment and construction, enhancing financial matching capabilities and so on. The new engine for global innovation embodies notional innovation in ideological public products, technological innovation in material public products, managerial innovation in organizational public products and regulatory innovation in institutional public products. The new engine for global governance implies the making of rules for peaceful and stable international security and order; for fair and efficient international economic competition; and for shared cooperative and win–win international governance. These new engines will prove to be of primary significance to global economic governance and growth.

The CPC Central Committee, with Xi Jinping as its core, has come up with the overall layout of "five in one" and "four comprehensive" strategy, calling on the Chinese people to firmly establish and carry out the development philosophy of innovation, coordination, greenness, openness and sharing; accommodate the new normal of economic development; and endeavor to push the constructive cause of socialism with Chinese characteristics to new heights. All this has created unprecedented opportunities and conditions for Chinese economists, who should base themselves on China's modern practices, absorb the essence of Chinese civilization, aim at the forefront of world academics and bring forward innovation and breakthroughs in economic theories so as to move toward the forefront of world economic theorization and lead its development.

Translators

Yong Heming is Professor and President of Guangdong University of Finance.

Peng Jing is Associate Professor at Guangdong University of Finance and Economics.

Chen Dinggang, PhD, is Lecturer at Guangdong University of Finance.

Chen Zimin is a member of GDUF Translation Team of Financial and Economic Works.

1 Regional government

1.1 Regional government: a demarcation

1.1.1 *Nature of regional government*

"Region" is a multi-faceted, multi-layered and highly relative concept and can be interpreted from various perspectives. The perspective of politics refers to a region as an administrative unit under national jurisdiction; the sociological perspective regards it as a community of human beings with the same language, belief and ethnicity in a society; and the geographical perspective defines it as a geographical unit on the planet.

However, economics posits that a region is a relatively large territory with various types of resources for a range of productive and non-productive social–economic activities. This definition is three-pronged:

(a) Region is a relative concept. It does not exist unless an overall boundary is given. For example, relative to the whole world, all continents and nations can be viewed as regions. Relative to a nation, various localities within it can be viewed as regions, and so on.
(b) Region is not a natural object but a result of human perception upon natural objects: a conceptual representation.
(c) Regions share some common characteristics. They are divided according to their commonalities in certain aspects, and different criteria will lead to varied regional divisions.

"Regional government" refers to an organization which manages an administrative region of a nation. It is often used in relation to "national government" or, in a federal state, "federal government". Regional government (not including special administrative regions) in China is set at the provincial, municipal, county and township level. A fully functioning regional government should consist of three elements: (a) a relatively stable region, (b) a relatively concentrated population and (c) institutions that govern the region.

Government is characterized by publicity and coerciveness. The publicity of a government indicates that it is a formal representative for the whole society, representing all relevant tangible organizations and thus reflecting and representing the will and interests of the whole society. As an integral part of the multi-layered governance system, regional governments have one feature in common, i.e. serving the general public, whether they function as representative institutions set by the national government or as entities that possess relative administrative powers. In addition to "super-economic coercive" legislative, judicial and administrative powers, the coerciveness of government also resides in its "economic coercive" powers, which are embodied in the financial, administrative and resource allocating power of regional government.

The "super-economic coercive" power and the "economic coercive" power of regional government are contingent upon the game between the region and the nation and the region's social and economic strength of development. Therefore, regional government can exercise two types of power – political power, or the power of "quasi-state", and economic power, or the power of "quasi-enterprise". The former refers to regional government exercising the authorities granted by the state to oversee public expenditure and maintain market order within that region by means of taxation, business administration, public security and market regulation. It also guarantees justice, openness and fairness by means of legislation and jurisdiction. The latter refers to regional government gaining benefits through its financial, administrative and resource allocating power, which is achieved through such organizational forms as state-owned, state-controlling and state-holding enterprises; control of land, mines and resources; and policy implementation.

States all over the world fall into unitary and composite types. The functions of regional government vary with the structural type of the state. In a unitary state, sub-national units such as administrative regions and autonomous regions are established according to geography. The national government has the ultimate and supreme authority. Regional government exercises only the powers that the national government chooses to delegate, in accordance to its constitutions and laws. Regional government, under the leadership and supervision of the national government, has the right to administer local affairs. National government provides guidance and supervision over the regional government by means of policies and laws. Countries like the UK, France, China, Japan and Italy fall into this type. In a composite state, more than two member nations, states or provinces are allied by agreements or constitutions. The range of powers of the state and its member states are stipulated by the constitution. All regional governments enjoy a high degree of autonomy within the range of their powers. They exercise their powers directly upon their people without interference from other regional governments. Since each regional government performs its duties in accordance with its position in the overall system and its range of power, its interests and behavioral patterns and those of the national government may not be always consistent. They manage affairs out of their own interests. Countries like the USA, Australia, Canada, Germany and Brazil fall into this type. Whether in a unitary state or a composite state, it is difficult, technically speaking, for the national government to integrate all levels of administration at low cost.

Thus, it is necessary to take advantage of regional governments to look into regional needs and tackle regional problems. That gives regional governments greater importance and highlights their roles.

Relative to the national government and non-governmental entities in a region (including residents, enterprises and other organizations), regional government has two prominent roles to play: the representative for the interests of both the national government and regional non-governmental entities, and the intermediate agent or bridge for the exchange of information between the national government and regional non-governmental entities. Regional government serves in a "dual role" in between the national government and non-governmental entities. On one hand, regional government acts as the agent of the national government, exercising macro-level regulation on regional economy, and plays the "quasi-state" role, acting on behalf of the state so as to guide and lead economic regulation and boost development. On the other hand, regional government acts as the agent of non-governmental entities in a region, striving for support from the national government, distributing local resources and maximizing the benefits of local economy by means of institutional, organizational and technological innovation – hence the "quasi-enterprise" role.

Regional governments have been transformed into relatively independent "stakeholders" as a result of a series of fiscal and financial reforms that aimed to delegate powers to regional governments in countries worldwide. Decades of market-oriented reforms have continuously enhanced the autonomy and financial status of regional governments. In fact, regional governments have already become relatively independent economic entities. The dual roles of regional governments put them in a unique position both of leading social economic activities and in being led. To one end, relative to the national government, regional governments serve as decision makers and quasi-micro entities, attempting to gain more economic benefits. To the other end, relative to the market and enterprises, regional governments serve as the first level of units in the administrative system of the state and executors of the national government, striving to maintain stability of macro-economy in the region.

1.1.2 Features of regional government

According to traditional western economics, the government, be it national or regional, is supposed to do only what the market cannot do, which means that the government exercises marginal regulation only in the case of market failure, and that the government exercises inactive regulation. The government's major responsibility is to maintain proper market order. However, practices in countries like China show that in today's market economy, the role of government is a composite – serving as both guardian of market order and participant in competition against other regional governments. As a single entity within its jurisdiction, regional government exercises macro-level regulation, and it becomes a participant of competition in a broader market when it deals with other regional governments – hence a competitive regional government system.

Competition between regional governments enriches government functions and does not prevent the market from becoming the decisive factor of resource allocation. A free market and a system of regional governments with composite roles constitute two pillars of the modern market economy.

The above analysis of the internal and external roles of regional government determines that regional government should be studied from both macro- and micro-level perspectives. From the macro-level perspective, the income of regional government should be addressed to see how it is influenced by various factors such as industrial structure, economic growth of the region and so on. From the micro-level perspective, its optimized performance, such as participation in competition, incentive policy-making and acting as an agent, should be analyzed. Given the special role of regional government, studies will be conducted concerning how regional government functions are to be enhanced, how a political system that facilitates GFL is to be fostered and how a comprehensive theoretical framework for regional government competition is to be constructed. This monograph puts forth four major theories to expound the special nature of regional government: the GFL theory, the "dual role" theory of regional government, the "dual-entity" theory of market competition and the theory of "double-strong mechanism" for effective allocation of resources.

1.1.2.1   Regional GFL

Let the market do what it can do and government do what the market cannot do or cannot do well; both of these should be put in place. GFL aims to give full play to government roles in economic guidance, regulation and warning and to take the lead in promoting scientific and sustainable growth in regional economy with recourse to market rules and forces; it does so by means of investing, pricing, taxation, legal and other measures and through innovation in notion, institution, organization and technology.

1.1.2.2   The duality of regional government role

Regional government plays both "quasi-state" and "quasi-enterprise" roles, acting on behalf of the state to exercise macro-level regulation in regional economy and on behalf of a region's non-governmental entities to participate in competition against other regions in order to maximize its economic interests.

1.1.2.3   The "dual-entity" system for market competition

Given the active competition between regional governments, two competing entities exist in the system of market economy – namely, "micro-level enterprises" and "regional governments". To put it another way, a natural person or a legal person of an enterprise may become a competitor in the market; so may regional government, though enterprises and regional governments compete at different levels.

1.1.2.4 The "double-strong mechanism" for mature markets

A mature market economy should be a combined economic system of "strong market" and "strong government". A strong market contributes to efficient resource allocation, whereas a strong government fosters and safeguards a sound market environment. A strong government does not mean replacing a strong market, as a strong market needs the support of a strong government. Only when the double-strong mechanism is in place can market failures be remedied and government malfunction be reduced.

1.1.3 Functions of regional government

An overview of national government functions all over the world shows that their major responsibilities are to maintain social stability, boost overall development and deal with emergencies. Their major obligations, as revealed by an investigation into regional government functions, are economic development, urban construction and livelihood improvement. China's reform and opening up demonstrate that regional governments have made significant efforts to perform the three functions and admirable contributions to the fulfillment of their obligations.

Regarding economic development, let's look at Shunde, Foshan (Guangdong Province, China) for an example. In 2005, the total output in Shunde District reached 60.1 billion RMB, with the secondary industry accounting for 61 percent. Household appliances and electronic products take up 70 percent of the total output of the secondary industry. In addition, the three electric tycoons in Shunde – Midea, Kelon and Galanz – nearly monopolized the household appliance industry. The Shunde District government was well aware that excessive reliance on one single industry, and possible poor performance by the key enterprises in that industry, might incur regional economic problems and even crises. In order to prevent that scenario from happening, the district government, proceeding from the industrial reality, proposed and implemented the "Triple-Three Strategy" for its industrial restructuring and overall industrial development. Specifically, this was three categories of industry (the coordinated development of the primary industry, the secondary and the tertiary industry); three pillar lines (no fewer than three pillar lines to be fostered and supported within each category of industry); and three leading enterprises (within each pillar line of industry, no fewer than three locomotive enterprises to be nurtured). The strategy aimed at fostering industrial chains, accumulating industrial clusters and achieving sustainable development.

Considering problems that arose out of weak industrial foundation and capital shortage in the development of its SMEs, the government of Shunde District innovatively established credit guarantee funds for its SMEs by setting up specialized fiscal funds in collaboration with underwriting institutions and commercial banks to offer credit guarantees and loans to the well-performing SMEs without adequate assets for mortgage. Practice has shown that the Shunde

District government's economic guidance, regulation and early warning contributed substantially to the more sophisticated development of the primary industry, the upgrading of the secondary industry and the speedy growth of the tertiary industry; to the transformation of traditional industries, the flourishing of emerging industries, the rapid growth of high-tech industries and a scalar formation of large, medium and small enterprises and the ensuing complementary industrial clusters; and, consequently, to the Shunde District's leading position among over 2800 counties in China in terms of economic growth over the past few decades.

Similar practices in western developed countries have also been conducted to steer, boost and adjust industrial development. For instance, the NNMI (National Networks of Manufacturing Innovation) is one key measure the US has taken to implement its strategy of "reindustrialization". Following the 2008 financial crisis, the US formulated "A Framework for Revitalizing American Manufacturing" and "Manufacturing Promotion Act". In June 2011, the "Advanced Manufacturing Partnership" (AMP) was launched, which was followed by the "National Network for Manufacturing Innovation" (NNMI) in March 2012. The NNMI consists of interrelated IMIs (Institutes for Manufacturing Innovation) with common goals but various focuses, and an investment plan for US $1 billion to build up 15 IMIs in different parts of the US. A more ambitious plan was made in July 2013 to build up 45 within ten years, and a budget was put in place in the 2015 fiscal year.

As is observed here, the program is, first of all, in line with the US's national strategies and concentrates on projects that accommodate the specific needs of regions and industries. Second, the program centers on resource optimization and restructuring and integrates existing resources of innovation by adopting a combination of "top-down" and "bottom-up" approaches. Third, the program operates with a public–private partnership guarantee, steady initial federal support and matching follow-up funding from universities and private institutions. Fourth, the program is managed through coordinated networks, with each IMI connecting the innovation resources of the region, the state and the world. The NNMI has established a committee to lead coordination and collaboration; this allows government, with its connection to the market and its role in optimizing government investment and balancing the interests of related parties, to play a guiding and leveraging role in investment, steer the direction of industrial R&D, improve high-end manufacturing layouts and accelerate innovation and commercialization.

The UK's Knowledge Transfer Partnership (KTP) is also worth mentioning here. In order to upgrade innovative capabilities of enterprises, the UK government implemented KTP to achieve the transfer of knowledge, technologies and skills from research institutes to enterprises and strengthen enterprise–academic partnerships, with personnel of expertise as the intermediary. The KTP program is funded by the government and public institutions as well as enterprises, which provide matching financial support. The UK government formulated application criteria and approval procedures and worked out assessment measures.

In so doing, the KTP program expanded government services for enterprises, stimulated enterprises' investment in innovation, integrated innovation resources of talents, enterprises and institutions and upgraded industrial structure.

Regarding urban construction, let's take China as an example. As of 2006, against the backdrop of reform and opening up in China, Foshan, Guangdong Province has achieved 30 times the economic growth with only three times the construction land, as land shortage has posed a harsh challenge to its future development. The Foshan Municipality issued in 2007 *The Provisions Regarding the Acceleration of Transformation of Old Towns, Factory Sites and Countryside Residences* (abbreviated as "three-outmoded transformation"). In 2009, *The Plan for Three-Outmoded Transformation* (2009–2020) was passed, releasing 253,000 acres of land, following the principle of government making policies, land users/owners providing land and developers making investments. A total investment of 35.7 billion RMB was drawn into the plan in the first three years, and that activated over 730 projects of three-outmoded transformation, taking up 30,000 acres of land with an increase in construction area of 23.99 million square meters. The model of "government facilitation, market operation and enterprise participation" for three-outmoded transformation, which effectively addressed the issues of regional construction, drastically raised the efficiency of land use and promoted industrial restructuring; it was summarized as the "Foshan Experience" and recommended as a role model for other regions to follow by the Guangdong provincial government and the central government of China. In 2010, Foshan Municipality government proposed the notion of "fourizations and smart Foshan", i.e. strengthening the comprehensive competitiveness of Foshan by means of industrialization, urbanization and internationalization through informationalization; this would enable Foshan to become safer, greener, more efficient and more harmonious through greater efforts in developing smart traffic, smart environmental protection, smart land control, smart security system, smart city regulation, smart education, smart medical service, smart cultural service, smart business service, smart administration, etc. Consequently, industrialization will be transformed, urbanization will be expedited and internationalization will be enhanced in Foshan. It turns out that the government has a significant role to play in figuring out modern approaches to city governance; this is also true of western developed countries. The revival of the "industrial toxic city" in Germany is a good example here. The Ruhr industrial region made great contributions to German economy, but serious pollution problems arose out of it. To address the problems, the Nordrhein-Westfalen government put forward a long-term scheme from 1968 to 1979 and then to 1989 that started with industrial restructuring and the development of emerging industries and was followed by ecological transformation of industrial legacies, ecological restoration and environmental improvement. As a result, the region was renewed as one that featured good cultural preservation, industrial upgrade, better infrastructure, rapid growth of the city and sound environments for living, business and development.

Regarding livelihood improvement, let's use as an example the scheme of livelihood improvement of the Guangdong provincial government, China. This was proposed in 2016 and covers the following ten aspects of people's livelihoods: (1) raise the basic standard of livelihood; (2) enhance poverty-relief efforts; (3) reinforce housing services to low-income groups; (4) improve living and manufacturing conditions in rural areas; (5) improve medical service in rural areas; (6) promote fair distribution of educational resources; (7) boost entrepreneurial activities and employment; (8) tackle pollution and build ecological environment; (9) consolidate public security; and (10) beef up disaster prevention and relief efforts. Every aspect was quite to the point and was put into place to guarantee public satisfaction.

Another good example is the New Village Movement in South Korea in the 1960s, at which time farmers accounted for 70 percent of its total population and agriculture was on the verge of collapse. Under those circumstances, the South Korean government campaigned for the New Village Movement by means of policy orientation and concrete measures. The movement endeavored to build up new villages by supporting rural construction projects and cooperative financing managed by agricultural associations. It brought forth an economic boom in South Korea, known as "Miracle on the Han River". It has become an exemplary case of how developed countries improve livelihood by resolving the imbalance between urban and rural regions.

1.1.4 Economic goals of regional government

Consumers and enterprises, in the role of micro-economic entities, are mainly concerned with prices. Regional government can guide family consumption and enterprise production decisions by resorting to price signals in order to achieve the greatest possible utility of consumption and profits of production. In reality, the scope of concern on the part of families or enterprises as micro-economic entities falls into micro-economics; those outside their scope of concern, which are not controllable by prices, do not belong to micro-economics and are categorized into market failure as externalities.

As macro-economic entities, governments are chiefly concerned with aggregate economy – the status of national income and its accrual. However, a macro-economic perspective fails to capture the concrete operation of a region, industry or regional bloc. The economic links between regions and industries often go beyond the control of enterprises but fall short of national regulation because regional behaviors and economy are not subject to the laws and principles of macro-economic management. Those behaviors that lie beyond national government control should be considered government malfunction. This demonstrates that there is a blind spot that skips the notice of both micro- and macro-economic entities, as it is somewhat too "broad" or "high up" for individual enterprises and too "regional" or "local" for national government. This blind spot lies in between micro- and macro-economic regulation and in between aggregate and individual economy; it is a collection of individual economies as well as a decomposition of aggregate economy, and that is where regional government should have a role to play. Therefore, in between these areas, regional economic growth can be achieved beyond individual enterprise behavior and more concrete macro-level regulation, and that is exactly where the economic goals that regional government strives to achieve reside.

It becomes obvious that regional government should address issues concerning the production and consumption of a region, industry or production bloc on the level that lies beyond individual enterprises and the level that goes beyond regional contributions to the nation. It follows that regional government must be involved in economic competition against the backdrop of the broader market, while exercising macro-level regulation on local issues such as price, employment, economic growth, etc.; hence its dual role – one that is similar to that of a producer or "quasi-enterprise" and one that is similar to that of national government or "quasi-state", which connects macro-economy and micro-economy and positions regional government as the entity that fulfills mezzo-economic goals. More specifically, the economic goals for regional government involve optimal distribution and utilization of regional economic resources, which affect regional competitiveness and sustainability.

1.1.4.1 Gaining regional first-mover advantages and optimizing resource allocation

Regional economic development goes closely with regional government competition. Regional government spares no efforts in establishing specialized markets, restructuring industries, introducing advanced technologies, organizing R&D projects, building infrastructure, guiding business investment, attracting foreign investment and so on; these are basically motivated by competition between regional governments. However, this will not happen if the market mechanism has not been applied to regional government behavior and if market competition mechanisms have not been applied to competition between regional governments in China.

Market competition between regional governments is to a great extent reflected in their planning and guidance, which pose serious challenges to the regional government's capacities of strategic positioning, resource mobilization and coordinated planning. Regional government planning and guidance differ totally from the in-process and post-process intervention advocated by laissez-faire government, government interventionalism and Keynesian government intervention. They stress foresighted pre-process analysis, prediction, planning and regulation of economic activities, which are based on the government's thorough consideration and judgment of the market and on how to give full play to market mechanisms in resource allocation.

1.1.4.2 Ensuring the stability and effectiveness of overall economic development

By exercising foresighted leading, regional government embodies long-term strategic visions, manageable internal competition and effectiveness of enhancing sound economic development. A regional government system of foresighted leading and orderly competition frees national government from the laissez-faire regulation and micro-economic intervention that were needed under a planned economy. Therefore, national governments have much more leeway to focus on macro-level planning and regulation for regional and industrial development and to formulate national strategies for long-term development and policy implementation. Issues concerning the development and regulation of particular regions and industries are left to regional government, a mezzo-economic entity, which is in a better position to more accurately and effectively exercise micro-level administration and regulation while also taking into consideration the stability and flexibility of overall economic development.

1.1.4.3   *Promoting scientific and sustainable growth of regional economy*

Regional government tends to be proactive and responsive. When economic turmoil arises, regional government can "cushion" their impact level by level and thus mitigate the effects to the least extent. When harbingers of poor economic performance occur at the micro-level, regional government can conduct timely interventions, which will remedy the oversights caused by macro-level regulation. In addition, regional government can help to improve the operation of the national economic control system, in the sense of mitigating the risk of centralized control. Experience of reform proves that the mezzo-economic regulative system plays an irreplaceable role in the overall national economic system. According to the control theory, the multi-objective optimization of a national economic system is to seek the maximum function. However, in the case of centralized control, the number of variables will increase drastically, which means the sharp increase of dimensions to be considered for the optimization of the system eventually causes formidable difficulties for an accurate calculation. Meanwhile, centralized control has a high degree of rigidness, as the center for control is the only unit that responds to random changes and environmental changes. Centralized control enhances the long-term stability of the system, but sharp conflicts will inevitably arise between the unchanged structure of the system and the innovatively changing parts thereof. Moreover, it may also reduce the operational reliability of the system. When something goes wrong with the center, it will be difficult for each sub-system to take preventative or remedial measures so that systemic deterioration will ensue. On the contrary, if control is delegated to various entities at different levels, sub-systems will have a certain degree of autonomy, hence multi-level (or decentralized) control, which allows the separation of power in a multi-level control system that may tackle the above-mentioned problems of a centralized control system. The multi-level control system is capable of adapting to environmental and internal changes as its sub-systems are independent and adaptive. In addition, each sub-system, which operates effectively according to the rules of a larger system, will have its control efficiency considerably improved, with the addition of self-received and self-processed information; overall efficiency will thus be greatly enhanced, so that regional government realizes its goal of sustainable economic growth.

1.2 Basics of regional government competition

1.2.1 *The concept of dual-entity competition between regional governments*

The dual-entity theory for market competition posits that two competing entities exist in the market – enterprises and regional governments. Competition between enterprises must abide by market laws. Such competition also exists between regional governments, who should obey similar laws. It follows that a double-layered system of competition exists in the market, each layer independently of each other. No competition takes place between enterprises and regional governments, but their roles in the market are complementary.

The dual role of regional government determines the dual-entity mechanism in the market system. Regional government per se constitutes the subjective entity of regional competition, whereas objective entities are the objects for which regional governments vie in the market, including a wide range of tangible and intangible resources in the region. Regional government competition targets optimizing resource allocation, enhancing efficiency of regional economy and gaining more benefits for the region. The competitive behaviors of regional government include providing enterprises with technological, personnel and financing services, promoting cultural programs, mobilizing innovation, offering policy guidance, building infrastructure and safeguarding market competition mechanisms.

1.2.2 *Relatedness and differences in competition between enterprises and between regional governments*

Competition between enterprises takes place in their fight over industrial resources, while regional government competition targets urban resources. The two types of competition are relatively independent and yet complementary. Their relatedness and differences can be summed up as follows:

First, they differ in the fields of competition. Enterprises are micro-economic entities. They mainly compete for commodity markets and focus on industrial resources allocation. Market equilibrium theory, which takes manufacturers as its main subject, occupies a dominant position in western classical economics. Enterprises regard the pursuit of profit maximization as a precondition and assume competitive forms of supply, demand, market equilibrium prices, perfect market competition, monopolistic competition, oligopolistic market, different market structures and competitive strategies, etc. Enterprise competition is the precondition and basis for regional government competition.

Regional government is the subject of mezzo-economics. Competition between regional governments focuses on factor markets and city resources allocation. Factor markets include land, capital, labor forces, property rights, and hardware and software markets such information. Regional government improves its competitiveness through the quantity, quality, structure and layout of urban resources. Regional government can also make policies and initiatives to regulate the allocation of regional factors, to attract and influence the direction of factor flow outside the region so as to optimize the allocation of resources and eventually enhance regional competitiveness. Factor market competition affects enterprise commodity market competition.

Second, they differ in means of competition. Enterprises seek to maximize profits mainly by increasing labor productivity – to effectively influence costs, prices, supply and demand and scale – and by optimizing the allocation of corporate resources to promote their cost minimization. Regional government makes every effort to increase total factor productivity as its chief means of sustainable growth. After simple dilatation through competing for tangible factors, such as land, projects and capital, the bottleneck of diminishing capital profits makes extensive economic growth difficult to continue. When nothing more can be added to regional input of all tangible factors, regional government will have to depend on the investment, increase and improvement of intangible factors such as technological advancement (with innovation as the core), resource allocation optimization and structural adjustment as well as institution, organization, legislation, environment, etc. as the new driving forces of regional economy development and urban construction.

Third, they differ in paths of competition. Enterprises are investment-growth oriented. The continuous improvement of business performance comes from the constant input of production factors, including capital, labor, land, technology, entrepreneurship and so on. The initial strategy for businesses investment is mainly extensive expansion of quantity, followed by the quality-enhancing stage and then the stage of business management. In all these stages, sustained and effective inputs become critical. Regional government is efficiency growth-oriented. In light of the experiences of regional economies in the world, their economic growth path starts from the factor-driven stage (also known as the resource allocation stage), to the investment-driven stage (also known as the efficiency improvement stage) and then to the innovation-driven stage (also called the sustainable growth stage). Regional government makes efforts to optimize the combination of tangible and intangible factors, with efficiency improvement as the focus of its growth.

Fourth, they differ in orientations of competition. Enterprises regard demand-side expansion as their orientation. Business competition starts from market demand, demand quantities, demand structure, corporate strategies and tactics. The ability to adapt to market requirements becomes essential to their survival and success. Regional government regards supply-side optimization as its orientation. Regional government's determined direction for economic development, urban construction and facilitation of people's livelihood is to promote supply-side structural reforms by effectively allocating the supply of land, capital, projects, technology, work forces and other tangible resources, by effectively regulating the supply of prices, taxation, interest rates, exchange rates, law and other intangible resources and through innovation in institution, organization and technology.

Finally, they differ in modes of competition. Enterprises adopt the ERP mode to exercise effective and integrated management of materials, finance, information and customer resources and to achieve inter-regional, inter-sector and inter-industrial coordination and effective allocation in terms of logistics and personnel, financial and information flow. Guided by market demands, enterprises will strive for effective integration of resources, adjustment of functions, improvement of production efficiency and eventual enhancement of competitiveness. Regional government, however, may establish the DRP mode to effectively allocate resources such as land, population, finance, environment, technology and policies, design layouts and make appropriate arrangements according to regional planning and strategies. Equipped with systematic management notions and approaches, regional government employs layout design and planning as the basis to make judgment upon market changes, deploy regional resources, enhance regional competitiveness, realize the best regional TFP and achieve sustainable economic and social development in the region.

1.3 DRP model of regional government resource allocation

1.3.1 *The concept of resources*

According to *Cihai* (online), a large-scale authoritative Chinese dictionary and encyclopedia, 资源 (resource) is "a source of material, often referred to as a natural source of fortune". In *MBA Think Tank Encyclopedia* (online), the United Nations Environment Program (UNEP) defines a resource (in particular a natural resource) as an environmental element or condition from which economic values can be generated at a certain time and location to improve the wellbeing of humankind at present and in the future. These two definitions interpret resources in a narrow sense and confine the term to the category of natural resources. The term is defined by Bergstrom and Randall (2016) as material that humankind discovers and finds usable and valuable. Their definition is so broad as to cover all useful and valuable materials. Yang and Pu (1993) propose the following definition in *Resource Economics: An Economic Analysis of Optimal Resource Allocation*: a concept relative to a particular time and location and a sum of input or potential input of factors in economic activities at that particular location in conformity with the preference of consumers and the sophistication of science and technology during that period.

Our understanding treats "resources" as, first and foremost, a type of existing or potential input factor, including natural and social resources, which forms the basis for all human activities. Second, resources have values in themselves which can be turned into social wealth through human activities. Lastly, the term "resource" is a holistic concept that should be defined with reference to the economic activities of a state, region, department or other economic entities over a certain period.

1.3.2   *Resource allocation and its stratification*

Resource allocation is a common issue in economic management; it refers to a rational distribution of limited or relatively scarce resources so that products and services can be generated with the least consumption of resources and maximum gain of benefits. Appropriate resource allocation makes it possible to manufacture more products; provide more services with limited resources; realize the supply–demand equilibrium; and ensure that resources are effectively utilized in accordance with different categories of products and services, the sub-categories of the same products and services and the different producers concerned.

Resource allocation can be conducted at the micro, mezzo and macro level. Micro-allocation is the most basic; it examines how entities such as enterprises, universities, research institutions, regional government, etc. distribute and utilize their resources internally to yield desired results in a more efficient manner. It helps to increase economic and social wealth. It is the most basic level because it is based on the operation of individual entities and considers resource synergizing and utilization as its major concern and the heightening of output level as its major objective. This level of allocation chiefly investigates the direct benefits of resource utilization and regards the most effective utilization as its objective; it is the initiatives of generating effects, and the capabilities of resource organization and employment on the part of entities of economic activities, that turn out to be determinant to the effects of resource allocation.

Mezzo-allocation lies at the intermediate level of a department or a region. Entities at this level consider the conditions of a department or a region from the perspective of the market and regional government. They give full play to regional advantages and intensify the association between resources and production so as to gain a higher level of overall benefits for the department or region. The mezzo level may allocate resources within a broader scope and in a more direct and concrete fashion, serving as an intermediate link or a bridge between macro- and micro-economic regulation, with a high degree of independence. Mezzo-allocation may exercise impacts upon the efficiency of allocation at both the micro- and macro-levels. Mezzo-level allocation in the context of regions is the main focus of this book.

Macro-allocation lies at the highest level. It deals with how state departments, proceeding from the global economic outlook, allocate resources – for regions, sectors, industries, operating entities, projects and programs and scientific fields – with a view to achieving sustainable development, social stability and prosperity and conducting directional regulation on micro- and mezzo-allocation through laws, mandates, market parameters and administrative directives.

The three levels of resource allocation are inseparably connected. They have their respective roles to play but form an integrated organic whole.

Macro-allocation is concerned with planning and guidance, mezzo-allocation with adjustment and optimization and micro-allocation with implementation and enforcement. Rational planning and regulation at macro and mezzo levels can exert directional influence and provide solid assurance upon micro-level implementation and enforcement. The difference between macro- and mezzo-allocation is that the latter tends to be more technical and more susceptible to micro-level factors. Macro-level planning and guidance tend to appear in the form of laws and policies and are hardly susceptible to micro-level factors – and are therefore highly independent. Mezzo-level regulation and optimization not only affect macro-level planning and regulation but also exert direct impacts upon micro-allocation. Given a fixed volume of resources, the rationality of mezzo-allocation will directly affect the efficiency of resource utilization at the micro level. In a similar vein, the rationality and efficiency of micro-allocation will directly affect the full utilization of limited resources and the mezzo- and even macro-allocation of overall resources.

1.3.3 Categories of regional government resources

1.3.3.1 Direct resources and indirect resources

From the perspective of regional government's control, resources can be divided into two types: direct resources and indirect resources.

Direct resources are directly allocated by regional government, including state-owned resources, fiscal revenues, civil servants, policy resources, etc. Regional government possesses absolute authority over these resources and can allocate them directly according to their will.

Indirect resources are not directly allocated by regional government, but their allocation can be guided and regulated through policy-making. These resources include privately owned capital, labor, land, entrepreneurship, etc. These resources are at the disposal of their owners. What regional government can do is to regulate their flow and enhance their efficiency of use through fiscal, income, currency and other policies and exert indirect influence on the efficiency of their allocation.

1.3.3.2 Tangible resources and intangible resources

From the perspective of whether they are visible and whether they can be evaluated with currency, resources can be divided into tangible and intangible types.

For enterprises, tangible resources mainly include material and financial resources. Material resources consist of land, factories, production facilities, raw material and so on which belong to the physical resources of an enterprise. Financial resources refer to capital that is used for investment or production, including receivables, securities and so on. Intangible resources include patents, technology, knowledge, network, culture, reputation, skills and so on. They fall into the category of scarce resources. They represent the necessary input of an enterprise to create economic value.

Whether in the long or the short run, enterprises allocate resources according to the principle of maximum profits. They need to calculate the long- and short-term total costs, total income, average cost, average income, marginal income and marginal cost. Then they decide on the output, following the principle of maximum profits in the long term and the short term. Certainly, the principle may vary with different types of markets, but it presupposes the efficient allocation of resources. The more complete the market competition, the more efficient the allocation of resources.

Among the material resources at a regional government's disposal are land, minerals, forests, population, etc. Financial resources can be used by regional government for investment. Intangible resources include those humanistic resources that are immaterial and invisible, such as regional culture, regional policy systems and supporting measures, distribution of regional industries and their development, regional scientific and technological development, administrative skills of regional government, etc. Intangible resources are more influential than tangible resources and can be essential to success in regional competition. Tangible resources, such as materials and capital, are to some extent intrinsic, and their scarcity can be rather confining. In contrast, intangible resources, which undergo a long process of formulation, can be exploited without limit and have advantages that are difficult to emulate and surpass. Regional government's administrative skills constitute the most crucial part of intangible resources. Their values reside in linking value chains of various intangible resources. They play a vital role in the efficient allocation of both tangible and intangible resources and determine the output competitiveness and regulative competitiveness of a region.

Resource allocation determines the output level of a region. Regional government regards effectively allocating regional resources, striving for the greatest efficiency of production and developing regional productivity as its fundamental responsibilities.

1.3.3.3 Mobile resources and non-mobile resources

From the perspective of mobility, resources can be divided into mobile and non-mobile types.

Mobile resources flow between regions and include financial capital, human resources, technological resources and so on. The flow is driven by high profits or low costs, which will eventually contribute to the balanced development of the regions concerned. However, it may temporarily cause a new imbalance of development between regions. The direction of flow, which has proved extremely crucial to the competitiveness of a region, therefore becomes the primary focus of regional competition. As for human resources, as the most important platform for personnel training and employment, developed countries draw in top talents from around the world and thus boost their best human resources.

However, with rapid economic growth and the improved social environment, developing countries are becoming increasingly appealing to talents from different parts of the world. As some developing countries begin to implement policies to attract talent, the direction of talent flow will be reversed. In terms of technological resources, patent applications happen mostly in the US, Japan, Europe, China and South Korea. Exchanges and transfers of technology between regions are becoming more frequent. Capital flows from developed countries to developing countries, where the cost of labor is lower. Recently, it has begun to flow back to developed countries as labor cost in countries like China has increased.

Non-mobile resources, such as land, mine, forest, etc., cannot circulate, as they belong to part of the natural endowment of a region. Admittedly, when land property rights are clear and transferrable, land resources do become transferable to some degree, which is conducive to efficiency and output of land resources.

1.3.3.4 *Operational resources, non-operational resources and quasi-operational resources*

The twenty-first century witnesses the simultaneous development of economy, urban construction and social welfare. Viewed from the global perspective, national governments worldwide regard ensuring stability, boosting development and handling emergencies as their fundamental responsibilities; regional governments regard their major functions to be developing the economy, facilitating urbanization and improving livelihoods.

The three functions of regional government embody its allocation, management and policy-making for regional resources; these imply regional government's economic classification, optimized allocation and policy matching for natural, labor, capital, industrial and urban resources, and so on.

Resources that are associated with economic development are called operational resources in market economy, and the major type is industrial resources. Different regions may choose to be oriented towards one of the three categories of industry according to their special economic, geographic and natural conditions. However, there are quite a few cases in which the primary or secondary industry develops along with the tertiary industry, such as logistics, exhibition, finance, tourism, intermediary services, commerce and retail, etc. In the west, institutions that manage operational resources are mainly businesses. In China, such institutions and agencies include those that administer development and reform, statistics and commodity price; public finance, taxation, commerce and industrial and commercial administration; industry, transportation, security, energy and tobacco; science and technology, information, communications and property rights; business, customs, maritime affairs, ports, postal service, quality inspection, foreign affairs and tourism; and auditing, land administration and food and drug administration, etc. Government organizations administering operational resources may vary in different countries, but their policies for the allocation of such resources focus on how to use them to invigorate economy through planning and guidance, support and regulation and supervision and administration, which is well accepted now.

Resources that are associated with public livelihood are called non-operational resources in market economy and cover social welfare and public goods in the following fields: economy, culture, science and technology, history, geography, environment, public images, notions, emergency treatment, security, relief and other social needs. In the west, responsible agencies are chiefly social organizations. In China, however, non-operational resources fall under the administration of governmental institutions involving the following areas: public finance, auditing, authorized strength, literature and history, counseling, documentation, civil affairs, social security, poverty relief, woman and child affairs, DPF (Disabled Persons Federation), Red Cross, ethnic affairs, religion, overseas Chinese affairs; ecology, earthquake, meteorology; and emergency, safety, public security, jurisdiction, supervision, firefighting, armed police, border defense, coast defense and anti-smuggling. Countries may have different names for organizations in charge of these affairs, but they allocate resources basically on the same principle of "social provision, general underpinning, fairness and justice, and effective promotion", which is also generally accepted.

Resources that are associated with urban construction are called quasi-operational resources in market economies and are mostly city resources used to form a public service system that ensures the normal operation of social and economic activities in a country or a region. They are also used to provide hard and soft infrastructure for social production and public livelihood, including traffic, postal service, electricity and water supply, greenery landscape, environmental protection, education, science and technology, culture, sanitation, sports and other public facilities. The level of such infrastructure determines the image, attributes, taste, function and influence of a country or a region. Sound infrastructure will advance all-round development of the region and optimize its spatial design and structure. These resources are so called because they are in the "borderline areas" in western economics or, in traditional economic terms, in the "overlapping areas" between government administration and market operation, where they can be managed by both the market and government to serve social development and welfare. In China, quasi-operational resources are administered by government organizations responsible for the following areas: state-owned assets and key projects; land, environmental protection and urban and rural construction; labor force and public resource transaction; education, science and technology, culture, sanitation, sports, news and publication, radio, television and film and research institutions; agriculture, forestry, water conservancy and maritime fishery; and so forth.

1.3.4   *The theory of efficient regional resource allocation*

1.3.4.1   *Total factor productivity (TFP) as a test criterion for the effect of regional resource allocation*

First, productivity is the ratio of total national output to the total input of various factors over a certain period of time and, together with the input of capital, labor and other factors, contributes to economic growth. It reflects to what extent a nation or a region can cast off poverty and develop its economy over a certain period and how technical progress impacts on economic growth. TFP, in economic terms, refers to the efficiency of utilizing resources such as labor, material and capital. It is a variable which accounts for effects in total output growth relative to growth in traditionally measured inputs of labor and capital. It is calculated by dividing output by the weighted average of labor and capital input, with the standard weighting of 0.7 for labor and 0.3 for capital. If all inputs are accounted for, then TFP can be taken as a measure of an economy's long-term technological change or dynamism. So TFP is a measure of productivity that concentrates on efficiency promotion, technical advancement and scale effects. It is only a relative measurement of how technological progress improves efficiency.

TFP originated from the Cobb–Douglas equation. In 1928, after analyzing a great amount of historical data, Paul Douglas, Professor of Economics at Chicago University, in collaboration with mathematician Charles Cobb, proposed the well-known Cobb–Douglas production function, or the C–D production function.

They investigated the impact of capital and labor on output in the US between 1899 and 1922 on the basis of data from relevant historical literature. They posited that, provided the unchanged technical conditions, the relation between output and input of labor and capital could be represented by the formula:

$$Y = AK^{\alpha}L^{\beta} \tag{1-1}$$

In the formula, Y represents output, A technical level, K capital input, and L labor input; α and β are the output elasticity of capital and labor, respectively.

α is output elasticity of capital, which means when the input of capital increases by 1 percent, the output increases by α percent. β is output elasticity of labor, which means that when the input of labor increases by 1 percent, the output increases by β percent. A is a constant, or efficiency coefficient. Under normal circumstances, $\alpha + \beta = 1$. In the description of C–D production function at the early stage, A is considered a constant. In fact, the most straightforward interpretation is that the C–D production function is the relation between output and input at a certain time. Therefore, on condition that α is known, the technical level represented as A can be measured as follows:

$$A = Y / (K^{\alpha}L^{\beta}) = Y / (K^{\alpha}L^{1-\alpha}) \tag{1-2}$$

The proposition of the C–D production function marks a turn in production theory from pure theoretical deduction to empirical analyses of production, thus laying a solid foundation for the development of modern economics. However, it is not without defects. Some hypotheses of the equation are at odds with reality. For example, technical progress may have different impacts on different samples. In addition, in the study of production function, sample data are often collected in the light of time sequence. Different samples represent different times. However, technical progress is closely related to time. Thus, the conclusion is not valid if the impact of technical progress on productivity is not taken into account.

Due to the above defects, researchers made substantial modifications to the C–D function which rendered it more applicable. Its theoretical value and applicability were becoming more widely accepted. J. Tinbergen, R. M. Solow, E. Denison and Dale W. Jorgenson all made significant contributions in this aspect.

In 1942, J. Tinbergen, a Dutch economist, argued that a time exponent should be added to measure technical progress. Then the constant A in the C–D production function is replaced with a time-varying parameter A^t. The exponential form is: $A^t = A_0 e^{rt}$ (A_0, r are constant). Meanwhile, the input of capital and labor are marked with the time as in $K(t)$ and $L(t)$. The original C–D function is revised as follows:

$$y(t) = A_0 e^{rt} K(t)^\alpha L(t)^\beta \tag{1-3}$$

Equation (1-3) is Tinbergen's dynamic C–D production function. The new model changes the initial function, in which the relation between input of production factors and output should be measured on condition of unchanged technical level, which makes it possible to measure technological dynamism in production.

In 1957, Robert M. Solow introduced a technical coefficient into the production function, thus generating an explicit formulation of technical progress. He established the residual method for measuring technical progress. Based on the hypothesis of neutral technical progress, he further develops the well-known formula of growth rate:

$$\frac{\dot{y}}{y} = \frac{\dot{A}}{A} + \alpha \frac{\dot{K}}{K} + \beta \frac{\dot{L}}{L} \tag{1-4}$$

The formula suggests that the growth of output is dependent on the increase of input of capital and labor as well as technical progress.

Solow (1957) offered a unifying account of economic theories of production and proposed an econometric approach to production function. It was the first time that the factor of technical progress was considered in a model of economic growth. In quantitative studies, Solow considered the technical progress rate as the reason for the part of growth that cannot be explained through capital accumulation or increased labor. The number is later came to be called "growth residual" or "Solow residual". In his 1957 paper, Solow proposed a revised model of the C–D production function:

$$Y = A(t) K^\alpha L^\beta \tag{1-5}$$

There are two forms of $A(t)$:

$$A(t) = A_0 (1 + \lambda)^t \tag{1-6}$$

$$A(t) = A_0 e^{\gamma t} \tag{1-7}$$

In Equation (1-6), λ has explicit economic significance, representing the rate of technical progress, while γ in Equation (1-7) does not. However, if the rate of technical progress is extremely low, even when $\lambda \to 0$, on the condition that $\ln(1+\lambda) = \lambda$, it follows that:

$$\ln\left(A_0(1+\varphi)^t\right) = \ln A_0 + \ln(1+\varphi)^t = \ln A_0 + t\varphi \tag{1-8}$$

$$\ln\left(A_0 e^{\gamma t}\right) = \ln A_0 + t\varphi \tag{1-9}$$

Therefore, γ in Equation (1-7) can also be regarded as the rate of technical progress (in fact, in addition to technical progress, γ also represents other determinants, including policies, education, brand and so forth). A revised C–D production function is shown below:

$$Y = A_0(1+\varphi)^t K^\alpha L^\beta \tag{1-10}$$

$$Y = A_0 e^{\varphi t} K^\alpha L^\beta \tag{1-11}$$

Apart from the two models above, there are other revised forms of the C–D production function. Derivation is as follows: log the two sides of Equation (1-11) such that:

$$\ln Y = \ln A_0 + \varphi t + \alpha \ln K + \beta \ln L \tag{1-12}$$

Take the derivative of t at two sides of Equation (1-12) such that:

$$\frac{dY}{Ydt} = \varphi + \alpha \frac{dK}{Kdt} + \beta \frac{dL}{Ldt} \tag{1-13}$$

Because the time of the data is disperse, on condition that the time span is short, a difference equation can be used to approximate a differential equation:

$$\frac{\Delta Y}{Y\Delta t} = \varphi + \alpha \frac{\Delta K}{K\Delta t} + \beta \frac{\Delta L}{L\Delta t} \tag{1-14}$$

In Equation(1-14), $\dfrac{\Delta Y}{Y\Delta t}, \dfrac{\Delta K}{K\Delta t}, \dfrac{\Delta L}{L\Delta t}$ can be calculated with the observed value of samples. Then φ, α, β can be calculated by Multiple Linear Regression. The result may diverge greatly from that calculated with Equation (1-12). It is found that the data in reality are inconsistent with the result of the non-linear regression Equation (1-14) because the value of t is one year. The time span is so long that there might be considerable technical change, which may lead to inconsistent results. That is why there are limitations in partial differential equations.

Back to Equation (1-14): let $\dot{Y} = \dfrac{\Delta Y}{Y\Delta t}, \dot{K} = \dfrac{\Delta K}{K\Delta t}, \dot{L} = \dfrac{\Delta L}{L\Delta t}$. Solow's residual value growth equation can be transformed as:

$$\dot{Y} = \varphi + \alpha\dot{K} + \beta\dot{L} \tag{1-15}$$

In the Equation (1-15), $\dot{Y}, \dot{K}, \dot{L}$ represent the growth rate of output, the growth rate of capital input and the growth rate of labor input, respectively. α, β are elasticity of output to capital input and labor input; φ is the growth rate of TFP. The growth rate equation can be rewritten as $\varphi = \dot{Y} - \alpha\dot{K} - \beta\dot{L}$, denoting that TFP is the balance of the weighted linear combination of the growth rates of output, capital input and labor input. Solow calls it "growth residual"; it is also known as "Solow residual". Solow believes that growth residual is brought by technical progress.

The significance of Solow residual is that it expands the notion of the production function by introducing the production factor of technical progress into productivity analysis. A new model of TFP growth rate is thus established, which makes it possible to measure the relation between the output growth rate, TFP growth rate and input growth rate of various production factors. And the contribution of the input of production factors to economic growth can also be measured by the growth equation. To sum up the above theories, the notion of TFP suggests that the regional government should focus on quality rather than quantity in resource allocation. It becomes a practical test criterion for the effect of resource allocation. The technical progress that drives TFP consists of innovation in notion, institution, organization and technology, as well as specialization and production innovation.

1.3.4.2   *Pareto optimality as the theoretical parameter for effects of regional government resource allocation*

Pareto efficiency or Pareto optimality is an ideal state of allocation of resources, from which it is impossible to reallocate so as to make any one individual or preference criterion better off without making at least one individual or preference criterion worse off. A Pareto improvement is a change to a different allocation that makes at least one individual or preference criterion better off without making any other individual or preference criterion worse off, given a certain initial allocation of goods among a set of individuals. An allocation is defined as "Pareto efficient" or "Pareto optimal" when no further Pareto improvements can be made. There are three aspects of Pareto optimality: (a) efficiency in production, (b) efficiency in exchange and (c) efficiency in production and exchange. The required conditions for the three aspects are: (a) the marginal rate of substitution between any two products must be the same; (b) the marginal rate of technical substitution (MRTS) between any two factors must be the same; and (c) the marginal rate of substitution (MRS) between two products must equal the marginal rate of transformation (MRT) between them.

Pareto optimality measures effects of resource allocation from the perspective of efficiency and fairness from the perspective of social welfare. Hence, Pareto optimality seeks fairness in the sense of efficiency. However, the absolute Pareto optimality does not exist in reality. The prerequisite for Pareto optimality is a free market system and the identical and yet unchanged preference of each consumer. A free market system does not exist in reality. And every consumer has his own preference, which may change over time. Therefore, Pareto optimality is only a theoretical assumption. But it could be approached indefinitely through raising efficiency. In this sense, Pareto optimality is of vital significance in judging whether an economic institution or policy in a region is conducive to resource allocation. Take Pareto optimality of resource allocation without constraints as an example.

Assuming in one economy, the number of consumers is M; the number of resource types is K; the cost of the kth type of resource is C_k, such that the quantity of the kth type of resource allocated to the mth consumer is X_k^m ($m = 1, 2, \cdots, M, k = 1, 2, \cdots, K$), which is a decision variable. The utility of the mth consumer is U^m, expressed as $U^m = U^m\left(X_1^m, X_2^m, \cdots, X_K^m\right)$, such that the sufficient condition (second order condition) for Pareto optimality in resource allocation is: $\mathrm{d}^2 U^m < 0 (m = 1, 2, \cdots, M)$, and the necessary condition (first order condition) is: $\mathrm{d}U^i = \mathrm{d}U^j = 0 (i, j = 1, 2, \cdots, M)$, or:

$$\frac{\partial U^i}{\partial X_l^m} \Big/ \frac{\partial U^j}{\partial X_n^m} = C_l / C_n = -\frac{\mathrm{d}X_n}{\mathrm{d}X_l} = MRS_{X_l^i X_n^i}^i = MRS_{X_l^j X_n^j}^l \tag{1-16}$$

In Equation (1-16), $i, j = 1, 2, \cdots, M$, $i \neq j$, $l, n = 1, 2, \cdots, K$, $l \neq n$. It means that when the resource allocation reaches Pareto optimality, the marginal utilities of the same type of resource for different consumers are the same.

Pareto optimality represents the maximum fairness in resource allocation. It is an important theory for measuring the effect of regional resource allocation.

1.3.4.3   A comparative analysis of TFP in a region

Table 1.1 shows TFP and average annual growth rate of some major countries (1999–2006) according to Equation (1-16).

The average of TFP in major countries from 1999 to 2006 reveals that northern European countries like Norway and Sweden rank highest, while the ranks of countries in Europe and the US are above 20. Brazil, Russia and China are at the bottom. The TFP of China is only 1.194. It indicates that the cutting-edge technologies and mature institutions in European countries and the US play a critical role in boosting economic growth. Economic growth in China is merely driven by external expansion without much impact from technical progress. In terms of average annual growth rate, Hungary, Russia and Korea are the fastest, with rates over 5 percent. For most of the developed countries, the steady-state economy makes it difficult to spur economic growth, which largely depends on the speed of technical progress. Those that cannot achieve technical innovation

Table 1.1 TFP and average annual growth rate of some major countries (1999–2006)

Country/Year	1999	2000	2001	2002	2003	2004	2005	2006	Average	Average annual growth rate (%)
Norway	31.005	30.649	31.587	35.815	41.383	42.178	42.405	40.136	36.895	3.279
Sweden	30.422	26.361	24.820	27.149	33.833	37.060	35.524	35.131	31.287	1.815
England	28.821	26.947	25.861	27.010	30.808	33.754	34.074	33.874	30.144	2.040
US	28.429	28.507	29.078	30.663	30.817	30.469	29.806	29.846	29.702	0.610
France	28.377	23.518	22.514	24.062	29.781	32.406	31.522	31.010	27.899	1.116
Germany	24.756	21.369	21.629	24.079	29.297	32.534	32.442	31.698	27.225	3.138
Japan	28.343	29.362	25.692	25.297	27.010	28.351	26.995	24.477	26.941	-1.816
Netherlands	22.529	19.854	19.982	21.642	28.169	31.498	30.854	30.389	25.615	3.812
Italy	24.100	20.348	19.536	20.659	25.966	28.847	28.740	28.669	24.608	2.194
Canada	21.017	21.999	20.876	20.875	23.260	24.514	25.547	26.364	23.057	2.874
Australia	19.194	18.773	16.556	16.443	20.267	22.874	23.524	23.010	20.080	2.293
New Zealand	17.322	15.220	14.528	15.666	19.423	21.676	22.838	21.158	18.479	2.532
Portugal	12.915	11.155	11.161	12.345	16.240	18.284	18.680	19.222	15.000	5.096
Mexico	12.130	13.060	14.175	14.327	13.400	12.885	13.632	13.278	13.361	1.137
South Korea	9.768	9.914	10.118	10.790	11.496	12.162	13.725	14.649	11.578	5.196
Hungary	8.689	7.805	7.905	9.141	11.551	13.286	13.712	13.620	10.714	5.780
Brazil	3.030	3.660	3.364	3.188	3.659	4.204	3.792	3.628	3.566	2.280
Russian Federation	2.331	3.367	3.134	3.203	3.233	3.526	3.521	3.615	3.241	5.640
China	1.154	1.159	1.181	1.166	1.189	1.198	1.227	1.278	1.194	1.287

Source: Wu et al. Calculation of TFP in major countries around the world based on panel data [J]. *Mathematics in Practice and Theory* 2011(7): 11–28.

to extend their PPF (production-possibility frontier) would fail to maintain appropriate growth. This is why France, the US and Japan are at the bottom in the ranking of growth rate. The rate of Japan even goes below zero, to -1.816 percent. The growth rate of China is 1.287 percent, which is not a very high number. Judging from TFP over the years, the value is not stable. It seems to be related to the lack of government leading in institutional, organizational, notional and technical innovation. Therefore, an efficient resource allocation by the government may significantly improve TFP.

1.3.5 *Design of DRP based on regional government competition*

Regional government competition aims to raise TFP through optimizing regional resource allocation. Regional government competition is, in essence, the competition of GFL – the regional government's decision-making capabilities in resource allocation. The increasing amount of information makes it more difficult to make decisions. The previous "wading across the stream by feeling stones" approach becomes inappropriate in today's management, which calls forth a data-driven and scientific approach. The DRP (distribution requirement planning) provides such a theoretical framework for decision-making in regional administration.

1.3.5.1 *The rationale for DRP design*

The DRP of regional government aims at improving TFP. Therefore, how to raise TFP is the basic concern in the design of DRP. The increase of TFP can be driven by innovations in notion, institution, organization and technology. The four types of innovation have different orientations. For example, technological and organizational innovation is oriented towards enterprises and concerned with the allocation and management of operational resources. Institutional and notional innovation, on the other hand, is oriented towards government and concerned with the allocation and management of non-operational resources. Hence, regional government should conduct institutional and notional innovations and lead enterprises to make technological and organizational innovations as well so as to achieve rapid growth of TFP.

1.3.5.2 *The criteria for DRP design*

DRP is a systemic approach to regional resource allocation, which can be used to collect and process resource information inside and outside the region and to conduct targeted analysis and management over regional resources. The approach helps to achieve projected goals and benefits by optimizing resource allocation and enhancing regional administration. Therefore, the design of a DRP model should aim at improving the region's mode of administration, administration level, comprehensive capacities and economic benefits.

The evaluation standard refers to a series of principles and criteria which are used to judge whether a project is a success or not. Stakeholders refer to the individuals or organizations who are actively involved in the project. They are the individuals or organizations whose interests are positively or negatively impacted by the implementation of the project. Different stakeholders might have varied demands and expectations for the project, which might sometimes run against each other. Therefore, to achieve a successful project, one needs to weigh up all these demands and expectations and formulate an evaluation standard that is acceptable to all stakeholders.

The design of a DRP model should take into consideration the following four criteria. The first should be a more integrated management system. DRP provides a technical solution to the integration of regional administration. DRP is software that enables integrated management on material resources, capital, institutions, policies and information in a region. The application of the software extends across multiple sectors and even various regions. To achieve the projected goal, the basic requirement is that the software should take effect as expected. It is used to establish a database for decision-making and information sharing for the region. All the data that are used in DRP should be timely, accurate and effective, with an accuracy rate over 95 percent.

The second criterion should be a more rationalized operation flow. DRP is a solution for improving management efficiency. The prerequisite for DRP to take effect is that it should be used to manage the operating process in the region. The regional government should use DRP to conduct effective planning and regulation on every single link in the supply and demand chain of resource allocation. It reveals whether GFL of regional government has been brought into full play. Therefore, the application of DRP will bring a more rational administrative operation flow and thus ultimately achieve the following goals: (a) drastically enhanced regional competitiveness; (b) significantly improved regional administrative efficiency; (c) a regional administration that is more adaptive to the market change; and (iv) more effective GFL.

The third criterion is a more dynamic performance monitoring system. DRP contributes to the effectiveness of regional administration and decision-making. DRP offers rich information for regional administration. Whether the information could be utilized to promote the promptness and effectiveness of government decision-making is considered a criterion to evaluate the design of DRP. If government fails to utilize the data offered by DRP to establish a monitoring system on its performance, it means that DRP has not been adequately applied.

The fourth criterion is a continuous administrative improvement system. The establishment and application of DRP will eventually be reflected in the obvious improvement of regional administration. A comprehensive evaluation of regional government performance may be conducted in the light of regional evaluation criteria so as to determine the extent of improvement of regional administration. The real value of evaluation resides in setting up a mechanism for continuous self-assessment and administrative improvement.

The application of DRP will bring significant improvement and innovation in the following aspects: administrative methods, mechanisms and foundation, operating process, organizational structure, scale economy, input and output, profit, regional competitiveness and adaptability, regional labor force, regional image, scientific decision-making and information-based construction.

The application of DRP generates economic benefits by bringing improvement to the following areas: regional government's financial analysis, regional economic growth, market prediction, foresighted leading of enterprises, resource allocation, TFP promotion, pollution reduction, resource waste reduction, budget management enhancement, cost reduction of resource allocation, output quality improvement and regional influence extension.

The application of DRP enhances the overall assessing capabilities of regional government in economic growth rate, resident consumption level, resident income level, fixed asset investment, financial balance, import and export, unemployment rate and price level in the region. Government can thereby optimize resource allocation and upgrade the goals and benefits of regional administration.

1.3.5.3 *The framework for DRP design*

Internally, DRP integrates various types of resources for the region. It enables optimal planning and allocation for the effective utilization of resources. It also brings more transparent and automatic management through real time processing of resource information. Easy access to information of the region will enhance the adaptability of regional government.

Externally, DRP enables the exchange of information with economic entities outside the region via its network. A larger regional community can thereby be established through horizontal or vertical integration. DRP is used for internal integration of resources and external exchange of resource information, though the former is its major function. The system runs without limit of time and space and thus empowers government to exercise fast and effective administration.

In sum, DRP is an information-based system that links resources within and outside of the region. It helps prevent unwanted waste of management and resources. With fast access to proper information, administrators can make correct decisions. The system of DRP cannot be put into place without Internet and big data technologies.

Let us discuss the development of DRP based on big data. Big data is an Internet-based system of enormous and diversified data sets. It is a modern data processing application. Great value hides underneath data which may be of strategic significance to economic development, environmental protection, social management, scientific research and many other fields. Big data will play a significant role in regional economic development.

Regional government can establish a DRP system based on big data. By exploiting some crucial information hidden in the data within and outside the region, the government can better allocate resources, reduce waste, increase efficiency of economic activities, lower the cost of economic development, promote industrial upgrade and achieve sustainability. The DRP system therefore injects new driving forces into the economy.

In today's fast-changing information age, big data empower regional government to respond to the changing environment accordingly by processing massive amount of real time information, making accurate predictions and thus establishing a sophisticated warning system. Big data enhance the government's responding capabilities and transform the management from a static into a dynamic one.

Now let's come to the framework for DRP design. According to the strategic goals of regional government, DRP can be designed as illustrated in Figure 1.1. DRP provides a model of resource allocation for a relatively long period (e.g. three or five years). In this model, government is supposed to formulate strategic goals at the beginning of the period. In order to make the goals more scientific, rational, mobilizing and feasible, government should do the following: (a) conduct an analysis on macro-environments, e.g. current economic conditions, national policies and so on; (b) conduct a survey on society, people's lifestyles and the trend of technological development; (c) make a comparative analysis of regional advantages and disadvantages against comparable neighboring regions in the following aspects: humanities, social administration, city regulation, economic development, population, education, etc.; and (d) make an analysis of various types of resources owned by the region, including personnel resources, financial resources, material resources, land resources, energy and so on.

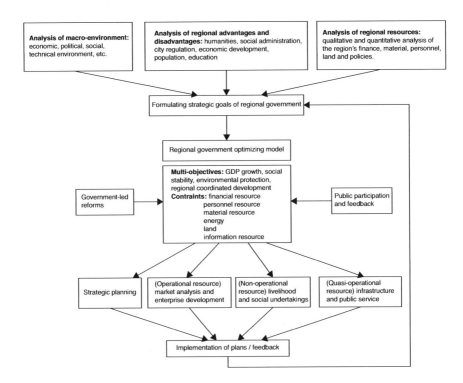

Figure 1.1 A DRP model for regional government resource allocation

After setting strategic goals, government exercises resource allocation in accordance with the regional government optimizing model. In this model, resource allocation is a multi-objective plan concerning a wide range of resources. The objectives include economic growth, employment, enterprise development, environmental protection, natural conditions, information resource, energy, land, policies, etc. In addition, public participation, support and opinions on resource acquisition should be taken into account to ensure democracy, rationality and fairness.

The regional government optimizing model can be further applied to map out the plan for "three categories of resource" and relevant measures. More specifically, the government drafts rules for enterprises, residents and regional government, which are entities in market competition, social affairs and regional competition, respectively. Government may revise strategic goals and plans according to the feedback in implementation.

1.3.5.4 *The optimization of regional government resource allocation (DRP) based on the linear programming approach*

Linear programming (LP) is an important approach in operational research. As one of the earliest approaches, it has developed quickly and generated sophisticated methods. It is a mathematical method that assists people in achieving scientific management. More specifically, linear programming is the mathematical theory and practice for the optimization of a linear objective function, subject to linear constraints. The method has been extensively applied to military operations, economic analysis, business management and engineering. It proves useful in achieving the best decision-making in the allocation of limited labor forces, materials and financial resources.

It usually takes three steps to construct a mathematical model to solve a problem in practice: (a) seek decision variables according to the elements that might affect the objective; (b) determine the objective function by the relation between the decision variables and the objective; and (c) determine the constraints over the decision variables by the conditions that the decision variables are subject to.

The mathematical model thus established has the following features. First, every model has several decision variables ($x1$, $x2$, $x3$, . . . , xn), in which n denotes the number of variables. Every decision variable represents one solution, and the value is usually not negative. Second, the objective function is the linear function of decision variables. It can be maximized or minimized depending on the specific issue, both of which can be called optimization. Third, the constraint is also the linear function of decision variables.

After a brief discussion of the linear programming approach, let's come to the parameters, model construction and case analysis. Parameters: $M \rightarrow$ the number of types of government tasks, e.g. the growth rate of GDP, national income level, employment, education, medical service, environmental protection, social stability, etc.; $N \rightarrow$ the number of types of resources, e.g. fiscal revenue, land, personnel, information, policies, etc.; $X_m \to$ the objective value of the mth task, e.g. maintaining 10 percent GDP growth, increase 8 percent of net national income; $\Upsilon_n \to$ the limit of the nth resource; $a_{mn} \to$ the quantity of the nth resource needed for the mth objective; $X_m^0 \to$ the minimum number for the mth objective; $p_m \to$ the value gained by the government through achieving the objective of m. $c_{mn} \to$ the cost of the nth resource to achieve the mth objective. Conditions: in the parameters above, $1 \le m \le M$, $1 \le n \le N$, the range of time should be the medium or long run plan of the government, e.g. annual budget or a five-year plan; the unit of all parameters is 1. Thus, all parameters could be calculated by elementary arithmetic.

Now let's construct a model in which the objective of each task is a decision variable:

$$\max f\left(X_1, X_2, \cdots, X_m\right) = \sum_{m=1}^{M} p_m X_m - \sum_{n=1}^{N}\sum_{m=1}^{M} c_{mn} a_{mn} X_m \tag{1-17}$$

$$s.t. \begin{cases} \sum_{m=1}^{M} a_{mn} X_m \le \Upsilon_n, 1 \le m \le M, 1 \le n \le N. \\ X_m \ge X_m^0 > 0, 1 \le m \le M. \end{cases} \tag{1-18}$$

Illustration of the model: $X_m (1 \le m \le M)$ is the decision variable; the rest is constant. What the model implies goes as follows: given the resource, price and cost needed for the objective of each mission, let us work out the value of the objective to maximize the benefit. Equation (1-17) represents the objective function for maximization of benefit. $\sum_{m=1}^{M} p_m X_m$ denotes the total value the government can gain by realizing the objectives of all the tasks. $\sum_{n=1}^{N}\sum_{m=1}^{M} c_{mn} a_{mn} X_m$ denotes the total cost after using all the resources to achieve the objectives. In Equation (1-18), $\sum_{m=1}^{M} a_{mn} X_m \le \Upsilon_n$ denotes the limited number of each resource to achieve the objectives. $X_m \ge X_m^0 > 0$ denotes the minimum objective value in each task. If the value is expected to be small, the equation above comes through transformation. Equations (1-17) and (1-18) generate the optimized objective value and the necessary resources of each task. Now let's construct a model in which each item of resource allocation is a decision variable:

$$\min f\left(a_{11}, a_{12}, \cdots, a_{mn}\right) = \sum_{n=1}^{N}\sum_{m=1}^{M} c_{mn} a_{mn} X_m \tag{1-19}$$

$$s.t. \begin{cases} \sum_{m=1}^{M} a_{mn} X_m = \Upsilon_n, \\ a_{mn} \ge 0, \\ 1 \le m \le M, 1 \le n \le N. \end{cases} \tag{1-20}$$

Illustration of the model: $a_{mn}(1 \le m \le M, 1 \le n \le N.)$ is the decision variable; the rest is constant. What the model implies goes as follows: provided the objective value of each task, the unit cost of each resource and the limit of resources, work out the consumption of each resource in each task to minimize the total cost of resources. In Equation (1-19), $\sum_{n=1}^{N}\sum_{m=1}^{M} c_{mn} a_{mn} X_m$ denotes the total cost of all resources paid for the projected goal. In Equation (1-20), $\sum_{m=1}^{M} a_{mn} X_m = Y_n$ denotes the limited number of each resource to fulfill the objective. Equations (1-19) and (1-20) generate the optimal arrangement of each resource in each task.

Calculation: the basic method to solve the linear programming question is the simplex method. To increase the speed of calculation, other methods are employed, such as the revised simplex method, the dual simplex method, the decomposition algorithm and various polynomial time algorithms. The above model can be solved when the value of each parameter is determined.

Now let's make a value analysis. Assume that the government sets two tasks, and there are two items of resources available. Now the value of related parameters are as follows: $p_1 = 9, p_2 = 12, c_{11} = 2.5, c_{12} = 2, c_{21} = 1.5, c_{22} = 1, a_{11} = 1, a_{12} = 2, a_{21} = 3, a_{22} = 4, Y_1 = 60, Y_2 = 80, X_1^0 = 10, X_2^0 = 10.$

In a model in which the objective of each task is a decision variable (X_1, X_2 are decision variables, and the rest is constant),apply the above numbers to Equations (1-17) and (1-18). A simplex method comes in the form:

$$X_1 = 20, \ X_2 = 10, \ \max f(X_1, X_2) = 85$$

That is: under the constraints of cost and resources mentioned above, let the objective of the first task be 20 and that of the second task be 10; the maximum benefit for the region is 85.

In a model in which each item of resource allocation is a decision variable ($a_{11}, a_{12}, a_{21}, a_{22}$ are decision variables, and the rest is constant), apply the above numbers to Equations (1-19) and (1-20). A simplex method comes in the form:

$$a_{11} = 0.3, a_{12} = 0.2, a_{21} = 0.9, a_{22} = 1.9, \ \min f(a_{11}, a_{12}, a_{21}, a_{22}) = 55.5$$

That is: let the first type of resource in the first task be 0.3 and the second type be 0.2. Let the first type of resource in the second task be 0.9 and the second type be 1.9. The minimum cost government pays is 55.5.

The case analysis above demonstrates that the regional government resource allocation model helps government to determine the objectives of various tasks and achieve minimum cost by proper resource allocation. Therefore, DRP is a vital tool for effective resource allocation (achieving regional economic growth). It provides an important rationale for a regional government to formulate sustainable policies and initiatives.

2 Three categories of resources

2.1 Theories of government resource allocation

2.1.1 *Marxist economics and resource allocation*

In Marxist economics, the theory of resource allocation mainly deals with the value distribution of resources and their categorization. The theory of labor value elaborates on the nature (quality and quantity), the representation and the operating law of value. It discusses the resource allocation model in a commodity economy from the perspectives of labor time, exchange of equal values and market demand. The theory of production focuses on surplus value of production. Surplus value production is the basic characteristic of capitalist commodity production. In fact, it explains the allocation of production factors. Whether the allocation is rational depends on whether it contributes to surplus value or profits. It is rational when it does and vice versa. The theory of circulation concerns individual capital circulation and social capital circulation. The discussion on capital flow in the individual capital circulation is actually a demonstration of rational allocation of capital factors. The discussion concerning social capital illustrates that allocation of social resources should be market-oriented so that production can be developed in an appropriate and coordinated manner, and resources can be properly utilized. The theory of distribution examines how surplus value is turned into profits and average profits, interests and land rent. Capital flows into sectors with high profit rates. Currency owners gain interests by lending while land owners earn rent by selling the use right. They emphasize efficiency in utilizing capital and land. Therefore, profits, interests and land rent are powerful economic leverages for resource allocation.

Although Marxist economics fails to explicitly discuss the issue of resource allocation as modern schools of western economics do, the theories proposed therein are indispensable parts of the overall resource allocation theory.

2.1.2 *Externality, public goods and government resource allocation*

The term "externality" was originally proposed by Alfred Marshall (1842–1924), one of the founders of neoclassical economics, in 1890. The term "external economy" occurred for the first time in his book *Principles of Economics* (1890).

In 1920s, Arthur Cecil Pigou (1877–1959), a student of Alfred Marshall's and a founder of public finance, further investigated the issue of externality in his famous book *The Economics of Welfare* (1920). Pigou accepted the notions of internal economy and external economy proposed by Marshall and established the theory of externality from the perspective of optimal social resource allocation and marginal analysis. Pigou maintained that in economic activities, if a factory causes some undesirable loss to other factories or the entire society, that is external diseconomy. When it occurs, the market cannot correct the impact. Thus, the government's interference is needed.

The analysis of externality goes as follows: (a) externality is produced by not only production activities but also consumption activities. For example, when production of one product is involved with positive externality, the output determined by the market would be too low and the price would be too high. The government would try to expand its supply. Otherwise, the government would reduce the supply; and (b) externality refers to the spillover return or cost of private consumption or production. That is, the externality drives resource allocation away from Pareto optimality in complete competition. "Public good" is the extreme case of externality. In his classic paper *The Pure Theory of Public Expenditure* (1954), Samuelson defined a public good, or as he called it in the paper, a "collective consumption good", as follows: "[goods] which all enjoy in common in the sense that each individual's consumption of such a good leads to no subtractions from any other individual's consumption of that good". This is the property that has become known as non-rivalry. In addition, a pure public good exhibits a second property called non-excludability: that is, it is impossible to exclude any individuals from consuming the good. Because, for a pure public good, the marginal cost of marginal consumption is zero, it is technically impossible or extremely costly to prevent any consumer from enjoying a public good. Therefore, the government should use the power commissioned by the public to provide public goods such as defense, security and public facilities. There are some quasi-public goods of different degrees of rivalry between public goods and rivalrous goods. This type of goods is often offered by government investment or by co-investment of government and private investors.

Generally speaking, if competition is not free, or there is externality, or there are public goods, or there is a lack of market, or information is limited, resources cannot be allocated effectively. Even if the economy is in complete competition, as long as there is externality or public goods, the resource allocation cannot reach Pareto optimality. In this case, the government needs some role to play in resource allocation. Because the market cannot effectively offer public goods and services to the society, government needs to use its authoritative power to regulate resource allocation so as to promote the efficiency of various social resources and factors.

2.1.3 Development economics and government resource allocation

Between the 1950s and 1970s, the first generation of development economists advocated that for government to dominate resource allocation through plans and planning guidance. In the 1950s, the government's plan was highly advocated, while the market price system was downgraded by structuralism. The development economists at this stage (1950–1975) believed that developing countries don't rely on the market price system. With a limited number of entrepreneurs, these countries need to forge ahead with major reforms, with government as the implementer. The theory of development economics at this stage is characterized by pessimism over external economy and optimism over internal economy. Based on observations on developing countries, they posit that the governments of these countries should achieve economic restructuring and growth by means of promoting capital accumulation, utilizing surplus labor reserve, exercising import substitution, deregulating foreign exchange and planning resource allocation.

The economic models which propose the above policies include the Rostovian take-off model, Ragnar Nurkse's "balanced growth" model, Rosenstein-Rodan and Mandelbaum's "theory of the big push" and Lewis's "Economic Development with Unlimited Supplies of Labour" model, all of which are centered on capital accumulation. They hold that capital accumulation ensures GDP growth, increase of per capita income in growing population and development. Some structuralists are more concerned with the rigidity of demand and supply, lagging indicators, shortage and surplus, systemic inflation and export disadvantages. They criticize the market price system and call for government intervention in resource allocation through planning.

Between the 1960s and the 1970s, attention was turned from tangible capital to human capital, thus generating doubts of and criticism on the theories of development economics. In the 1960s, people began to realize that labor plays a decisive role in development. A combination of good knowledge, good health and skills would also contribute to the increase of TFP. Despite the optimism of development economists over their theories, some developing countries, guided by their theories, were still unable to get rid of high unemployment, poverty and uneven distribution of income. To explain these phenomena, some began to criticize policies that brought bad consequences. For example, some public policies incur non-market failure, negligence over agriculture, low efficiency of state-owned enterprises, negative impacts of export substitution and deficit of international payment.

From the late 1960s to early 1970s, the defects of industrial planning and comprehensive planning became more prominent. Criticism was targeted towards government failures such as defects of planning, insufficient information, unexpected disorder of national economic activities, defects of institutions and deficiencies of public policies. In the 1990s, Paul R. Krugman criticized development economists for pushing their theories out of the mainstream of economics. In 1952, Arthur Lewis explained the practice of developing countries as follows: governments of the underdeveloped countries need to make efforts in establishing industrial centers, regulating foreign exchange, formulating laws concerning public service and economy, etc. Governments of developed countries, on the other hand, could have entrepreneurs do the job. In addition, developing countries need to rely on a system of civil servants, which is worse than that of developed countries, and with limited abilities, they are faced with too many tasks.

Since the 1980s, second-generation neoclassical development economists have advocated that government should play effective roles in remedying market failures and in correcting new market malfunctions. From 1975, second-generation development economists considered development economics as an applied science based on neoclassical economics. The focus shifted from macro-level modeling of the overall economy to micro-level modeling of production units and families. They emphasized human capital, considered technical progress as supplementing the Solow Model of capital accumulation and showed more interest in varied modes of development in different countries.

As for the relation between government and market, development economists now believe that it is not an "either/or" option in the mechanism of resource allocation. Government is an essential factor in the formulation of an economic system. It may substitute or supplement other institutional factors. Government should do the best it can in the domain where it may play a role. The challenge is how to gain the greatest benefits from government behaviors at the lowest cost. Government may function in the following aspects: dealing with market failure (incomplete information and high cost, incomplete market, turbulent externality, increase of marginal profits, multiple equilibriums and path dependence, transaction cost, etc.), providing public goods, reducing poverty, improving income distribution, building infrastructure, protecting environments and so on.

Now let's come to the transaction cost theory in institutional economics and resource allocation. Before the 1960s, under the influence of Pigou's traditions, economic theories generally hold that government's intervention should be employed to deal with externality, for example, imposing tax or giving subsidies on external causers. This tradition was later revised by Ronald Harry Coase (1910–2013), the 1991 Laureate of the Nobel Prize in Economics, in his paper "The problem of social cost" (1960), which proposed the formalized "Coase theorem", which suggests that well-defined property rights are the prerequisite for market transaction. Coase argues: (a) if property rights are well defined, and all transaction costs are zero, then efficiency of resource utilization is irrelevant to who owns the property; (b) if property rights are well defined, and all transaction costs are zero, then Pareto optimality (or economic efficiency) could be achieved.

It follows from the Coase theorem that we could use market transaction rather than legal procedures to solve external problems. In spite of some limitations, the Coase theorem is of vital significance because it tackles the problems of externality in resource allocation by clarifying the relationship between property rights and economic efficiency. That paper points out that on the condition that the transaction cost is positive, efficiencies of resource allocation will vary from one institution to another. Douglass C. North (1920–2015) neatly summarizes that when transaction cost is positive, institutions matter. This observation reflects the basic notion of institutional economics: institutional structures and change are important factors that affect economic efficiency and development.

2.2   Categories of allocation in the "dual role" theory of regional government

Theories in the west have conducted a great deal of discussion concerning the functions and the boundary of market and government in resource allocation. And the discussion has not been finalized. Some theories may overemphasize functions of the market and exclude the active role that the government can play. Some theories highlight the function of the government, which violates the law of the market. In mainstream western economics, the government's role in resource allocation often finds no theoretical rationale. However, there are more government behaviors involved in resource allocation in practice. Therefore, it is necessary to expand traditional economics to better account for government resource allocation. The role of government in resource allocation should be revisited.

In their book *Mezzoeconomics* (2015), Chen and Gu establish a theoretical framework that accounts for the relations between externality and internality, private goods and public goods, resource allocation and institutional defects and market failure and government failure. It is suggested that regional government is the object of research in mezzo-economics. Regional government competes against other regions while exercising macro-regulation over the region. It sustains regional growth through foresighted leading in fostering core competitiveness. It is in this sense that regional government plays the role of "quasi-state" and "quasi-enterprise". That latter role leads to the existence of dual competing entities in modern market economy – that is, enterprises and regional governments compete with their counterparts at different levels in the market so that the allocation of private goods and public goods as well as quasi-public goods will be optimized. The mezzo-economic theory offers a better perspective on the issues of externality, internality, government failure and market failure.

2.2.1   *The dual-entity theory of market competition*

Let us begin by discussing the defects of market theories in traditional western economics. Competition, price, supply and demand are factors that determine how the market works. The relations between them are issues that will continue to be discussed in the market theory of micro-economics. Traditional western economics posits that the competition structure of the market is the exogenous variable that determines prices, whereas supply and demand are endogenous variables. The objective of market equilibrium is price equilibrium. At the price equilibrium point, all economic entities can achieve maximum profit or utility. In different structures of market competition, models that determine the price equilibrium point vary, and so do the ways of seeking excess profit. In a completely competitive market, the only way to seek excess profit in a short period is to lower production cost. In a monopoly market structure, the key to gaining excess profit is to acquire the "monopoly power".

Under the condition of complete competition, supply and demand are without constraint. Curves of supply and demand fluctuate freely. The reach of market equilibrium price is not affected by exogenous variables, only subject to the influence of "complete competition". Hence, "complete competition" drives all enterprises and consumers to accept the equilibrium price. But they cannot influence or determine the price. The price, therefore, indicates the upper limit of an enterprise's marginal cost. The enterprise that cannot produce at or lower than the marginal cost will be excluded by the market and eventually eliminated in the "complete competition".

When the competition is constrained, monopoly occurs. From monopolistic competition, oligopoly, to complete monopoly, curves of supply and demand are increasingly "controlled". In this case, price is no longer determined by the free flow of supply and demand curves but maneuvered by monopolistic power. Those enterprises with monopoly power will "manipulate" supply and demand for excess profit. In a monopolistic competition market, monopoly power comes from product differentiations. Some enterprises rely on product or service differentiations to affect consumers' preference. They are empowered to move the demand curve to a certain extent over a certain time span. They have the ability to determine the market price, thus gaining excess profit. In a monopolistic competition market, a few enterprises manipulate the supply curve via conspiracy, thus affecting the price and gaining excess profit. In this case, the key is conspiring relations between the enterprises concerned. However, the process of conspiracy is a complicated game. In a market of complete monopoly, a certain product is provided by only one enterprise, who possesses the greatest monopoly power. It can manipulate supply and demand at will, thus controlling the price for excess profit.

The above analysis offers a splendid theoretical landscape: under the condition of complete competition, all parties in the market gain maximum benefits or psychological utilities; under the condition of monopoly, the key to gaining excess profit is monopoly power. However, the most obvious defect of this theory is that it considers the enterprise as the only competing entity in the market. The government is overshadowed as merely the exogenous variable rather than the competing entity that affects the market. The government does not enter the market and does not participate in market competition. This assumption oversimplifies matters in reality. In fact, the government is not a type of force that stands outside the market but rather is one involved in market competition. That is, competition takes place between enterprises and between regional governments. In fact, the success of China's economic model is the result of two-layered competition in the market. It is therefore necessary to revisit market competition theory.

It is now time to discuss the dual-entity theory for two-layered market competition, which suggests that there are two types of competing entities that do not compete with one another: enterprises and regional governments. Competing relationships only occur between enterprises and between regional governments, but not between enterprises and regional governments. The competition between enterprises follows the law of market economy, whereas that between regional governments follows the law of super-economy. Enterprises compete for economic benefits, the pursuit of which is constrained by the law of economy; this has been well explored in traditional western economics. Then, according to the super law of economy, the ultimate goal of regional government competition is more than just economic benefits. The multi-objective competition at this level is not merely subject to the law of economy. It is a new subject that deserves serious investigation.

Regarding enterprise-level market competition, its modes and degrees are closely related to market types. Under the condition of complete competition, there are plentiful economic entities in small scales. Thus, they are not in a position to affect the supply–demand relationship through buying and selling, nor can they affect the market price. Every one of them is a passive recipient of the market price. Meanwhile, market products are the same quality – products do not vary from one producer to another. Because a product of any individual seller is the same as that of other competitors, there is no way to manipulate the price. Various types of resources circulate freely without constraints in a market of complete competition. Labor also circulates without obstacles across regions, sectors, industries and enterprises. Any owner of production factors cannot monopolize input of factors. New capital flows into the market freely and the existent capital can withdraw from the market without difficulty. Market information is complete and balanced. That means both enterprises and residents can gain complete market information without deceit. As a result, competition between enterprises is chiefly realized through reduction of cost. In the long run, enterprises can only gain average profit rather than surplus profit. The market is the most effective when the enterprise is in the long-term equilibrium. However, this kind of market with complete competition is so idealized that non-differential products will not be able to meet diversified demands of consumers. Therefore, a market of complete competition is an idealized proposition and can only serve as a frame of reference for actual market analysis.

A monopolistic market is a market structure in which only one enterprise offers all products and services to the market in one industry. The products cannot be substituted by other products. There are barriers for other enterprises to enter such an industry. Monopoly occurs for several reasons. First, material and technical conditions are the major reason why only a few or one enterprise is present in an industry. Second, some man-made or legal factors constitute entry barriers of an industry. Finally, some enterprises possess scarce resources due to their geographical advantages. Monopolistic enterprises gain long-term excess profit. Monopoly leads to poor output, high market price and low efficiency of resource allocation. Therefore, governments should adopt anti-monopoly policies.

Numerous consumers and enterprises exist in a monopolistic competition market. Manufacturers sell products that are differentiated from one another but are substitutable to a great extent. Thus, competition and monopoly co-exist in the market. In the long run, enterprises can enter or exit an industry freely. In the short run, however, enterprises of monopolistic competition can only adjust the variable input of production factors, and there is no enterprise that enters or exits the industry. The economic efficiency of a monopolistic competition market is intermediate between that of complete competition market and that of a non-monopolistic competition market. It is considered to be the market type that is most conducive to technical progress. In a complete competition market, there is no protection over technical innovation, and thus there is no motivation. In a monopolistic market, on the other hand, there is no competition and thus no pressure for technical innovation. In a monopolistic competition market, there is protection over technical innovation, e.g. property rights, and there are products of the same kind competing with each other in the market, producing external pressure for innovation. Therefore, enterprises of monopolistic competition are believed to be the major driving force for innovation.

In an oligopolistic market, a market or industry is dominated by a small number of sellers. Means of competition are varied and the market price is relatively stable. The greatest difficulty facing an oligopolistic enterprise is that it does not know how its competitors may react when making decisions. Generally speaking, in an oligopolistic market, the market price is higher than marginal cost and the minimum average cost. Hence, an oligopolistic enterprise is lacking in the efficiency of promoting output and technology. However, due to the fact that there is competition in an oligopolistic market, and it is fierce sometimes, the efficiency is higher than a monopolistic market. On the other hand, in an oligopolistic market, products are differentiated to meet various preferences of consumers. Moreover, due to its large scale, an oligopolistic enterprise is in a better position to use advanced technologies. Fierce competition will speed up production and technical innovation. Therefore, a certain degree of efficiency can be found in oligopoly. In many countries, people attempt to resolve the low efficiency of oligopoly to encourage its competition.

Now let's turn to market competition at the level of regional government. Competition is an essential attribute of market economy. Competition between regional governments is also based on market economy. Regional government takes on a "dual role" in a country or a region of market economy. Its dual role determines the dual-entity competition mechanism in the market system.

Market competition at the level of regional government occurs between regional governments. Competition should be prevented between regional governments and enterprises. In other words, the competition between enterprises and that between regional governments are at two levels. There are no cross-cut competitive relations, so that regional government will not use its power to seize market resources which should have gone to enterprises. The independent operation of enterprise competition should be maintained at the micro level and full play should be given to the market mechanism. In this regard, there exists no essential conflict between the government positioning advocated by mezzo-economists and that by micro-economists, for both respect the free competition between enterprises and oppose any damages to enterprise competition by government.

As one of the competition entities, regional government is required to have the following features. First, a regional government is a formal organization that has a name, governance framework, rules and regulations. It is established in accordance with the principles and procedures prescribed by national laws and regulations. Its functions and their fulfillment must conform to national laws and regulations.

Second, regional government is a social organization under the condition of market economy. Different from macro-level government that purely performs macro-level administration and regulation, regional government has a dual identity of "quasi-enterprise" and "quasi-state", which gives it the dual attributes of the economic nature of enterprises and the public welfare nature of government. As one of the regional competitors, regional government requires a primary focus on their "quasi-enterprise" role, i.e. their economic nature. As a "quasi-enterprise", regional government will center on regional economic activities, implement all-round economic accounting and pursue and commit itself to the continuous enhancement of regional economic benefits. The pursuit of regional economic benefits is the major motive and purpose for the competition between regional governments.

Third, regional government with "dual role" characteristics is administratively subordinate to its higher-level institution and enjoys some independence in legal and economic affairs within its region as a unit to own independent property rights of clear-cut boundaries. Regional government has full capacity for economic conduct and independent regional economic interests; implements independent economic accounting within an administrative region; makes its own decisions; and exercises autonomy, self-administration, self-discipline, self-reliance, self-restraint, self-motivation, self-transformation, self-accumulation and self-development. As a whole, it is fully independent externally and socially, which means that it independently exercises administrative powers and assumes administrative obligations and responsibilities according to law. In economic interactions, regional government should water down the awareness of administrative levels and subordinate relations so as to be fully equal in their economic standing.

As a competitor, regional government has diversified goals, such as maintaining stability, increasing employment, promoting growth, reducing inflation, seeking regional financial revenues, pursuing departmental interests and maximizing the political and economic interests of government officials.

Certainly, a competitor faces constraints: competition is not unconditional and a competitor is fettered by many constraints in competition. Objective constraints include location of jurisdiction; political, economic and cultural foundations; rules and regulations of higher governments, etc. Subjective constraints include the preferences of voters and the revelation thereof. Preferences and revelation of competitors indicate that different competitors have different subjective values for one and the same public product, thereby forming their different preferences for different public products.

In terms of preferences, there exists the problem of information asymmetry. On the one hand, not everyone is willing to reveal their genuine preferences, and there is a possibility of purposeful concealment of preference information; on the other hand, the revelation of preferences may be through an entrusted agent, who may distort the revelation. Cognitive pattern and learning of competitors show that cognition is the intangible construction of reality based on the perceptions that arise in the mind. It operates almost imperceptibly in the way of thinking to help people explain reality.

Meanwhile, cognition is restrained by culture to some extent. Therefore, people from different cultures make different explanations of reality. That is to say, human knowledge is determined by social experience: one competitor may understand the same reality in a way different from another competitor with different experiences. So, the performance of functions by regional governments and the pursuit of personal interests by competitors are accompanied by a series of cognitions or perceptions of their own environment. This is why the economic competition of regional governments itself may be deemed as a dynamic process of spurring participants to continuously learn and change their mode of cognition.

The objects of competition between regional governments are the targets of such competition through the market. Under the conditions of market economy, the objects of competition are the tangible and intangible resources in a region. The former includes material resources (land, mines and forests), human resources and financial resources; the latter includes regional cultural quality, policy system, supporting measures, industrial distribution, state of development, status of scientific and technological development and the management capability of regional government. Because of the natural attributes of tangible resources, competition between regional governments should be more reflected in intangible resources; these not only are more flexible and creative in market value but also enable the competition between regional governments to get rid of the fetters of natural resources, ensure fairness to some extent and facilitate the innovation spirit and capability of regional governments.

The purpose of competition between enterprises is the maximization of profits, and that of competition between regional governments is the optimal allocation of regional resources and the continuous enhancement of the efficiency and revenues of regional economy. The purpose of competition between regional governments provides them with the initiative in developing regional economy, limits the scope of competition to specific regions and intensifies the primary task of regional governments, which is to focus on the overall regional interests and achieve the balanced development of regional economy.

In fact, the purpose of competition is determined by the "quasi-enterprise" characteristic of regional government, but the other identity of regional government, the quasi-state role, requires regional government to allow for the administrative obligations stemming from higher-level government in the national governance hierarchy rather than focusing only on economic interests in the same way as enterprises. Therefore, the final establishment of the competition objectives of regional government actually involves the setting of indexes for its performance appraisal. How its performance should be evaluated plays an important role in guiding the conduct of regional government and its final achievement of the purpose. So, the government at a level higher than regional government must follow market laws, make good use of market competition mechanisms and objectively draw up the plan for evaluation of the performance of regional government from a broader perspective. Only by doing so is it possible for competition between regional governments to develop in an orderly manner and meet the goal of facilitating the overall allocation of resources.

Micro-economics discusses the different forms of competition under different market types, e.g. cost competition, product differentiation competition and the balance of power between several large oligopolistic enterprises except for consumers. What lies behind these forms of competition is the contest of enterprises in technical and human resources, financial strength, market understanding, innovation capabilities and management level.

In their capacity as "quasi-enterprise", regional government also implements financial budget control, which is similar to the management of enterprise costs, and aims at the highest revenues at the lowest cost. An enterprise uses different forms of competition when confronted with different types of market. Likewise, regional government adopts corresponding guiding means under the general trend and follows the status quo of the market and enterprises to achieve the growth of regional economic interests and carry out the competition with different regional governments. Under the precondition of enhancing tax utilization efficiency, everything provided by regional government for enterprises – including good technical services, talent services, fund services, cultural atmosphere, innovation support, policy guidance and infrastructure – and all the efforts they make to break the obstacles against market competition will become the major aspects of competition between regional governments. The entire competition shall be based on the highly efficient use of the financial budget.

Some discussions should be conducted concerning the relation between the two-layered competition types in the dual-entity system. Comparison is first to be made of inter-enterprise competition and the economic competition between regional governments.

The purpose of competition is to obtain the objects that are supposed to meet common needs. In other words, competition is the result of needs, without which competition will not be generated. For both enterprises and regional governments, the original drive of competition is to satisfy "needs". Inter-enterprise competition differs from the economic competition between regional governments in types, process, entities, objectives, types of market, types of products and institutional arrangement, as shown in Table 2.1.

Although market competition can be analogous to the economic competition between regional governments to a great extent, the two types differ considerably in many ways, for example, in objective functions, constraint conditions and relevant variants of the competitors. The starting point of both is the maximization of interests, but for enterprises, interests include "profits" only, while for regional governments, interests include both economic benefits and political benefits. For regional government, the means of competition is to provide public

Table 2.1 Comparison of inter-enterprise competition and the economic competition between regional governments

Items	*Enterprises*	*Regional governments*
Competition process	Economic process	Political process
Types of market	Four types of market	Similar to monopolistic competition and oligopolistic market
Types of competition	Competition of products and cost	Competition of resources and institution
Market players	Entrepreneurs	Regional governments
Goals of competition	Maximization of profits	Multiple goals including maximization of regional revenues
Types of products	General products and services	Formal institution
Failures of competition	Market monopoly	Power monopoly (centralized power)
Institutional arrangement	Anti-monopoly, upholding market competition	Anti-power centralization, upholding institutional competition

products, and the mode of action is to use illiquid economic elements to boost or constrain liquid economic elements. The economic competition between regional governments propels them to provide better regional public products and services – e.g. building good infrastructure for transport, communications and energy, simplifying administrative formalities, enhancing administrative efficiency and safeguarding the economic order. That means that regional governments need to continuously increase the input of illiquid elements to attract the inflow of scarce elements, such as funds, technology, talents and information; enable enterprises to take part in economic competition at lower business cost; intensify the industrial concentration and upgrading within the region; and promote the prioritized development of regional economy. Meanwhile, the excessive and even vicious competition between regional governments will also cause regional protectionism and the use of administrative power to restrict the outflow of economic elements. Therefore, the rationale for the economic competition between regional governments has its distinctive characteristics.

The dual-entity competition is a two-level competition system consisting of competition between enterprises and that between regional governments. The two systems are mutually independent and yet related to jointly constitute a dual-entity competition system in market economy.

First, enterprise competition and regional government competition are mutually independent double-loop operational systems. The former takes place only between enterprises, in which case government may only function as the maintainer of market competition environment and its fairness through policy-making, institutional arrangement and environment, instead of being an equal subject like enterprises to get involved in enterprise competition or directly intervening in the micro-economic affairs of enterprises. The latter unfolds only between regional governments, which are market players engaged in equal competition to compete in the capability of allocating regional resources and the created efficiency and benefits of regional economy. With the basis of respecting market competition laws, it will not incorporate inter-enterprise competition into the system. Thus, they are competition systems operating at two levels, independently of each other.

Second, the competition system of regional governments is based on the competition system of enterprises and plays the role of maintaining and guiding the latter. Enterprise competition is the fundamental attribute of market economy and a major factor for market economy to become revitalized. An economy without enterprise competition cannot be called a market economy, so enterprise-level competition is the foundation for market competition. The system of competition between regional governments also has as its basis the competition between enterprises within the region and centers around services for it. Without inter-enterprise competition, the competition between regional governments will evolve into a power struggle and be completely devoid of the basic attributes of a market economy. It follows that under the market economy system there is bound to exist enterprise-level competition, which in turn drives the competition between regional governments. All this stems from the operation of market mechanisms. Obviously, the competition between regional governments highlights "foresighted leading" in such aspects as institution, policy-making, environment creation and competition purposes. Therefore, the competition between regional governments takes place on a level higher than inter-enterprise competition, playing definitive roles in guiding and helping the latter. The two are not completely separate or cross-relations but form a close connection of mutual underpinning and influence on the basis of the "foresighted leading" mechanism of the former. Instead, they are two independent competition systems of seamless connection, which signifies that the "boundary delimitation" between them has become a crucial issue for successfully handling the two systems.

2.2.2   *The dual role theory of regional government*

The conceptualization of dual-entity in market competition originates from the "dual role" theory of regional government. The dual role theory suggests that regional government plays the quasi-state role, representing the national government and conducting macro-level administration and regulation of local economy within the region; it also plays the quasi-enterprise role, representing non-governmental social entities in the region in allocating local resources, contending for the support of higher-level government and competing with other regional governments through institutional, organizational, technological and notional innovations to maximize local economic benefits.

Regional government plays the dual role in the market. As a participant, its direct participation in economic activities or its indirect participation in non-governmental organization have played a significant role in national economic development, for which ample effective evidence can be found over the past decades. As a regional policy maker and executor, it directly affects the competition pattern and development ecology of some industries. As the reform for fiscal decentralization goes deeper, regional government is now more than ever pursuing its own benefit maximization as independent economic entities. There has been an obvious tendency toward "enterprise-like government". While representing the central government in macro-level administration and regulation of local economy, regional government represents local non-governmental entities in implementing the decisions of the central government and seeking its support to maximize local economic interests. That has given rise to the multi-dimensional roles of regional government, i.e. as an agent of higher-level government, as a representative of the interests of regional NGOs, as an administrator within its jurisdiction, as a provider of public goods, and finally as an economic organizer in its own right to seek maximized interests. The multi-dimensional status creates different target functions and constraint conditions for regional government.

Finally, let's try to define the three categories of resources that are to be allocated by regional government. Maintaining stability, fostering development and tackling contingencies are the three critical tasks facing countries across the globe. To the end of fostering development, government must perform its functions in economic growth, urban construction and social welfare. In economic terms, the performance of the functions in these three areas is explicitly manifested in how the government aligns its policies with the categorization and allocation of tangible and intangible resources, including resources that are already at the country's disposal and resources that are potentially up for grabs.

Category A: resources that are pertinent to social welfare, referred to as "non-operational resources" in a market economy. Resources in this category exist mainly in the form of social public goods, which cover a wide range of dimensions, including social security, culture, science and technology, history, geography, environment, images, spirit, ideas, emergency response, safety, assistance and other social needs. Policies and principles for the allocation of resources in this category can be encapsulated with the following words – "providing social security, guaranteeing basic needs, ensuring equity and fairness and striving for improvements".

Category B: resources that are pertinent to economic growth, referred to as "operational resources" in a market economy. Such resources exist mainly in the form of industrial resources, including resources in the primary, secondary and tertiary industries. Given the differences in economic, geographic and natural conditions, countries might vary greatly in the level of development in these three types of industries, although success stories are often recorded in countries that have opted to refine the primary industry, optimize the secondary industry and expedite the tertiary industry. Policies and principles for the allocation of resources in this category can be summed up as follows: "planning and guiding; supporting and adjusting; regulating and managing".

Category C: resources that are pertinent to urban construction, referred to as "quasi-operational resources" in a market economy. Such resources exist mainly in the form of urban resources, including public service systems (for keeping national economic and social activities running on a day-to-day basis) and software and hardware infrastructure (for providing public services necessary for productive and living activities). Specific examples include public utilities, transportation, postal and telecommunication services, power and water supply, gardening and greening, project development, education, science and technology, culture, sports, press and publication, radio and cable broadcasting, etc. Such resources are deemed as "quasi-operational resources" in that they can be developed and managed by the government, in which case they are non-operational and not for profit, or placed into the invisible hand of the market, in which case they are operational resources and for commercial purposes. Whether they are developed and operated by the government or by the market can be determined by these three key factors: the government's fiscal standing, market demand and the level of public acceptability.

2.3   Operational resources

2.3.1   *Implications of operational resources*

Resources that are associated with economic development are called operational resources in market economy, and the major type is industrial resources. Different regions may choose to orient towards one of the three categories of industry according to their special economic, geographic and natural conditions. Admittedly, there are cases in which the first and second sectors develop in one region along with prosperity in the third sector, including logistics, exhibition, financial service, tourism, agent service, retail sales, etc. It is another way of indicating goods, industries and their matching services. Therefore, operational resources should cover three aspects: (a) products or goods; (b) sector or industry (industrial chains); (c) facilities and institutions related to those products or sectors. Allocation of this type of resources can be optimized via market mechanisms, that is, through the operation of enterprises, hence the term "operational resource".

In the west, institutions that manage operational resources are mainly commercial businesses. In China, such institutions and agencies include those that administer development and reform, statistics and commodity price; public finance, taxation, commerce and industrial and commercial administration; industry, transportation, security, energy and tobacco; science and technology, information, communications and property rights; business, customs, maritime affairs, ports, postal service, quality inspection, foreign affairs and tourism; auditing, land administration and food and drug administration, etc. Government organizations administering operational resources may vary in different countries, but their policies for the allocation of such resources focus on how to use them to invigorate economy through planning and guidance, support and regulation, and supervision and administration, which is well accepted now.

For example, consumer goods and production materials as well as such services as general telecommunications and transportation can all be gained through market choices on the part of enterprises, families and individuals, which suggests that those goods and service providers have to survive through market competition. It is through this competition mechanism that the market drives the optimal allocation of operational resources, thus maximizing utility for consumers and profits for enterprises.

The household appliance industry is a typical example of how operational resources are allocated through market mechanism. Household appliance manufacturers continuously press ahead with technical innovation and control their costs in order to gain competitive advantages and greater market share. The industry also spurs other industries like artificial intelligence and environmental protection, which trigger another round of reform in business concepts, technologies and business modes. These examples show that only when operational resources are allocated by the market can their potential be fully unleashed and more value created.

2.3.2 *Principles for operational resource allocation*

The competitive nature of operational resources suggests that the resources should be allocated in accordance with market rules. The market offers or allocates the resources with a certain price, ensuring that people will make decisions on production and product use in consideration of cost and benefit. The allocation of competitive resources is left to the market to increase economic efficiency. Exclusiveness of operational resources means that enterprises can gain the benefits from the resources and the market is willing to offer them. In sum, operational resources such as commodities, industries and their related service sectors should be allocated and managed in conformity with the market mechanism and laws.

Operational resources belong to private goods rather than public ones, so regional government should not interfere in their operation. Rather, government should exercise regulation on operational resources in the region by means of capitalization, letting the market, society and various types of investors inside and outside the region operate them. The resources should be invested in accordance with market demand, social supply and trend of global economic development. What government should do is to optimize the market structure, promote comprehensive development of a market-oriented system and prevent market turbulence in light of predictions.

Operational resources should be allocated by the market. Hence, government should follow market rules. In so doing, government needs to formulate some basic principles or policies that conform to the market rules and specify what type of policy should be made, e.g. policies of deregulation, supportive policies, anti-monopoly policies, emergency-relief policies, etc. All of these policies will combine to form a policy ecology in line with the market rules.

There are three points that regional government should accomplish in allocating operational resources: it should (a) plan and lead the industry; (b) support and regulate the market and enterprises as a whole; and (c) exercise supervision and management over the region and local markets.

2.3.3 *Policy support for operational resource allocation*

Regional government should make industrial policies that plan and guide the use of operational resources. For example, in 2013, the CPC Central Committee pointed out that government should forge ahead with the reform of the economic system and make the market the decisive factor in resource allocation. More specifically, government should adhere to and improve the basic economic system; speed up the improvement of the modern market system, macro-control system and an open economic system; and accelerate the transformation of economic development modes and the construction of an innovative country. As for the market allocation of operational resources, government should take a non-intervention policy.

Another case in point is that in 2005, the Shunde District government proposed the "Triple-Three Strategy", namely three categories of industry (the coordinated development of the primary industry, the secondary and the tertiary industry), three pillar lines (no less than three pillar lines to be supported within each category of industry) and three leading enterprises (within each pillar line of industry, no less than three locomotive enterprises to be nurtured). The Shunde District government was in a position to support and encourage the development of some industries. When the industries were adjusted back onto the right track, the government began to take a non-intervention policy. This strategy helped Shunde District to become one of the most economically developed regions in China.

For the market and enterprises as a whole, regional government should not impose direct intervention but rather give full play to its role of support and regulation through policy-making. Take risk-management policies, for example. A case in point is the US government's response to the 2008 financial crisis. To deal with the crisis, the Federal Reserve and the US Treasury issued a series of policies rarely seen in history. The Federal Reserve implemented seven new liquidity management measures to adjust the discount window loan policy and offered bailouts to financial institutions. The US Treasury Department implemented a fiscal stimulus package of US $150 billion in January 2008 and took over FreddieMac and FannieMae in July 2008. In October 2008, it launched the largest ever financial rescue plan of US $700 billion. Another example is the ownership reform of state-owned enterprises in China. The carriers of the existing assets were transformed into ones which could better utilize the capital market. The carriers were restructured into enterprises of public–private partnership, stock-holding, joint venture and cooperation, and then sold to private investors at auction. In this way, they became carriers of operational projects in the form of sole proprietorship. As for some new operational projects, which were the carriers of the incremental assets, the government paved the way for their development according to regional plans. When there was a temporary shortage of capital or investors, the government offered loans to establish a governmental enterprise. Then the enterprise would be restructured in due course to prevent the incremental assets from being managed in the system of state-ownership.

The supervision and management of regional government over enterprises and local markets is also a vital link in the policy support of operational resource allocation. The US government, more often than not, issues anti-monopoly policies to ensure that resources are allocated under market rules. For example, the *Sherman Antitrust Act* in 1890, *Federal Trade Commission Act* in 1914 and *Clayton Antitrust Act* also in 1914 all prohibit monopoly agreements and behaviors and curb market centralization and enterprise mergers for the purpose of protecting consumer rights and interests and forbidding unfair competition.

2.4 Non-operational resources

2.4.1 *Implications of non-operational resources*

Resources that are associated with public livelihood are called non-operational resources in market economy and cover social welfare and public goods in the following fields: economy, culture, science and technology, history, geography, environment, public images, notions, emergency treatment, security, relief and other social needs. In the west, responsible agencies are chiefly social organizations. In China, however, non-operational resources fall under the administration of governmental institutions involving the following areas: public finance, auditing, authorized strength, literature and history, counseling, documentation, civil affairs, social security, poverty relief, woman and child affairs, DPF (Disabled Persons Federation), Red Cross, ethnic affairs, religion, overseas Chinese affairs; ecology, earthquake, meteorology; and emergency, safety, public security, jurisdiction, supervision, firefighting, armed police, border defense, coast defense and anti-smuggling. Countries may have different names for organizations in charge of these affairs, but they allocate resources basically on the same principle of "social provision, general underpinning, fairness and justice, and effective promotion", which is also generally accepted.

2.4.2 *Principles for non-operational resource allocation*

As for non-operational resources which go beyond the market, it is government's responsibility to manage their allocation in accordance with the guideline of "general underpinning, fairness and justice, and effective growth". That is why fiscal revenues, which come from the people and serve the people, should weaken its constructive function and strengthen its public welfare nature.

The principle for non-operational resource allocation is to guarantee the provision of "social public goods", viz. to enforce the principle of "livelihood underpinning, fairness and justice, and social welfare". Due to their non-exclusive and non-competitive nature, social public goods cannot be exchanged in the market according to the basic principle of "whoever produces gains". Enterprises, whose main task is to seek maximum profits, can hardly be motivated because they cannot gain market recognition by offering social public goods. These goods, however, are relevant to livelihood and public interests. They are of great strategic significance to the whole society and the national economy. Therefore, the allocation of non-operational resources must be done by government. In other words, government is responsible for providing free public goods or services via public production or provision.

In regard to non-operational resource allocation, government needs to formulate a series of laws, regulations, mandates and plans to form a policy ecology that is oriented toward public interests. The policies should aim at addressing public issues, reaching public goals, achieving public interests and guiding behaviors of related organizations and individuals. Government should ensure fairness, social stability and social security. The most fundamental policies should cover public goods investment, transfer payment, pricing of public goods, etc. Policies concerning public goods investment stipulate that government should invest in public infrastructure and public services, providing financial support to ensure their operation. Policies concerning transfer payment stipulate that monetized investment should be made in projects of social safety and social welfare through social security and financial subsidies. Government should also adopt policies of tax reduction to ensure social stability and basic welfare in case of crises. These policies should function in the same way as the national government functions by its nature. Policies of public goods pricing vary depending on the purposes of their provision. They may also be influenced by their categories, operations and management. For example, in the fields of national defense, diplomacy, jurisdiction, public security, administration and environmental protection, government should adopt the zero-price policy so as to provide pure public goods and cover all their cost with tax revenues.

2.4.3 Policy support for non-operational resource allocation

As indicated above, the making of policies concerning non-operational resource allocation should follow the guiding principle of "general underpinning, fairness and justice, and effective growth", with focuses on distributing social resources, regulating social behaviors, addressing social issues and boosting social development.

The principle of fairness, justice and effective growth calls for GFL in social resource allocation from the perspective of long-term development. For example, government should make strategic planning for land resources to ensure their effectiveness and sustainability. The regulation of social behaviors requires that policies be made to protect property rights, guarantee contract implementation, provide and monitor public goods and services and encourage infusion of correct social values.

The principle of general underpinning requires that government should formulate policies that address the basic issues of livelihood such as social security, pension insurance, medical insurance, unemployment assistance, personnel training, maternity, work injury insurance, disaster relief, salvation, etc. Government should consciously steer social resources into establishing a platform for social development and stability. The policy support for social development should proceed from a global vision, aiming to establish a human welfare society that features sufficient nutrition, no disease, ample opportunities for business, education and employment, active participation in communities, self-realization, etc. Government should focus on comprehensive social development rather than merely economic growth.

The "scientific outlook on development" in China represents a political theory that aims at promoting social development, reinforced by the implementation of a strategy of rejuvenating the country through science and education; a strategy of strengthening the nation with talented personnel; and a strategy of sound, rapid and sustainable development, on the basis of the law of development, innovations in thinking, transformation of development modes, cracking of hard issues and promotion of quality and efficiency, so that a solid foundation is laid for developing socialism with Chinese characteristics.

2.5 Quasi-operational resources

2.5.1 Implications of quasi-operational resources

Resources that are associated with urban construction are called quasi-operational resources in market economies and are mostly city resources used to form a public service system that ensures the normal operation of social and economic activities in a country or a region. They are also used to provide hard and soft infrastructure for social production and public livelihood, including traffic, postal service, electricity and water supply, greenery landscape, environmental protection, education, science and technology, culture, sanitation, sports and other public facilities. The level of such infrastructure determines the image, attributes, taste, function and influence of a country or a region. Sound infrastructure will advance all-round development of the region and optimize its spatial design and structure. These resources are so called because they are in the "borderline areas" in western economics or, in traditional economic terms, in the "overlapping areas" between government administration and market operation, where they can be managed by both the market and government to serve social development and welfare. In China, quasi-operational resources are administered by government organizations responsible for the following areas: state-owned assets and key projects; land, environmental protection and urban and rural construction; labor force and public resource transaction; education, science and technology, culture, sanitation, sports, news and publication, radio, television and film and research institutions; agriculture, forestry, water conservancy and maritime fishery; and so forth.

2.5.2 *Principles for quasi-operational resource allocation*

Regional government competition may have a two-fold implication. From the broad perspective, it means competition of regional total factors, embodied in operational, non-operational and quasi-operational resources and their matching policies. From the narrow perspective, it means the exploitation, operation, maintenance and policy support of quasi-operational resources. Therefore, the system of DRP may also be defined from broad and narrow perspectives. From the broad perspective, it concerns the allocation of the three types of resources, whereas from the narrow perspective, it only concerns the allocation of quasi-operational resources.

The conceptualization of "quasi-operational resources" and its analysis highlight the originality of this monograph and a major breakthrough in its theorization, as regional government competition mainly centers round quasi-operational resources rather than operational resources and non-operational resources. Despite the fact that both types are economically motivated, regional government competition concentrates more on the effective allocation of quasi-operational resources. The DRP model and the innovation in regional government competition fall exclusively on quasi-operational resources.

Whether quasi-operational resources should be allocated and operated in the same way as operational resources or as public welfare resources is determined by a variety of factors, such as regional development, financial status, capital flow, market needs, social acceptability, etc. Generally, there are three principles to follow. The first is the principle of market rules. Quasi-operational resources have a dual property of being allocated either by the market or by government. They form a cross area in which both market and government mechanisms may come into play. Likewise, regional government plays a dual role of "quasi-state" and "quasi-enterprise". The latter role determines its competitive behaviors in the allocation of quasi-operational resources.

However, regional government should allocate quasi-operational resources in full considerations of the market, as the market plays a critical role in resource allocation. Government should exercise its administration according to market rules and strengthen its adaptability to the market. Competition between regional governments should be benign and contribute to market efficiency, economic growth and social benefits. The role of regional government, therefore, should be shifted from an administrator that stays away from market competition to a quasi-enterprise that participates in competition and promotes management efficiency.

Both regional government and the market may be engaged in the allocation of quasi-operational resources. That is to say, they are substitutive for each other, forming a type of "either this or that" relationship. When regional government performs its function, the market mechanism will lose part of its impact. Likewise, when the market comes into play, government function will lessen its effects. This substitutive relationship gives rise to the question of how to achieve optimal combination on the government–market interface. The optimal point is determined by the point of contact between the equal-production curve and the equal-cost curve, which is the point where the output is maximized at a given cost or the cost minimized at a given output. It thus conforms to the principle of maximizing resource allocation efficiency.

The second is the principle of regulating market operations. There are two concerns in the allocation of quasi-operational resources: determination of carriers and capital operation. As for the determination of carriers, in order to allocate, operate and manage quasi-operational resources via market mechanism, regional government can establish the project carrier by means of sole proprietorship, joint venture, cooperation, joint-stock and even public–private partnership. The carrier will make effective investment, optimize structures, and boost social development in light of the market demand, social supply and trends of economic development. It can conduct effective regulation according to predictions over the market.

In the past, government merely focused on providing public services and goods, neglecting the benefits and returns of the input, thus leading to waste of resources. The carrier will help improve urban administration and prevent possible damages and losses. Therefore, regional government should transform the carriers of the existing assets into ones which can utilize the capital market. The carriers should be restructured into enterprises of public–private partnership, stock-holding, joint venture and cooperation, and then auctioned to private investors. In this way, they become carriers that follow the market rules and participate in market competition. As for some new operational projects, which were the carriers of the incremental assets, they should be established in the form of sole proprietorship, joint venture, cooperation or shareholding. Conditions should be created for them to become competitors in the market, and government should be prevented from becoming the sole carrier of those resources.

As for capital operation, in order to allocate and exploit quasi-operational resources via market mechanism, regional government should raise funds in capital markets by means of issuing bonds or convertible bonds, issuing shares, establishing project funds or taking advantage of some domestic and overseas investment projects, backdoor listings, securitization of project assets, projects merging, bundling operation, leasing, mortgage, replacement, auction, etc. Regional government can also raise capital through concessions such as DBO (design–building–operation), BOT (building–operation–transfer), BOO (building–owning–operation), BOOT (building–operation–owning–transfer), BLT (building–leasing–transfer), BTO (building–transfer–operation), TOT (transfer–operation–transfer), etc. Regional government may also adopt a certain mode of operation or combine various modes according to the features and conditions of a "quasi-operational" project. For example, regional government may establish a carrier with the 3P mode (Public+Private+Partner, also known as the PPP mode), operate on the concession of BOT or TOT or restructure a project into a listed enterprise in due course. In this way, government can resolve the capital bottleneck and achieve the sustainability of city resources.

And the limited public finance can be leveraged to meet the increasing demands for public goods and public welfare.

The third is the principle of participating in market competition. The enterprise-like nature of regional government determines that it can participate in market competition in quasi-operational resource allocation. In terms of its internal management, regional government can learn from the fruitful theoretical models and practical experience of business management and establish an efficient mode of management. Government may become important drivers of institutional, organizational, technological and managerial innovation. In the meantime, regional government is characterized by strong economic independence. To achieve maximization of economic benefits, government is motivated to carry out institutional and technological innovation. The executives in the region gain the reform courage and foresighted thinking, displaying a type of, as Schumpeter calls it, political entrepreneurship.

To conclude, the guiding principle of "government promotion, social participation and market operation" is followed in the process of quasi-operational resource allocation, exploitation, operation and management. It suggests that regional government is one of the competitors in the market, that it must follow market rules and that it is a guide, a coordinator and a supervisor, performing macro-economic functions. Regional government should provide policy support for quasi-operational resource allocation according to this principle.

2.5.3   *Policy support for operational resource allocation*

Operational resources are allocated by market mechanisms, whereas non-operational resources are allocated by regional government. It is the quasi-operational resource allocation that reflects foresighted leading on the part of regional government. The policy support for quasi-operational resource allocation includes a series of foresighted leading initiatives, among which the PPP model is the most significant.

The PPP model arose initially from the new public management movement that aimed at enhancing the role of market in public service provision. It called for the introduction of private sectors in the operation and construction of public projects. In fact, the PPP model is a quasi-public goods provision system that connects public departments of the whole society, enterprises, professional organizations and other public entities. The system addresses the problem of capital shortage and raises operation efficiency of public projects. Notably, the transaction cost theory and the principal–agent theory provided impetus for this reform. In the early eighteenth century, the PPP model was applied to the construction of the toll road in Europe. In the 1970s, countries like the UK and the US started to invite private entities to participate in the construction and operation of public projects. In the meantime, the PPP model was applied to public administration, thus generating a series of policies that promoted public–private partnership. In the mid-1980s, some moderately developed countries and developing countries began to adopt the PPP model. One typical example is the construction of Sha Tau Kok Power Station B in Shenzhen by Hopewell Holdings Limited, a Hong Kong–based enterprise. Later, the application of this model was soon extended to other modes of business such as concessions, O&M, leasing, etc. Countries and regions around the world attempted to use PPP to build major infrastructure projects. Now PPP has become one of the most important operating models for multi-principal cooperation in the international market.

Focusing on projects of quasi-operational resources, policies regarding the PPP model should ensure the cooperative relationship between governments, profit-making enterprises and non-profit organizations. While consideration should be given to the investment objective of the private sectors, all partners should share responsibilities and financing risks to provide the society with public goods and services. In this way, full use will be made of limited resources. In a word, to provide policy support for the PPP model, government needs to consider how to formulate policies of partnership, profit-sharing and risk-sharing and how to exercise foresighted leading.

First, a law and regulation system must be established. The allocation of quasi-operational resources demands both market and regional government involvement. The boundary between the two sides and the mode of partnership must be ruled by laws and regulations. In practice, the operation of quasi-public projects is more complicated when the market comes into play. More uncertainties may occur because of the massive amount of investment, the long-term partnership, the combination of private and public capital and the interaction between regional government administration and market cycles. Hence, a sound contract system and a good dispute resolution mechanism should be in place for the long-term operation of a project. There is the definite need to speed up the establishment of relevant laws and regulations, with priority given to those that regulate government behaviors, and to formulate laws and regulations for the purpose of protecting rights of non-governmental entities. Without these laws and regulations, it would be difficult to promote the PPP model. Only when the rights of non-principal entities are protected by legislation can more private capital be drawn into projects of quasi-operational resources.

Judging from the legal system concerning PPP in China, there is a lack of state-level policies for quasi-operational resource allocation, and some local or industrial measures or regulations are far from authoritative. Therefore, regional government is supposed to bring its foresighted leading into play in this aspect by formulating a unifying, fundamental and justifiable legal system that addresses issues such as delimiting roles of departments, coordination, approval, supervision, etc., and by mapping out comprehensive regulations that cover all links in a quasi-public project such as approval, bidding, construction, operation, management, quality supervision, fees and its adjustment, exclusiveness, dispute resolving mechanism, transfer, etc.

Second, an institutional system of contractual culture should be set up. In order to introduce market mechanisms into quasi-operational resource allocation, there is the necessity of upholding the contract spirit, which is an essential component of the market economy and of establishing the contractual partnership between regional governments and non-governmental entities with the principles of freedom, equality, mutual benefit and rationality. The contractual relationship may be established between regional government and the public, between regional government and private entities and between non-governmental enterprises and professional and social organizations which are involved with quasi-public projects. The relationship between regional government and private entities are of particular importance, as it is realized in the form of contracts through negotiation of the two parties on specific items or issues, through cooperation of government departments and private sectors for the provision of public goods and services, and with credit-based business culture and contract spirit serving as its foundation, which poses a great challenge to government administrative power. Therefore, a high level of government by law is needed in the first place. Then regional government must strengthen its institutional constraints, recognize the importance of contract spirit and contract binding and infuse the contract spirit into the whole society.

Third, innovation and foresighted leading become crucial in the creation of financing models. Regional government needs to accelerate the improvement of policy support for the financing of quasi-public projects. Consideration should be given to building a government-led fund which provides financing services to those PPP projects that are not able to raise money from the capital market. The investor repays the fund after the project has gone off to a success. In this way, the capital raised by regional government can flow back to the pool and run into recycling. Consideration should also be given to taking advantage of the extant policies, such as setting up specialized funds for PPP projects or establishing exchange platforms for investments in PPP projects.

In addition to financing policy support, regional government should encourage financial institutions to create financing products and new modes of financing management. For example, a project financing channel can be established to offer multiple choices of financial instruments, such as commercial bank loans, trusts, funds, project income bonds, asset securitization and so on. By so doing, the appropriate mode of financing can be chosen for a project so as to lower financing costs, increase capital operation efficiency and thus give full play to the PPP model.

Finally, foresighted leading and the improvement of supervising mechanisms must be put into effect. Projects of quasi-operational resources are public goods in nature and pertain to public interests. Hence, regional government is obliged to protect public interests by supervising their operation. In the PPP model, regional government is a contract performing party as well as a supervisor. On the one hand, it ensures that market participants will gain rational returns, and on the other hand, it must represent the interests of the public and regulate the profits gained by non-governmental entities. Therefore, government responsibility must be strengthened for supervision to prevent potential financial risks.

3 Resource allocation in "the four phases"

Regional government competition, which is achieved through the effective allocation of regional resource factors, can be interpreted in both the broad and narrow sense. The former covers competition in the allocation of total factors, i.e. operational resources, non-operational resources and quasi-operational resources, while the latter tends to take place in the structural adjustment and effective allocation of quasi-operational resources.

The realization of corporate profits and the growth of regional income are both issues of input and output and cannot do without the investment and allocation of resources, but the ways that resources are defined and allocated have become dynamic processes of constant adjustment and change. On the one hand, the concept of resources has transitioned from traditional physical resources to the expanding scope of intangible resources. On the other hand, the dominant factors affecting their allocation are constantly shifting from simple factors to total factors such as technology and innovation. Porter (1990) points out that a country's economic development undergoes four phases, which are characterized as factor-driven, investment-driven, innovation-driven and wealth-driven. From the perspective of the development of global economies, the resource allocation pattern of regional government has also experienced dynamic changes from factor-driven, investment-driven, innovation-driven and to wealth-driven. The policy eco-environment of regional government may vary with these phases, and so will the resource allocation means depending on the particular time given, so regional government must effectively judge the core driving force of economic growth over a given period of time and adopt a series of resources allocation means to guide the ecology of policy.

3.1 Features of resource allocation in the factor-driven phase

3.1.1 Factor-driven resource allocation: its implication

Any output requires the input of resources, and their allocation paths determine the extent of output efficiency. Resources generally appear in the form of factors of production in the production process, and production functions are generally defined as follows: in the given conditions of production technology, the material numerical relationship of the input combination of production factors to the maximum production output over a certain given period is a technical expression of the relationship between input and output in production, which can be shown:

$$Q = f(\mathrm{l},\ K,\ E,\ N)$$

Q stands for production output, L for labor, K for capital, E for a variety of natural resources headed by land and N for entrepreneurship, which may also represent the administrative capabilities of regional government.

In the initial phase of economic development, technology may remain at a low level, and no significant improvement may be foreseen in the near future. Lack of capital is often commonplace due to ineffective and inadequate accumulation. As a result, economic growth tends to be achieved and sustained simply through the increasing input of labor, land, natural resources and other production factors. This mode of economic growth is simple and easy and can be highly productive in the short run. However, the bottlenecks in capital and technology will inevitably appear in the long run so that marginal productivity will decline, and its potentials and sustainability for development will become limited. Therefore, this factor-driven approach may only work in the early stage of economic development.

3.1.2   Characteristics of land resource allocation

In the agricultural society, land is considered a primary factor that affects economic growth; those regions that are economically well developed are mostly endowed with rich natural resources and abundant labor forces and land supply, while those with limited land and sparse population tend to be economically underdeveloped. This can also be said of a region or an enterprise, the development of which depends on the enormous input of production factors and their scale expansion in the short run. But in the long run, such factor-driven growth is not sustainable and can only be a preliminary means of short-term expansion. In the industrial society, land is easily superseded by capital, and constraints in land input are more readily overcome by technological progress. As a result, the impacts of land factors on economic growth gradually fade away, which has been evidenced by the gradual declining role of land investment in western developed economies. However, land resources have a significant role to play in regional government competition in China, without which rapid industrialization and urbanization will become impossible. Land expansion has become the chief instrument for China's regional government to conduct urban operation and seek economic growth. China's economic growth over the past decades has relied heavily upon the utilization of land development by regional government in China.

Land transfer has always been a major form of competition for regional governments in China. The fierce competition for it has forced regional governments to seek the initiative of land management and development in a more active manner, as land is not simply "land" but has its own roles to play in attracting investment, financing and revenues. Regional government can maximize the output of land resource allocation by implementing a series of operational mechanisms such as expanding its scale, mode, price and income distribution, and thus attract more investment, achieve urban expansion, maintain fiscal balance and ultimately exercise the mode and path of economic growth. Land is no longer merely a production factor in the traditional sense as far as regional government competition is concerned. It has become a strategic resource that regional government can operate by means of land transfer, which amply demonstrates its nature as quasi-operational resources.

It has become apparent from the empirical study of China's inter-provincial spatial data (1998–2012) that there are three ways that the allocation of quasi-operational land resource may affect economic growth. First, it exercises its impacts upon economic growth not only as an instrument of investment but as an institutional instrument as well; the scale of land transfer, the income derived from it and the competition for it may all have significant positive effects on economic growth. Second, judging from their characteristics in different regions, its impacts turn out to be most obvious in the eastern coastal regions, as the revenues from land transfer have had greater favorable effects than land factor inputs. Third, urbanization and industrialization are the two probable channels through which land resources may affect economic growth. Revenues from land transfer can propel urban construction, urbanization and eventually economic growth, and low-cost land transfers for industrial development can attract investments, facilitate regional industrial development and ultimately drive regional economic growth.

3.2 Features of resource allocation in the investment-driven phase

3.2.1 *Investment-driven resource allocation: its implication*

Investment-driven resource allocation, also known as efficiency-driven resource allocation, is a mode of economic growth through capital generated by investment. Capital is one of the factors of production, and the separation of the investment-driven mode from the factor-driven mode is due to the fact that the force that drives economic growth has undergone a gradual shift from resource endowment to capital advantage, whose power, relative to those of other factors of production, has become more outstanding and even predominant, without temporal and spatial constraints. In addition, the investment-driven mode gives greater prominence to efficiency.

Practices have shown that the simple investment expansion of natural and labor resources in the long run, given that capital input remains basically unchanged, will inevitably lead to capital bottlenecks and the decline of marginal productivity, so capital investment must go alongside labor input with a certain proportion of growth. Thus, the "long-term production function" is derived, assuming that technical sophistication is given, operations are sound and all the input of factors are effective; capital must go along with labor and other factors so as to achieve the maximum long-term output. The optimal approach should be a series of tangent links of isocost curves and isoquant curves through a combination of capital and labor, called production expansion lines.

3.2.2   Characteristics of infrastructure investment and allocation

Infrastructure, which is a typical type of quasi-operational resource and the major object of competition for regional government, can be distinguished in the broad and the narrow sense. The former mainly refers to economically related facilities, including transportation, telecommunications, electricity, water supply and drainage and other public works, while the latter, in addition to what is mentioned above, covers education, public health, law and order, administration, etc. Infrastructure is characterized by its fundamentality, investment- and time-inseparability, spatial dependence, monopolization, externalities and publicity. As a major public product of regional government, infrastructure is one of the fundamental conditions for regional economic development. Similarly, education, scientific research and technological development are all major regional public products, serving as important resources and bases for maintaining and promoting regional economic competitiveness.

Both government and the market can be participants in the competition of some infrastructure projects. Government should permit corporate groups and qualified private enterprises to invest in profitable public welfare and infrastructure projects. In his analysis of the formation and growth of public investment in the US, Holtz-Eakin (1994) divides public investment into four categories on the basis of its final purpose, i.e. education, roads and highways, sewage treatment facilities and public utilities, while Etsuro-Shioji (2001) combines the last three into one category of infrastructure public investment, hence only two categories. According to Holtz-Eakin's estimate, the proportion of the four public investments above in total government investment in 1988 went as follows: education 20.2 percent, roads and highways 34.5 percent, sewage treatment facilities 7.5 percent and public utilities 13.2 percent. In Japan, public investment is defined so broadly as to include a total of 14 categories, which Etsuro-Shioji (2001) restructured into four, i.e. education, infrastructure (including public housing, sewage treatment, waste disposal, water supply, urban parks, roads, ports, airports, industrial water treatment), state-owned land protection (including mountains, rivers and coasts) and agriculture and fishing. Its corresponding proportion in public investment in 1990 is 12.1 percent, 60.6 percent, 13.5 percent and 13.7 percent respectively.

Justman, Thisse and Ypersele (2002) believe that in terms of competition in infrastructure services, regional government competes, more often than not, for diversification. Diversified infrastructure can not only reduce the waste of financial expenditure but also, more importantly, make it difficult for rivals to imitate, which contributes to the inter-regional differentiation of competitive advantages, the satisfaction diversified regional needs and the formation of a virtuous circle by stimulating other regional governments to enhance their infrastructure diversification.

Bucovetsky (1982) makes an analysis of government competition based on the investment public goods. He thinks that government infrastructure investment can produce agglomerated productive effects; that is to say, sound infrastructure and public environment will be conducive to the mobility of skilled labor forces in the region, while competition of investment in inter-regional public goods can be destructive. Through Nash equilibrium analysis of public goods investment models, he concludes that even if initial conditions of each jurisdiction are the same, the equilibrium may not be symmetrical. The problem is not just the excessive investment in public goods in each jurisdiction but rather the willingness of too many jurisdictions to invest. The stronger the mobility of factors in different jurisdictions is, the fiercer their competition becomes, for competition between regional governments for mobile factors may deplete the rents generated by investment in public goods.

Wilson (1999) investigated the impacts of public goods invested by regional governments with an inclination for self-interests upon public goods expenditure in the region. They argue that regional government officials are very much motivated to invest in public goods because it can exert a positive effect on the efficiency of its labor force and capital, and that more tax sources are available to regional governments. Consequently, the positive correlation between public goods input and tax revenues becomes intensified. Assuming that capital can flow freely between jurisdictions, regional governments will plunge themselves into "spending competition", thereby reducing the welfare of the residents of the region when capital cannot flow freely.

Fiva and Rattso (2007), using the methodology of space econometrics, make an empirical estimation of the consequences of welfare competition between governments. The competition for welfare between regional governments will not lead to the inadequate provision of public goods in a certain region, as regional governments' inherent motive and huge financial capacity often leads to excessive public goods spending.

Keen and Marchand (1997) examine the employment of infrastructure by regional governments to attract capital flows, which is thought to result in an oversupply of productive infrastructure and an inadequate provision of basic living facilities.

Chinese scholars Zhang Jun et al. (2007) make a careful study of the issues concerning infrastructure construction in China and find that after the supervision of economic development level, deepened financial reforms and other factors, the scale of competition between regional governments in "inviting investments" and the transformation of government governance is a major explanation for decision-making regarding infrastructure investment in China, which indicates the ultimate importance of decentralization, Tiebout competition and the transition to development-type government for the incentives for investments in government infrastructure.

American economists Richard Abel Musgrave (1910–2007) and Walt Whitman Rostow (1916–2003)believed that in the early phase of economic development, regional government investment occupies a higher proportion of total social investment, and the public sector provides social infrastructure for economic development, such as roads, transport systems, sanitation systems, law and order, health and education and other investments in human capital. These investments are essential to the countries' "take-off" in the early phase of their economic and social development and to their development in the mid-term phase. Regional government investment should continue in the mid-term phase, but only as a supplement to private investment. Whether in the early or in the med-term phase, there exist market failures and market imperfections, which hinder economic development. Regional government intervention must be in place to compensate for market failures and overcome market imperfections. Musgrave believed that the proportion of total investment in GDP is rising in the process of overall economic development, but that of regional government investment in GDP will decline. As an economy grows into maturity, the level of per capita income rises sharply. The pursuit of a better quality of life poses higher demands for regional governments, which force regional governments to provide better environments, more developed transport, faster communications and higher levels of education and health services, and thus a higher share of public investment. In addition, with the development of the economy, market failures are increasingly prominent, which requires regional government to implement legislation, increase investment and provide services to curb conflicts and contradictions. The consequence of these initiatives is the growth of public expenditure. In short, the rise and fall of public expenditure depends on the differences in the phases of economic development and the income elasticity of public goods provided by regional governments.

The US economy is already in its mature phase, so its regional government expenditure focuses on public service areas, such as national security, education, medical care and old-age pensions. China is still in the med-term phase of development, with some provinces and cities still in the early phase of their development, so regional government investment in economic construction has accounted for a relatively higher proportion in its expenditure.

3.3   Features of resource allocation in the innovation-driven phase

3.3.1   *Innovation-driven and total factor productivity*

Innovation-driven development revolves around the growth of TFP. When production efficiency of tangible resources, such as labor, capital and land, are released to the maximum and all show a trend of diminishing marginal productivity, what regional economic growth stems from this becomes a subject of great interest to economists. In the 1950s, Robert M. Solow, the Nobel Laureate in Economics, proposed the concept of "TFP". TFP growth, in essence, refers to the efficiency of technological progress, i.e. the growth of the productivity brought about purely through technological progress beyond all the factors of physical production (labor, capital, land, etc.). In a functional expression, the growth of TFP is the increase in the amount of production that is brought about by changes in intangible resources when the input of physical factors of production remains unchanged. The "total" in TFP does not mean the productivity of all factors but the part of economic growth that is not ascribable to the growth of tangible factors of production but ascribable to the productivity of intangible resources, such as pure technological progress, which is an important part of the source of long-term economic growth. The so-called pure technological progress includes the improvement of knowledge, education, technical training, scale economy, organization and management, but this kind of pure technological progress does not mean more investment of advanced facilities, higher-tech labor and more robust land expansion, and so on; these types of input are still capital, labor, land and other tangible factors of production, and "TFP" must be some non-specific technological progress brought about by the increase in productivity.

For regional government, the simple expansion of tangible factors such as land and capital creates a bottleneck of diminishing capital returns and makes the extensive mode of economic growth unsustainable. The establishment of long-term policies and institutional arrangements for sustainable growth becomes the source of economic growth; technological advancement, resource allocation and economic restructuring, which are TFP-oriented and innovation-focused, have inevitably become the new driving force for regional economic growth.

In the 1990s, Japan, faced with the challenges of its aging population, implemented the development strategy of more material capital investment. The constant increase in the amount of per capita capital of its labor force led directly to the decrease of TFP's contribution rate from 37 percent to –15 percent over the same period, as represented by technological innovation, which weakened the driving force for its economic growth and eventually pulled it into a long-term standstill. Evidently, with economic growth refined to its unprecedented level, the mode of economic growth has to shift its track from the increased investment of capital, land, labor and other factors of production to the enhancement of TFP. Innovation must become a more important source for TFP. Innovation driving means TFP driving, which means quality economic growth and the basic force to keep sustainable growth.

3.3.2 *Innovation-driven and regional government competition*

Innovation-driven economic development is based on the assumption that high-tech, management, organization and institution are primary resources. They can bring forth industrial aggregation by integrating science and technology and economy via marketization and networking, enhance production efficiency and transform management notions and means, organizational structure and patterns and institutional conceptualization and implementation. Innovation is, in essence, a process of "creative destruction". As Schumpeter once indicated, it is not merely external factors that push the economic system from one state of equilibrium into another. There exists within the economic system a source of energy that may achieve any state of equilibrium by means of automatic destruction.

Innovation is a new combination of factors of production by entrepreneurs. Currently, market competition is not that of prices but of innovation, the result of which is that entities with better productivity performance will grow stronger, while those with poor performance will be ousted from the market, and the entire economy will enter into total factor productivity (TFP) driving mode. What regional governments should do is create a sound "creative destruction" environment, which makes it possible to give full play to GFL while maintaining the decisive role of market. Regional governments will make competition entities well aware of the impetus for promoting TFP and allowing resource reallocation and technological advancement to play a dominant role in economic growth; this will be accomplished by adopting the principle of survival of the fittest, creating a favorable environment of fair competition and initiating a series of innovations in theorization, institution, organization, talents and so on.

Resources can be tangible and intangible, and innovative-driven resource allocation focuses more on the effective allocation of intangible resources. Innovation drivers to which regional government resort include innovation in science and technology, administration, organization and institution. Owing to competition in science and technology, administration, organization and institution, the allocation of resources in the innovation-driven phase actually refers to the allocation of "quasi-operational resources".

3.3.3 Characteristics of resource allocation in the innovation-driven phase

The resource allocation in the innovation-driven phase is mainly manifested by the inclination and aggregation of human resources, capital, technology, management, policy-making and others towards new technology, management, organization and institution.

The development in the US, Japan, Finland, South Korea and other innovative countries suggests that the innovation-driven phase generally needs the following conditions: the contribution rate of science and technology toward economic development exceeds 70 percent; the ratio of research and development in innovation investment to GDP exceeds 2 percent; original innovations should account for a great part, and the dependence index of external technology should go below 30 percent; there should be high innovation output and a large number of patents; in terms of industrial development, innovation should be embodied not only in the cutting edge of science and technology but also in the international competitive advantage of products or services as well, and in this phase will form better developed industrial clusters and stronger immunity against economic fluctuations and external impacts; in terms of social development, the driving force of innovation extends from economic growth to many other domains, such as social development, environment improvement, institutional optimization; and so on.

In terms of capital investment in global innovation in science and technology, the total R&D funding in 2013 amounted to US $1.3958 trillion, with an average growth rate of 5.2 percent between 2010 and 2013 and a steady growth trend. However, the global R&D funding remained concentrated in a handful of countries, with the US continuing to take the lead and accounting for 30.8 percent, followed by China (14.3 percent), Japan (11.1 percent), Germany (7.4 percent), France (4.3 percent), South Korea (4.1 percent) and the UK (3.4 percent). The total amount of investment in other countries and regions accounted for only 24.6 percent. In terms of its growth rate (see Table 3.1), the R&D funding in China and South Korea grew much faster than the global average, while that in the US and Germany had grown slowly, that in France and the UK had gone below the global average and in Japan the growth rate was negative.

Table 3.1 indicates that China's R&D investment continued to show an increasing trend over recent years and reached the level of medium-developed countries. In 2014, its total amount was over 1.3 trillion yuan, ranking second in the world. China's R&D funding intensity reached 2.05 percent, with an increase of 0.04 percent in 2013, an increase of 0.32 percent over 2010 and an increase of over 2 percent in the past two successive years, higher than the average rate of 1.94 percent in 28 of the EU countries. Although there was still a gap compared with the rates of 3 percent or 4 percent in some developed countries, a trend of steady growth was clear. A decomposition of the input shows that R&D funding from enterprises was 981.7 billion yuan, accounting for 75.4 percent of R&D funding. The financial technology allocation amounted to 645.5 billion yuan, accounting for 4.25 percent of total fiscal expenditure.

Table 3.1 R&D funding in major countries (2011–2014)

(in million dollars, prices for the indicated year)

Year/ Country	2011	2012	2013	2014	Growth rate per year
China	134443	163148	191205	211826	16.4
USA	429143	453544	456977	–	2.1
Japan	199795	199066	170910	164925	–6.2
Germany	104956	101993	109515	109941	0.16
France	62594	59809	62616	63826	0.1
South Korea	45016	49225	54163	60528	10.4
UK	43868	42607	43528	50832	0.5
Globally	1325026	1368363	1395802	–	5.2

Source: www.most.gov.cn/kjtj/, Ministry of Science and Technology, P.R. China.

According to the import and export statistics of China customs (Figure 3.2), the volume of China's high-tech products trade declined for the first time in 2014, with imports falling by 1.2 percent from the previous year. The exporting of computers and communication technology dominated the high-tech product trade, accounting for 69.4 percent of the total exports of high-tech products. The source of high-tech imports was mainly eastern and southeastern

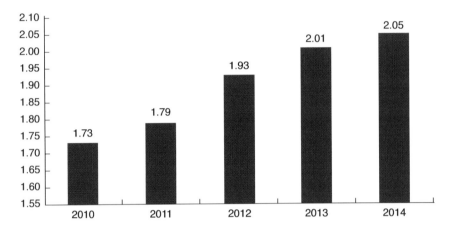

Figure 3.1 Investment intensity of R&D funds in China (2010–2014)

Source: www.most.gov.cn/kjtj/, Ministry of Science and Technology, P.R. China (in $100 million).

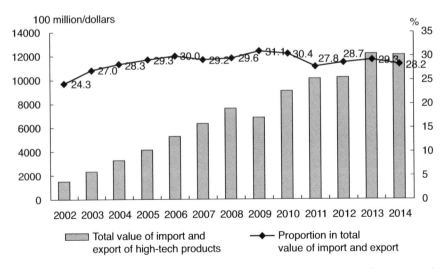

Figure 3.2 Total import and export of high-tech products and their share in total imports and exports (2002–2014)

Source: www.most.gov.cn/kjtj/, Ministry of Science and Technology, P.R. China.

Asia, and the main target markets for exports were the Hong Kong region, the US and the European Union. General trade exports accounted for a steady increase in the proportion of China's export trade in high-technology products, reaching 19.9 percent. The percentage from foreign-owned enterprises in China's exporting of high-tech products was still the largest, reaching 56.3 percent.

China's proportion of patent applications in 2014 amounted to 39.3 percent of the global total, with their structure being further optimized and the applications and authorizations of invention patents significantly increased over 2013. China's invention patent applications amounted to 801,000, 13.6 percent higher than in 2013, while its patents for utility models and image designs declined. Invention patent authorizations amounted to 163,000, an increase of 13.3 percent over

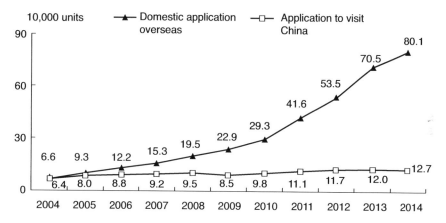

Figure 3.3 Applications of invention patents at home and abroad (2004–2014)
Source: www.most.gov.cn/kjtj/, Ministry of Science and Technology, P.R. China.

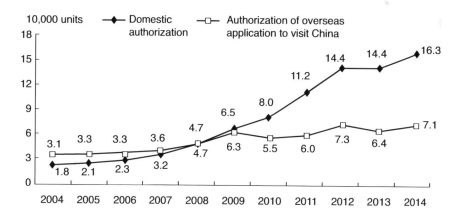

Figure 3.4 Authorized invention patents at home and abroad (2004–2014)
Source: www.most.gov.cn/kjtj/, Ministry of Science and Technology, P.R. China.

the previous year. Enterprise invention patent applications continued to grow rapidly, taking up 60.5 percent of domestic invention patent applications and 56.5 percent of total patent authorizations, and the top ten were all domestically funded. In 2014, China reached 4.9 patents per 10,000 people, and that number increased to 8.9 by June 2017. In 2014, China's PCT international patent applications reached 26,000, keeping its international rankings in third place, and the three-party patent ownerships reached 1897, maintaining sixth place in the international ranking.

In terms of the scale of human resources in the field of science and technology, its growth continued to maintain the advantage of scale internationally. Its scale reached 75.12 million in 2014, going up by 5.7 percent from 2013. Among them, university degree holders or above totaled 31.7 million, and that number was 21.1 million in "The Science and Engineering Indicators 2016" released by the US government. According to the full-time equivalent statistics, China's R&D personnel totaled 3.711 million per year in 2014, an increase of 2.7 percent from 2013, and the total number of researchers was 1.524 million per year in 2014, a 2.7 percent increase over 2013. In developed countries, the US boasted the largest scale, which amounted to 1.265 million per year in 2012. It turns out that China's input of R&D personnel has become the largest in the world in terms of both headcounts and full-time equivalents, and it is still on the rise. According to the OECD statistics concerning 41 major countries and regions, its proportion went from 18.4 percent in 2009 to 21.4 percent in 2014, while that of the US fell from 19.9 percent to 17.8 percent.

However, viewed globally, indicators of China's input intensity of R&D personnel are still falling behind the international level. In 2014, the number of R&D personnel in China was 48.0 persons per year/million, and the number of R&D researchers went down to only 19.7 years/per year/10,000, but in 2010 it had already reached 15.9, which shows that its growth was slow. An international comparison indicates that China was a little bit higher than

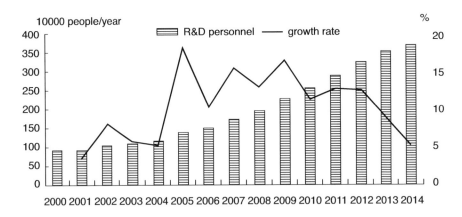

Figure 3.5 The trend of total R&D personnel in China (2000–2014)

Table 3.2 Countries with a total R&D population of over 100,000 per year

Country	Year	R&D population (in 10,000 per year)	R&D population per 10,000 employees (people per year/10,000 employees)	R&D researchers (10,000 per year)	R&D researchers per 10,000 employees (people per year/10,000 employees)
UK	2014	38.8	126.3	27.4	89.0
Canada	2013	22.7	125.6	15.9	88.2
USA	2012			126.5	87.4
Netherlands	2014	12.3	140.9	7.6	86.4
Germany	2014	60.1	140.7	36.0	84.2
Spain	2014	20.0	111.1	12.2	68.0
Russia	2014	82.9	115.9	44.5	62.2
Poland	2014	10.4	66.4	7.9	50.0
Italy	2014	24.6	101.2	12.0	49.3
Turkey	2014	11.5	44.5	9.0	34.6
Brazil	2010	26.7	21.7	13.9	11.3

Source: OECD, Main Science and Technology Indicators, January 2016.

such developing countries as Turkey and Brazil in terms of the ratio of R&D personnel per 10,000 employed labor force, which was over three times that of South Korea, France and other developed countries. China's ranking was the last but one in 2014, and that of the developed countries was generally more than four times that of China.

The above analysis shows that China has been fully prepared to undergo a major transition from the investment-driven to the innovation-driven resource allocation model. However, no innovation can maintain its momentum and sustainability without the underpinning and protection of organizational and institutional innovation. Innovation in the construction of policy ecology, which covers such factors as management, organization and institution, together with government leading, is the key to innovation driving.

3.4 Features of resource allocation in the wealth-driven phase

3.4.1 Wealth-driven resource allocation: its implication

Ecological economist Manfred Max-Neef (1995) proposed the "threshold hypothesis", which describes such a state of economic growth, i.e. every country undergoes a specific phase in which economic growth will lead to a threshold of improvement in the quality of life, and beyond this threshold point the quality of life may decline. This hypothesis actually raises suspicions concerning the meaning of economic growth, i.e. when economic growth causes environmental and social pressures, the region may experience a shift from the ecological surplus to the ecological deficit; social welfare will be hurt with continuing economic growth, which obviously goes against the original intention of economic growth. Sound economic development should bring increasing social welfare under the conditions of a constant ecological scale. That is the driving force in the fourth phase of economic development Porter proposed in his wealth-driven theory.

3.4.2   Resource allocation in the wealth-driven phase

Resource allocation under the wealth-driven model aims at the simultaneous promotion of economic growth and social welfare, taking the economic and social welfare generated through the unit natural capital consumption as the main measure index for the ecological performance; the social economic development derives its momentum from people's unremitting pursuit of good homes and happy life. As a result, the implication of wealth is further extended to include the experience of lives and the return of humanistic values beyond economic interest.

Research findings show that when wealth growth reaches a certain degree, people begin to pursue the all-round development of individuality, literary and art tastes, sports and health care, leisure and tourism and other enjoyments of life, which brings forth new economic models and new types of industries that match them and emerge as a new driving force for economic development. Economic development under the wealth-driven model tends to assume the following characteristics. First, traditional industries, which can absorb fewer and fewer labor forces, are unable to provide more employment opportunities for the fast-growing population, while the newly emerging service-oriented industries, which benefit enormously from their innovative development, can provide a great number of employment opportunities. Second, with the intensification of people's awareness of resources and environmental protection, the excessive consumption of natural resources and environmental damages caused by the traditional industry have become increasingly unacceptable to the public. Third, the market potential of traditional industries are basically stereotyped and thus unable to provide opportunities for new participants to accumulate quick wealth, while the profit-seeking motive of capital is constantly generating and triggering off new wealth-creating industries. Thus, the wealth-driven phase is also a phase for discovering new economic models that emphasize human enjoyment and development and the potential for wealth creation and space for full employment.

The prominent feature of resource allocation in the wealth-driven phase is the aggregation and efficient allocation of high-quality resources under new economic models and in newly emerging industries, including an enormous input of "quasi-operational resources", such as infrastructure investment, regional government administration, organizational models and institutional innovation.

The UK can be cited as a good example to illustrate this. By the end of the twentieth century, its traditional demand started to shrink, and capital intensification did not lead to faster economic growth. People began to find new economic models and create new industries. However, there appeared in the early years of the UK's wealth-driven economy such problems as too much reliance on mergers and acquisitions to create wealth; keener interest in foreign investment than domestic investment; and hedonism overriding hard work and enterprise, as well as high taxes, lower labor efforts and gradual labor confrontations. The occurrence of these problems shows that wealth-driven economic growth is a double-edged sword: it will lead to the ultimate goal of both economic and social development if it is well guided; otherwise it may easily fall into the vicious cycle of hedonism and economic stagnation. What is currently happening in Europe, especially Greece, Spain and Iceland, reveals that while chasing human enjoyments, these countries are losing their economic competitiveness and entrepreneurial spirit and have incurred huge financial and social crises. The UK later proposed the development strategy for "creative industry", which made full use of the knowledge and information platform provided by the computer and the Internet, grasped learning opportunities from the perspective of individual needs and acquired full information resources fairly. Revolutionary changes are taking place in new types of industrial creation and business models, which have become the major power for economic development. Practices in these countries and regions are worthy of serious attention and reference by other countries and regions upon their entry into the wealth-driven phase.

3.5 Resource allocation policies in the four phases

3.5.1 Resource allocation policies in the factor-driven phase

Smith's theory of absolute interest, Ricardo's comparative interest theory and Heckscher and Olin's production factor endowment theory all favor the factor-driven resource allocation mode. The theory of absolute interest holds that every region has certain absolute favorable production conditions, in light of which labor division and exchanges are made so as to achieve the most effective use of regional resources, thereby enhancing regional productivity and interests. However, no convincing solution is provided as to how regions without absolute advantages should develop. The theory of comparative advantages holds that there is no need to produce all varieties of goods in regions where there are absolute advantages in the production of all products and focus should be laid on the production of those goods with the greatest advantages of production, while in regions where the production of all varieties of goods is at a disadvantage, it is desirable to produce what is of the least disadvantage, rather than producing nothing at all.

These two types of regions can derive comparative advantages from this division of labor and trade. The theories of comparative advantage and absolute advantage are based on the premise that the factors of production do not flow and therefore turn out to be defective. Heckscher and Olin's theory of production factor endowment holds that factors of production may vary with regions, which result in regional differences in comparative advantages. That is also the fundamental rationale for regional division of labor. If impacts of demand are left out of account and there are obstacles to the flow of factors of production, regions should be in an advantageous position to produce with its relatively affluent production factors.

The factor-driven resource allocation model has made great contributions to economic growth in developing countries such as China over quite a long period of time. China has achieved rapid economic development by employing cheap human resources, and southeast Asian countries such as Vietnam and Thailand are becoming the centers of world manufacturing by capitalizing on their advantages of labor resources; enterprises in OPEC and African countries rely heavily on natural resources for economic support. Factor-driven resource allocation is essential in these regions for steady economic growth.

However, the factor-driven development model is unsustainable in the long run, owing to the diminishing marginal income of factors and decreasing productivity, along with rising factor cost and factor-driven dividend attenuation. The factor-driven model can easily lead to extensive development characterized by high input, high energy consumption, high emissions, high pollution, low economic efficiency and low labor returns. With mounting pressure from the decline in factor dividends, continuing international trade barriers and the rise of other emerging economies, this model proves feeble in pushing regions forward from the middle-income to the high-income stage. For example, some provinces in central and western China with a relatively unitary industrial structure have been experiencing an obvious trend of economic decline over recent years. Shanxi and Inner Mongolia are provinces with abundant resources, with a GDP growth rate of 4.9 percent and 7.8 percent respectively in 2014.

Shanxi was at the bottom of GDP national rating, and Inner Mongolia stood at twenty-second. Their GDPs fell by 4.0 percent and 1.2 percent respectively, compared with 2013. More seriously, economic collapses have repeatedly struck northeast China, where there used to be abundant resource reserves but which are currently nearly exhausted. These regions are faced with huge challenges. In 2014, the economic growth rate in Heilongjiang, Liaoning and Jilin Provinces continued to decline, with their GDP growth rates standing at 5.6 percent, 5.8 percent and 6.5 percent, respectively, and at the last but one, the second and the third from the bottom in national GDP ranking, with a decrease of 1.8 percent, 2.9 percent and 2.4 percent respectively, compared with that in 2013. Consequently, the factor-driven resource allocation model is coming to an end in these regions. However, it will not happen overnight that resource allocation in the factor-driven phase can develop its strong points, avoid its weaknesses and achieve a leap forward in shifting the driving mode, as regions and individual productivity differ in various ways and it requires some time for economic development modes to take a shift. Eventually, policy ecological leading will have a huge role to play in the factor-driven development model.

In the light of the predicament the factor-driven resource allocation model incurs, policy ecological leading should focus on the promotion of industrialization and urbanization, the consolidation of economic foundation, the adjustment of industrial structure, the reduction of production overcapacity, the monitoring of environmental pollution, the improvement of infrastructure and the input of public services. Measures must be taken to carry out the transformation of government functions, improve institutional efficiency and develop modern agriculture, new strategic industries and advanced equipment manufacturing so as to enhance TFP efficiency.

From the demand side, regional government should realize that demand gaps are unavoidable under certain economic circumstances and that failures to make up for the gaps may certainly affect the economic growth rate; the crux of the matter is how to make up for them. Demand gaps used to be remedied through regional government's unlimited investment, which in turn gave rise to problems such as excessive reliance upon investment stimulus and inefficiency. China's "4 trillion" economic stimulus program in 2008 led to the flow of a great part of capital into state-owned enterprises without shortage of funds, and that resulted in the accumulation of repeated and ineffective investments and the inadequacy in economic hematopoietic mechanisms. Statistics show that the comprehensive utilization rate of production capacity in China's industrial enterprises was generally below 80 percent by the end of 2013, and more than 30 percent of overcapacity existed in iron and steel, coal, electrolytic aluminum, cement, flat glass, shipbuilding and other industries in 2014 and 2015. Due to government subsidies and government-designated development routes, newly emerging strategic industries, such as wind power equipment, polycrystalline silicon, photovoltaic cells and many others, mushroomed overnight, causing serious overcapacity and slumping profits. This way of investment may easily self-circulate and accumulate capacity, for it uses growth to stimulate growth and resources to produce resources, merely for the sake of pursuing higher growth rates. Therefore, from the demand side, regional government must rationally guide investment directions and control investment scale, discard previous quantity and scale-oriented catch-up practices and shift its focus on quality and efficiency.

From the supply side, the core of policy ecology resides in activating production factors, enhancing TFP and ensuring continuous improvement of national income. Traditional policy subsidies distorted the price of factor market and depressed investment costs. This fundamental defect in institution caused the distortion of the investment behavior of regional government and state-owned enterprises, the widespread structural excess and the decrease in the efficiency of investment and resource allocation. Therefore, at the micro level, reform should focus on improving the quality and efficiency of supply, correcting the distortion of financial subsidies and stimulating the vitality of market entities so that all kinds of factors can easily get into and out of the market, create their values freely, realize their values independently and generate the inexhaustible impetus of sustained economic growth.

In other words, the supply-side reform should target fewer monopoly areas or monopoly links, fewer market access restrictions, lower entry barriers, more opportunities for social capital participation and more equal factor prices, including land, capital, labor, stronger resources and environmental constraints. Enterprise reforms should also be conducted, and regional competition awareness strengthened. The supply potentials of land need to be further tapped, the reform of the land approval system facilitated, the rise of land cost curbed, farmland renovation enhanced and the rural property system reform pushed forward. Regional government should undertake innovations in administrative management systems and macro-level management modes, create favorable environments for market entities to fully release wealth and its potentials, and employ policy tools with a view to facilitating the optimization and redistribution of stock resources and improving the overall quality of national economy and international competitiveness.

The policy matching for land and other resources should, first of all, deepen the reform of land use and its transfer system; further release "land dividends" by means of policies concerning capital attraction through land introduction, finance and competition; promote land marketization and capitalization; and improve the efficiency of land expansion, land introduction and land finance expenditure. Second, regional government should standardize the transfer of industrial land and prevent excessive industrial land transfer at low prices so as not to incur land use with low efficiency and extensive economic growth. Finally, regional government should standardize and coordinate local government competition for land transfers and avoid high resource costs and low social efficiency brought about by excessive competition in land transfers.

3.5.2   *Resource allocation policies in the investment-driven phase*

The development history of the driving factors of economic growth demonstrates that labor input is relatively easy to obtain and that there is always shortage of capital resources, especially when labor input begins to show a decline in marginal productivity, the strong demand for capital has accumulated to a certain extent and the driving force of capital investment has become increasingly powerful. Under such circumstances, investment naturally becomes regional government's most favored instrument for economic growth. Regionally, the growth of GDP stems mainly from consumption, investment, government expenditure and the pull of net exporting. Among these four driving factors, investment is the most powerful instrument and has the most direct effect. For regions where government enjoys greater power, investment-driven economic growth is the most convenient and rapid means.

In the US and developed countries in Europe, there has always been opposition to direct government intervention in economic regulation, but in the aftermath of the Second World War and with the outbreak of the economic crisis, there has been no hesitation in adopting direct government investment as a powerful economic stimulus lever to ensure that regional economy becomes stabilized in no time. Most of the countries and regions in southeast Asia are typical investment-driven economies, and regional government spares no effort in investment, which has been playing an active role in building up the economic foundation of these economies and opening up international markets. China is also a typical investment-driven economy with high savings rates, high investment rates and low consumption rates. According to estimates by World Bank economists, the contribution rate to labor productivity generated the investment-driven model reached 45.3 percent between 1978 and 1994 and 64.7 percent between 2005 and 2009.

This model of economic growth has continued in China for over three decades, but it must be noted that but the side-effects it has caused cannot be overlooked, though it can serve as some sort of stimulus for aggregate demand and GDP growth. Strictly speaking, investment-driven economic growth is by nature an extension of scale, without shaking off the basic framework of the momentum for economic growth driven by physical factors of production, which leads to unquenchable thirst for capital and eventually a series of financial crises. On the other hand, this model is susceptible to capital dependence, which brings about the extensive growth of economy, a great deal of repeated construction with low returns, and the probable cover-up and constant distortion of deep-seated contradictions concerning economic restructuring and optimization.

Ultimately, it hinders the growth of regional economies. The new normal economic growth model China proposed is a reflection upon the model of investment-driven economic growth, and investment must be efficient rather than simply pursuing scale expansion. The reason why investment has not been driven by efficiency is that it has failed to target effective social demands. Therefore, from the demand side, regional government should regard it as its primary task to stimulate effective demands, satisfy the structural shortage of market supply and create new demands, so it turns out to be of vital importance for regional government to exercise its leading role in policy ecological construction.

In terms of investment demand, regional government should try every means to crack down monopoly, further broaden private capital investment, allow private capital to invest and operate in monopolistic industries, promote and perfect the construction of the GSP financial system, reduce the financing cost of small and medium-sized enterprises, stimulate the growth of investment demand and thus effectively support the transformation and upgrading of real economy and industries.

In terms of consumption demand, regional government should strengthen its guiding role of consumer markets in innovation and allow products to be more personalized, services more customized, brands more competitive and consumer demands further expanded. Meanwhile, regional government needs to adapt its industrial structure to the demands of the current market.

Regarding the creation of the demand for people's livelihoods, regional government should increase investment in energy sources, radio and television, culture, medical care, pension, educational and cultural facilities; open up more such space for private capital; promote gradual industrial reforms; take appropriate measures to relax restrictions in industrial entry; reduce regulatory controls, introduce new investors through capital market and other channels; improve and ensure the capacity and level of public services; give outlets for consumer spending; strengthen support to the poor and those in difficulty; and strengthen environmental beautification in urban and rural areas. All this constitutes the starting point for regional government to expand effective demand.

In terms of tax policy-making, regional government should carry out differential reduction in taxation, arouse enthusiasm for production and consumption on the part of enterprises and inhabitants, reduce the tax burden of small and medium-sized enterprises, reform individual income taxes, real estate taxes, inheritance and gift taxes, heighten the overall income level of middle- and low-income population and narrow down income gaps.

In terms of supply-side adjustment, regional government should concentrate its efforts in planning the development orientations of regional industries and modifying the supply structure so that the supply derived from investment effectively meets and even leads the demand. In the cultivation of institutional environment, regional government should implement decentralization, clarify the major roles of entrepreneurs and researchers in scientific research and the transfer of its findings, create a relaxing social environment for innovation and entrepreneurial efforts, perfect the market mechanism and accelerate the pace of the transformation of scientific and technological accomplishments towards industrialization and commercialization.

In terms of financial means, regional government should enhance its capability of fund supply for enterprises; reduce their financing costs, and thus strengthen their controlling power for comprehensive operational costs; and create favorable conditions for the increase of industrial capital investment. At the same time, regional government should adopt such means as interest rates and exchange rates to slow down the speed of capital outflow, heighten the level of research and development of enterprises, promote R&D capabilities for scientific and technological innovation and revitalize domestic innovation and entrepreneurial stamina.

In terms of industrial restructuring, regional government should take effective measures to reduce substantially industrial overcapacity; improve industrial supply and its structure; promote market annexation and reorganization led by key enterprises; nurture new industries in the strategic directions of industrial Internet, intelligent manufacturing and other areas; and relocate government capital to the major industries and areas pertaining to regional security and economic lifelines and to forward-looking strategic industries so as to effectively upgrade and transform their core competitiveness.

3.5.3   Resource allocation policies in the innovation-driven phase

In terms of the policies regarding the allocation of resources for innovation in science and technology, regional government should increase the investment in innovation and improve the proportion of R&D expenditure in the total income and of R&D personnel in the whole staff. These two indicators are of paramount importance in determining whether an economy has entered into the innovation-driven phase of development and whether it has undergone the transition from the factor-driven and investment-driven phase to the innovation-driven phase. Investment in innovation of science and technology is more efficient than directly in production. Resources can produce extra benefits when they are used for innovation. In addition to the increase in the amount of investment, efforts should be intensified in the adjustment of investment structure, with inclinations toward human capital, especially high-caliber innovative entrepreneurial talents, and toward the incubation and R&D of new technology.

Only when these two major innovation-driven links are identified and emphasized can a steady stream of new technology be generated and investment be guaranteed, which will make it possible to transform into innovation-driven development. In the construction of scientific and technological innovation environment, it has become the fundamental guarantee for talent retention and innovation-driven development to provide sound living and development conditions for those creative talents. The environment thus created should be well suited for living, research and industrialized R&D, equipped with infrastructure and facilities for network information channels, platforms for R&D cooperation and production, good environments for innovative entrepreneurial talents, active risk and innovation investments, innovative culture, etc. Policies must be made to build up public environments that can revitalize innovation, with the maintenance of market competition and the continuous pressure of technological innovation. Moreover, regional government should allow a certain degree of monopoly on the basis of guaranteeing necessary competition mechanisms by means of intellectual property protection, such as patents, and recognize the rights of innovative enterprises and monopolize innovation-generated income for a certain period of time, which can fully compensate for innovation costs incurred by innovators and stimulate the continuous improvement in innovation output.

In relation to the policies for resource allocation concerning management innovation, it is important to make clear that supply-side management is the key for innovation. The analysis of the demand side and supply side shows that demand is endless. The effective demand under this umbrella only refers to what the power of payment can support, i.e. the demand that is underpinned by the willingness and the ability of fulfillment in total amount of flux. It follows that there is nothing like "innovation" in relation to the demand side, and "innovation" is essentially on the supply side. Supply must meet the effective demand and create new demands, so it must face a lot of specific uncertainties. Therefore, supply-related innovation needs policy incentives, and policies that guide the supply-side prove to be more prominent. Certainly, policies respecting supply-side–related innovation in management do not negate the short-term total demand management, which is dominated by monetary and fiscal policies. The supply-side reform, with the structural reform and marketization reform at its core, fall into medium and long-term policies, while the short-term total demand management based on monetary and fiscal policies fall into short-term policies. They are both complementary. The vigorous structural adjustment and the removal of overcapacity will aggravate the downward pressure on economy, which requires monetary and fiscal policies to be somewhat relaxed so as to release the pressure to some extent and create a favorable atmosphere for supply-side innovation.

Regional government's build-up of policy ecology should focus on the combination of both short-, medium and long-term policies, i.e. strengthening the supply-side structural reform while moderately expanding aggregate demand. The short-term policies are mainly monetary and fiscal policies, which are adopted to adjust anti-cyclic economic fluctuations. The medium-term policies focus on consumption stimulation and tax reduction for enterprises with an attempt to promote the balanced growth from both demand and supply sides and give strong support to innovation. The long-term policies undertake supply-side and marketizing reforms and employ innovation as the chief driving force for the purpose of activating the potentials of economic growth.

Regarding policies for resource allocation in organizational innovation, special attention should be paid to changes in governance structure and modes established as a result of new economy and new business modes, with all necessary support. For example, innovation in financial organization must give full play to the role of financial support in real economy. It should center around how to serve real economy, heighten the openness level of finance to the outside world, actively develop new business and new models, improve the multi-level capital market construction, promote the optimal allocation of resources, solve the problems of enterprise financing, enhance the efficiency of capital utilization and stimulate the new vigor of supply-side reform.

Regarding the layout of asset securitization, measures should be taken to effectively activate stock assets, enhance the liquidity of operating assets, reduce the financing cost of real economy and promote the adjustment and transformation of economic structure. As the link between real economy and capital market, financial trusts can also develop new technology, new industries and new business modes that are related to regional strategic development, and expedite the cultivation of new business fields. Meanwhile, financial investment should be in favor of high-tech industries, promote scientific and technological innovation, promote technological progress and eventually expand product supply boundaries. The facilitation of green, low-carbon and circular economic development may require the integration of creditors' rights, equities and other financial instruments to incorporate investors, enterprises and intermediary service agencies, together with other rights and interests of all parties into the trust platform, and direct financial capital into real economy and private capital into national strategic industries so as to promote the innovation and development of real economy. Innovation in trust policies is also reflected in the participation in the enterprise employee stock ownership plan, which allows employee shareholding through trusts, avoids the excessive distribution of stock rights and improves corporate decision-making efficiency. Besides, merger and acquisition funds may be established in case of need to assist in merger and reorganization, provide leverage for capital through structural design and bring social funding into enterprises. Private equity investment, PE products and other ways may also bring direct or indirect investment, along with investment returns, into enterprises.

Innovation in financial policies can also be embodied in the construction of multi-level capital markets, opening up new capital market transactions, promoting reforms in stock and bond issuing and trading systems, raising the proportion of direct financing, reducing leverage rates and implementing the registration system for new shares issuing so that capital market financing channels are opened up for pioneering and innovating enterprises, allocation structure is naturally optimized, excess capacity is discarded, new industries are selected and multiple channels for enterprise financing are created. Measures should also be taken to vigorously develop overseas business, achieve globalized asset allocation, implement internationalized development strategies, promote the transnational flow and market allocation of capital factors and improve the efficiency of financial asset allocation by constructing a more open financial system.

Regarding policies of resource allocation concerning institutional innovation, regional government should strive to create "regional innovation systems". The most important part of government involvement in innovation is integrating the two major innovation systems of enterprise technological innovation and university knowledge innovation, so that all links in the innovation systems gather, coordinate and interrelate around a core objective of innovation, forming the knowledge-based and application-oriented aggregation of innovative activities between enterprises and research institutions and gradually an internal set of mature innovation systems so as to cultivate regional innovation capabilities. In this regional innovation system, enterprises interact with scientific research institutions through flexible market mechanisms. The major role of government in the regional innovation system is to effectively perform its functions in providing innovative resources; cultivating innovation entities; and removing obstacles to knowledge flow by means of financial incentives, investment guidance and market regulation; playing an additional role of coordinating public organizations; and building research and production cooperation innovation platforms in the form of regional science commissions, technology promotion organizations, university science and technology parks, business incubation centers and so on in order to provide a bridge between "knowledge discovery" and "knowledge application" and help overcome market failures.

3.5.4   Resource allocation policies in the wealth-driven phase

The primary task in the wealth-driven phase is the construction of an ecological innovation system, which will provide support for the wealth-driven transformation. Innovation in this phase cannot just stop at the technical level and must be linked to eco-orientation, advocating ecological innovation, such as adopting the economic growth mode of low resource consumption and brand new products or services, process designs, marketing models, organizational structure and institutional arrangements so as to prevent damages brought about by economic growth to the environment. At the level of social management, emphasis should be laid on institutional innovation and systematic innovation, transformation of product structure, pursuit of alternative development paths through changing people's life and work objectives, avoidance of one-sided pursuit of high efficiency through sheer reliance on technological innovation, close attention to system innovation, transit from efficiency-leading to effect-focused and improvement in regional ecological performance.

What comes next is adjusting industrial structure, developing circular economy and low-carbon economy and creating a new type of industrialized mode of service economy so that all types of economic development are inclined toward the self-promotion of people, the harmony of external environment and the continuous intensification of momentum for economic growth. In addition, the structure of employment should be contingent upon the adjustment of industrial structure, from the simple productive or manufacturing creation of employment opportunities to the service- and performance-integrated creation, so that the traditional linear economic growth pattern undergoes radical transformation and a welfare society comes into being, characterized by green economy, as well as the promotion of life values, social harmony, environment friendliness and sound economic prosperity.

The third is to strengthen the provision of public goods and services on the basis of considerations of ecological scale, which is the due responsibility of government. The regulatory policy, market policy and public participation policy should be all fully enforced, and in consideration of the overall scale control of ecology, the infrastructure and public services that contribute to urban green transformation are to be provided; further measures should be put in place to control and close down environmentally damaging industries so that the level of social welfare is heightened. Through a series of incentive systems, regional government should urge enterprises to consciously assume the responsibility of the "cradle to cradle" product life cycle and take measures to implement resource-saving and environment-friendly product design, eco-technology, clean production and product recycling systems. The public should be encouraged to foster a new type of consumption based on ecological adequacy; strengthen the publicity and education of consumers through educational institutions, trade associations, non-profit organizations, mass media and public welfare activities; advocate healthy consumption concepts and life styles; and reduce resources and environment pressure.

Fourth, regional government should actively cultivate new consumption trends and open up new consumption markets. With the comprehensive coverage of the Internet in production and all walks of life, people's consumption patterns and consumption trends are changing fast, and the increasingly mature conceptualization of income and values also makes consumers more and more inclined to pursue the quality of life. Rather than simply pursuing material life, people begin to pay more and more attention to spiritual enjoyment, which is the source of wealth-driven power. Therefore, it is necessary for regional governments to make better policies regarding service consumption, such as pension, health, education and culture; to promote tourism consumption, domestic service and information consumption; to encourage enterprises to develop experiential consumption, shop-less consumption, customized consumption and other new patterns of consumption; and to promote green cyclic consumption of new electronic products, smart home appliances, energy-saving environment-friendly cars and environment-friendly home-building materials, so as to form an effective, sustainable consumption pattern, driving the development of related industries.

Finally, regional government must nurture the culture and values of the wealth-driven phase to guide the healthy and sustainable development of economy. The accumulation of wealth can not only make people more self-independent and entice them to pursue a higher quality of life, but can also degenerate them into idle lazybones. The driving force of economic development should continue to be dependent on financial gains. A correct understanding of wealth must be cultivated to turn people into owners of wealth rather than being caught in the bondage of wealth. Therefore, greater challenges are posed in the wealth-driven phase to the whole society's civilization and enterprising spirit. Regional government must take precautions to foster a healthy, positive and innovative cultural atmosphere, which requires a series of systems and sustained patience and perseverance.

4 The representations and effects of regional government competition

This chapter discusses various forms of regional government competition; discusses the attributes of resource allocation and policy matching in different phases through careful analyses of mechanisms of regional government competition for effectively allocating the three types of resources; and provides its manifestations within the market system.

4.1 Modern market system

The market system is an integrated body of various types of market with different functions, which are interrelated, mutually constrained and intertwined. It is a structurally complicated combined system that consists of various market factors and sound mechanisms which reflect and represent various economic relations.

A traditional market system can be interpreted mainly from the following perspectives. From the standpoint of transaction or circulation, it consists of commodity markets, which cover production material markets and consumption goods markets, and production factor markets, which cover land markets, labor markets, currency markets, technological markets, information markets, etc. From the spatial standpoint of market transactions, it consists of all local markets across different geographic regions, inclusive of local markets, regional markets, integrated national markets and cross-border world markets, which form a complex and gradually expanding continuum. From the standpoint of organizational governance and structural setup, it is composed of wholesale markets, retail markets, online markets and various types of intermediaries, which constitute a huge network connecting production and consumption, supply and demand, cities and countryside, domestic and international markets and online and offline markets. And finally, from the standpoint of transaction means and manners, it is composed of spot trading markets, forward trading market and futures markets.

The modern market system emphasizes both the systematicity of market composition and the structural integrity of market functions. A look at the relation between the function and structure of market reveals that the market system is first of all an interest-adjusting system, playing allocating, regulating and constraining roles in the distribution of interest on the part of market entities. Both parties in transactions or entities of competition must abide by market rules without infringement of transaction rules or interests that go beyond market rules. The market system is a system of competition which takes place between its entities by various means, through different processes and with varied outcomes. No matter what its nature is, all forms of competition must proceed in conformity with market laws and values so as to achieve optimal allocation of resources through the functioning of the market system. In addition, the market system is a system of information transmission. It conveys information concerning the supply and demand of transaction parties via prices and competition so as to lead the flow of resources and the transformation of production. As a result, transaction parties must always keep abreast of market changes and take information costs for the pursuit of the market.

As indicated above, a traditional market system can be interpreted mainly from four perspectives, i.e. transaction or circulation, space, organizational governance and structural setup and transaction means and manners. The modern market system emphasizes the systematicity of both market composition and structural functions. As far as structural functionality is concerned, a modern market system is first and foremost an interest adjustment system, a competition system and an information transmission system. Thus, according to theories regarding modern market systems, a modern market should encompass at least the following components, i.e. a market factor system, a market organizational system, a market legal system, a market supervising system, a market environment system and a market infrastructure system. All these combine to form a larger network of markets which comprehensively reflects its structural integrity and its functional completeness and provides guarantees for the normal functioning of market.

(1) A market factor system consists of practically all types of market and market factors, including commodity markets, factor markets and financial markets, as well as the most cardinal market elements, such as prices, supply and demand, competition, etc.

(2) Specifically speaking, a market organizational system consists of the organizers of market factors and activities and their gathering locations, covering all kinds of market entities such as retail markets, wholesale markets, online wholesale markets, personnel management organizations, labor markets, financial institutions and cross-border trade and investment organizations, as well as intermediary agencies such as consultancy, training, information, accounting, law, property rights, asset appraisal agencies and market management organizations such as chambers of commerce and industrial associations.

(3) A market legal system refers to an entirety of laws and regulations established and formed in accordance with cardinal market economic theories, including property rights economics, the economics of contracts and normative economics, with normative market value orientation, normative market trading behavior, contract behavior and property rights behavior as its objects of regulation. It encompasses legislation, law enforcement, judiciary and law-related educational institutions.

(4) A market supervisory system is a policy enforcement system built on the basis of the market legal system, consisting of supervisory bodies, contents and measures. Supervision in this regard covers the aspects of organizations, businesses, markets and policy and law enforcement.

(5) A market environment system mainly includes a well-designed real economic foundation, a corporate governance structure and a social credit system. As far as a social credit system is concerned, it is critically important to set up a full-fledged market credit system; regulate and restrain by legal means trust relations, credit instruments, credit intermediary agencies and pertinent credit elements; and put in place a social credit governance mechanism based on a market credit guarantee mechanism.

(6) Market infrastructure is an integrated system encompassing software and hardware facilities. Necessary components of a mature market economy include market service networks, supplementary equipment and technologies, market payment and clearance systems of all types and high-tech information systems.

Building a modern market system is a feat that can only be accomplished by incremental steps. In the early development phase of the US's market economy (in the post-independence period from 1776 to 1861 and the post-Civil War period from 1865 to 1890), laissez-faire economics was held in high esteem, and its operation in economy resulted in significant improvements of the US's market factor system and market organizational system, while fervid objection to government intervention was the prevailing sentiment of the time.

In 1890, the US Congress promulgated the *Sherman Antitrust Act*, which was the US's first federal statute to prohibit trusts and monopoly. In 1914, the *Federal Trade Commission Act* and the *Clayton Antitrust Act* were passed as complements to the *Sherman Antitrust Act*. Henceforth, the US's antitrust system and regulatory measures have undergone century-long evolution and perfection, with the country's market legal system and market supervisory system experiencing significant improvements and upgrading along the way. In other words, the market legal system and the market supervisory system emerged on a par with the market factor system and the market organizational system in the US, with the entire market system demonstrating a prominent pattern that featured coexistence between monopoly and competition and between development and supervision.

As of the 1990s, two predominant trends occurred. On the one hand, the US government, instead of confining its antitrust goals to simply preventing and clamping down on market monopoly and price manipulation, undertook effective measures to combat technical monopoly and Internet oligarchy beyond the realm of IPR protection, and on the other hand, against the backdrop of an explosive growth in ICT (information and communication technology) and network technology, market-driven innovation and system infrastructure regeneration became the prominent manifestations of market competition.

Remarkable achievements were then recorded in regard to market infrastructure and environment, including the enhancement of market infrastructural facilities pertinent to registration, settlement, trusteeship and backup, the increase of capabilities against disasters and technical malfunctions, the upgrading of market information systems and credit systems and the sharing of market regulation-related data. As a result, the US's market credit system and infrastructure were further optimized and enhanced, which meant that in addition to the market factor, organizational, legal and supervisory systems, market infrastructure and environment systems were also being constantly perfected, culminating in the creation of a mature modern market system in which market competition was driven by total factor productivity and system participation.

4.2 The external possibility and intrinsic necessity of regional government competition

Regions share commonalities, similarities and generalities, but are also characterized by their individuality, particularity and diversity. Regional government is a government organization which administers affairs within its own jurisdiction, with a relatively fixed area, a relatively concentrated population and institutional governance. Regional government has the attributes of publicity and coerciveness.

The publicity of regional management is mainly reflected in ensuring regional public spending and maintaining regional markets and social stability by means of taxation, industry and commerce, public security, and monitoring and supervision and in ensuring its openness, fairness and impartiality through administrative legislation and justice. The coercive power of regional administration is embodied not only in the three super-economy coercive forces of legislation, justice and administration but in the economic coercion derived from its financial rights and rights to administer its affairs. Superficially, regional government manages economic development, urban construction, and social livelihood, but in essence, its administration is reflected in its effective allocation of tangible and intangible resources of various categories, existing and potential, within its jurisdiction.

Two serious drawbacks reside in western market economics. On the one hand, government, market and society are considered independent, and government has been excluded from the market; on the other hand, government is deemed to have a single function of public administration and is deprived of the competitive function in economic development and urban construction. Regional government's basic policy of "general underpinning, fair play and effective promotion" of non-operational resources and the regulation, supervision and management policies for operational resources makes it the centralized agent of both the region and the central government. These also enable it to promote social stability through basic social guarantee and public services and to regulate regional economy through pricing, taxation, interest rates, exchange rates, and legal means. In practice, regional government achieves its publicity and coercive power by utilizing public revenues and expenditure and increasing taxes and other sources of revenue to provide budget arrangements for government administration, national defense and security, culture and education, science, health and utilities, etc. This is accomplished by providing social consumption expenses in the industrial, transportation, commercial and agricultural sector; by providing fiscal expenditure in government investments that cover infrastructure, scientific R&D and policy-oriented financial input in industries which need urgent development; and by providing transfer expenditure, mainly composed of social security and various fiscal subsidies. By so doing, regional government plays the "quasi-state" and "quasi-macro" roles.

Regional government's participation in the allocation of and competition for quasi-operational resources and its planning, guidance and support for operational resources make it the centralized agent of a non-government entity in the region and enables it to compete with other regions through innovation in institution, management and technology. Under such circumstances, regional government possesses management rights as its jurisdictional power, which allows it to allocate resources so as to maximize regional benefits, mainly through investment attraction, development, investment, operation and management of regional projects. Although this role of regional government differs from enterprises in objectives, development modes, regulatory factors and evaluation criteria, the competitive mechanism becomes the driving force for regional governments as the same agent of resources allocation as of enterprises within certain areas; their rules of behavior must meet the requirements of market mechanisms. Regional government then plays the "quasi-enterprise" and "quasi-micro" roles. Regional government's "dual role" and the competitiveness stemmed from it in practice remedy the drawbacks of traditional market economic theories. According to modern market economics, not only are enterprises the entity of market competition but regional governments are as well. The operating mechanisms of regional government explain the inherent inevitability of regional competition.

Enterprises generally compete for the allocation of industrial resources, and regional governments mainly compete for the allocation of city resources. Relative independence and complementarities exist between enterprises and regional governments, but they differ as follows:

(1) Differences in fields of competition. Enterprises are micro-economic entities. They mainly compete for commodity markets and focus on industrial resources allocation. Market equilibrium theory, which takes manufacturers as its main subject, occupies a dominant position in western classical economics. Enterprises regard the pursuit of profit maximization as a precondition and assume the competitive forms of supply, demand, market equilibrium prices, perfect market competition, monopolistic competition, oligopolistic market, different market structures and competitive strategies, etc. Enterprise competition is the precondition and basis for regional government competition.

Regional government is the subject of mezzo-economics. Competition between regional governments focuses on factor markets and city resources allocation. Factor markets include land, capital, labor forces, property rights, and hardware and software markets such as the information and big data market. Regional government improves its competitiveness through the quantity, quality, structure and layout of urban resources. Regional government can also make policies and initiatives to regulate the allocation of regional factors and to attract and influence the direction of factor flow outside the region, so as to optimize the allocation of resources and eventually enhance regional competitiveness. Factor market competition affects enterprise commodity market competition.

(2) Differences in competition means. Enterprises seek to maximize profits mainly by increasing labor productivity – to effectively influence costs, prices, supply and demand and scale – and by optimizing the allocation of corporate resources to promote their cost minimization. Regional government makes every effort to increase total factor productivity as its chief means of sustainable growth. After simple dilatation through competing for tangible factors, such as land, projects and capital, the bottleneck of diminishing capital profits makes extensive economic growth difficult to continue. When nothing more can be added to regional input of all tangible factors, regional government will have to depend on the investment, increase and improvement of intangible factors such as technological advancement (with innovation as the core), resource allocation optimization, structural adjustment as well as institution, organization, legislation, environment, etc. as the new driving forces of regional economy development and urban construction.

(3) Differences in competition paths. Enterprises are investment growth-oriented. The continuous improvement of business performance comes from the constant input of production factors, including capital, labor, land, technology, entrepreneurship and so on. The initial strategy for businesses investment is mainly extensive expansion of quantity, followed by the quality-enhancing stage and then the stage of business management. In all these stages, sustained and effective inputs become critical. Regional government is efficiency growth-oriented. In light of the experiences of regional economies in the world, their economic growth path starts from the factor-driven stage (also known as the resource allocation stage), to the investment-driven stage (also known as the efficiency improvement stage) and then to the innovation-driven stage (also called the sustainable growth stage). Regional government makes efforts to optimize the combination of tangible and intangible factors, with efficiency improvement as the focus of its growth.

(4) Differences in competition orientation. Enterprises regard demand-side expansion as their orientation. Business competition starts from market demand, demand quantities, demand structure, corporate strategies and tactics. The ability to adapt to market requirements becomes essential to their survival and success. Regional government regards supply-side optimization as its orientation. Regional government's determined direction for economic development, urban construction and facilitation of people's livelihood is

to promote supply-side structural reforms by effectively allocating the supply of land, capital, projects, technology, work forces and other tangible resources; by effectively regulating the supply of prices, taxation, interest rates, exchange rates, law and other intangible resources; and through innovation in institution, organization and technology.

(5) Differences in competition modes. Enterprises adopt the ERP mode to exercise effective and integrated management of materials, finance, information and customer resources and achieve inter-regional, inter-sector, and inter-industrial coordination and effective allocation in terms of logistics and personnel, financial and information flow. Guided by market demands, enterprises will strive for effective integration of resources, adjustment of functions, improvement of production efficiency and eventual enhancement of competitiveness. Regional government, however, may establish the DRP mode to effectively allocate resources such as land, population, finance, environment, technology and policies, design layouts and make appropriate arrangements according to regional planning and strategies. Equipped with systematic management notions and approaches, regional government employs layout design and planning as the basis to make judgment upon market changes, deploy regional resources, enhance regional competitiveness, realize the best regional TFP and achieve sustainable economic and social development in the region.

4.3   Forms of regional government competition

The relations and differences in competition between regional governments and enterprises reveal that competition between regional governments and that between enterprises are two systems of competition on different levels of the modern market economy. They are mutually independent but related, constituting the double entities of competition of the modern market economy. Competition between enterprises is the basis of competition in the market economy and leads to competition between regional governments. Regional governments compete for the optimization of resources allocation via systems, policies, projects and environment. It is a different kind of competition above the level of enterprise competition, which in turn influences, supports and promotes enterprise competitiveness. Enterprise competition takes place only across enterprises. Regional government can only act as a planner and guide of industrial development; an assistant and regulator of commodity production; and a supervisor and manager of market order. It has no right to exercise direct intervention in micro-level enterprise operations. Regional government competition takes place only across regional governments. It follows the rules of market economy and competes in terms of projects, policies and public affairs in relation to regional resource allocation, economic development, urban construction and people's livelihoods.

Regional government competition takes the following forms, depending on its focuses in different phases:

4.3.1 Project competition

There are mainly three categories of projects: national key projects, social investment projects and foreign investment projects. The first category includes special national key projects; major projects of national science and technology programs; major infrastructure projects of national science and technology programs; and major state-financed construction and industrial projects. The second category includes projects in high-tech industries, newly emerging industries, equipment manufacturing, raw materials, finance, logistics and other services. The third category includes projects concerning intelligent manufacturing, cloud computing and big data, networking, intelligent urban construction and so on.

Regional governments compete for projects in order to directly acquire capital, talents and industry; effectively solve regional financing, land acquisition and other issues through legitimate project policies and rational public services; guide, through project implementation, regional land development, urban infrastructure construction; increase investment; promote industrial development; optimize the allocation of resources; enhance policy capabilities; and facilitate the sustainable development of regional economy and community. Consequently, project competition becomes one of the key issues for regional government work that leads the direction for regional development. Awareness of the importance of projects, development, efficiency, advantages, conditions, policies and risks becomes an essential requirement for regional government in market competition.

In China, the system of project management is a major mode of economic administration after the implementation of the tax system reform, which extends from central government to local government and then to grassroots units. This system works through special transfer payments or special fund allocation for certain projects. Major national projects are classified into four categories: national major projects, major national science and technology projects, major construction and industrialization projects with national financial support and infrastructure construction for science and technology development, etc. These projects are generally endowed with special missions by different levels of government, giving support to national and regional science and technology projects or certain industries, such as major science and technology projects, high-tech industrialization projects, strategic development of emerging industries, equipment manufacturing projects, raw materials and consumer goods projects, distinctive industries projects, intelligent manufacturing projects, the Internet of things projects, cloud computing and big data projects, smart city construction projects, regional leading industrial projects, etc. The great majority of the projects launched through competitive bidding are selected in light of regional government performance. National special transfer payments increased from 15.98 percent in 1994 to 46.7 percent in 2012, an increase of 300 percent. That did not include special funds, which were far greater than special transfer payments, allocated through the budget departments within the public financial system, ministries and national commissions, and departments with budgetary and financial authorization. Along the vertical chain of government administration, provincial and regional governments also set up a series of local special funds. This system has become an important mode of economic governance at all levels of government, spurring and mobilizing grassroots units and local enterprises through project application for special funds.

Projects are important economic resources for regional governments in China. First, projects can directly provide funds. Regional governments at the provincial level can obtain all sorts of national project funds, while regional governments at the local level can obtain all sorts of provincial project funds, thus boosting the development of key industries and enterprises while accelerating the pace of infrastructure construction and the supply of public goods. For example, during the 13th Five-Year Plan, Anhui Province had 327 projects that were listed major national projects, with a total investment of 2 trillion yuan, as well as 877 projects that were listed as major provincial projects, with a total investment of 1.9 trillion yuan.

Second, in the light of the validity of project policies and the justifiability of public services, it is possible to expedite the procedures of project-oriented examination and approval from higher-level governments and the expropriation of land in rural areas; at the same time, it is also possible to enhance government credit and the qualifications of financing so as to help regional governments find solutions to fund-raising, financing and land requisition.

Third, with resort to the availability of projects approved by higher-level authorities, regions can turn project resources such as land development, infrastructure construction, investment attraction and industrial support into economic programs through corresponding policy resources. While promoting work in all areas by drawing upon the experience gained from key projects and pursuing guided development, the current regional government should lead the next to participate in project competition in an attempt to enhance their awareness for projects and competition. In order to fully leverage the market competition mechanism, governmental projects related to infrastructure and public facilities should be put into operation so as to boost regional development and improve the efficiency of resources allocation.

Project competition is initiated by way of longitudinal project applications, which entail not merely the renewed regional government examination and evaluation of development orientation, key areas of development, development advantages and conditions but, more importantly, also cultivate the awareness of projects, efficiency, risk and guidance among participants. Such competition is market-based, since regional government at all levels creates a project-oriented market within their jurisdiction for sub-national governments. In this process, lower-level governments become equal participants through project application, though superficially, regional government will leave no stone unturned to trigger off competition and contests for project resources, thus forming a complicated interest relationship.

In addition, the horizontal international flow of project investment has also become the main target of horizontal competition initiated by all regions.

4.3.2 Competition of industrial chain development

Generally speaking, each region has its own industrial foundation with its own characteristics, which are in most cases contingent upon natural resource endowments in the region. The crux of the matter lies in how to maintain and optimize regional internal resources endowments and how to synergize and obtain high-end resources from outside the region. The key is optimization of industrial structure and effective development of industrial chains, and the breaking point is developing towards high-end industries, form industrial agglomeration and lead industrial clustering.

Regional government competition for industrial chain development unfolds mainly in two aspects. The first is concerned with factors of production. Low-end or primary factors of production cannot form a stable and long-lasting competitive edge. Only by introducing, investing and developing high-end and high-level factors of production – such as industrial technology, modern information technology, network resources, transport facilities and professional personnel, research and development think tanks, etc. – can powerful and competitive industries be built up. The second is concerned with industrial clustering and industrial underpinnings. Regional competitiveness reveals that effective industrial clustering, employing the existing regional industrial base as the leading force, can reduce business transaction costs and improve enterprise profitability. The industrial smile curve makes manifest that the most valuable areas are located at both ends of the value chain – R&D and market. As a result, an important route for regional government to follow in achieving sustainable development is cultivating competitive industries, developing industrial chains and introducing "targeted" investment according to the structural requirements of the industry.

In China, governments at all levels are supposed to formulate their own development strategies for primary, secondary and tertiary industry, thus forging their own strategic industries. The realization of industrial strategy and industrial cluster and the development of strategic industry depend on the endowment of resources within the region, the convergence of foreign resources and the updating and positioning of technological structural standards. Due to the horizontal flow of resources in all regions and the vertical flow as a result of the vertical management chain, whether internal resources endowment can be maintained and the convergence of external resources can be achieved hinges on the competition between regional governments. Industrial chain supporting competition is of great significance to regional government's endeavor to make the best of current resources endowment and give full play to competitive advantages. Meanwhile, the convergence and integration of more resources can be realized by resorting to preemptive rights and policy-based advantages. Regional government that wins in the competition is in a better position to attract industrial investments and raise the level of industrial clusters as well as assist the regional government in completing established industrial goals. It is rather difficult for those who fail to win the competition to effectively invite industrial investments, obtain comparative advantages in the industrial chain, reach a high-end position of value chain or promote the concentration of industries and create reasonable industrial clusters.

It seems that Michael Porter's diamond model is formulated for the analysis of why a certain industry in a given country has stronger competitiveness in the world. In reality, it may also be extended to analyze the industrial competitiveness of regional government. In Porter's opinion, four factors may contribute to the industrial competitiveness of a region: (a) production factors, including human resources, natural resources, knowledge resources and capital resources as well as infrastructure; (b) demand conditions, namely the level of market demand and the demand structure that are determined by the level of economic development; (c) the basis of present standard regarding relevant and supporting industries and the level of labor division in the whole industrial chain; and (d) the performances of strategy, structure and competitor, namely the level and basis of strategy, structure and competitor. In Porter's opinion, the four factors are mutually influential, and their combination has a crucial bearing on the industrial competitiveness of regional government. Apart from the above-mentioned four factors, Porter also takes into consideration two major variations, i.e. government and opportunities. External opportunities are obtainable but hard to control. Likewise, government policies can be won over but require relevant parties to take the initiative.

According to the diamond theory, regional government competition for industrial chain matching can be carried out through production factors and through industrial chains and clustering.

First, Porter divides production factors into basic and advanced production factor. Based on Porter's idea and the reality of development, basic production factors refer to natural resources, geographic position, non-tech and low-end human resources and self-owned financial resources, etc., while advanced production factors refer to modern information technology, industrial technical conditions, Internet resources, traffic resources, labor forces with higher education, research institutes and think tanks, etc. However, the importance, demand and cost of basic factors are on the decline and their availability is relatively simple. By contrast, advanced factors have to undergo a difficult process of formation, with their importance, demand and cost of availability on the increase and the approaches to their availability unique in their dependence upon external channels and internal investment as well.

It is possible for high-end production factors to maintain steady and everlasting competitiveness while it is impossible for low-end production factors, as the shortage of low-end production factors can urge regional government to step up innovation and scale up the investment of high-end production factors. If regional government wants to create a strong and long-lived industrial advantage by resorting to production factors, it must develop advanced and professionalized production factors, such as the cultivation of high-caliber professionals, investment in research institutes and think tanks and the attraction of outward advanced production factors, rather than merely relying on low-end production factors, even though they turn out to be well-endowed.

Second, the industrial division of regional governments leads to the formation of industrial chains, but their values vary with sections of industrial chains. It can be inferred from the industrial smiling curve that sections with maximum values are highly concentrated in both ends of the value chain: research and development and market, and the production, assembly and processing of parts are distributed in the low-end section of the value chain. In this connection, competitiveness resides in industries that are developed at both ends of the smiling curve of the industrial chain or in self-completed industrial chains. Advantageous industries for regional governments do not exist by themselves. It is also of vital importance for the industrial "clusters", together with their matching industries, to form and develop.

For example, German-made printing machinery enjoys global industrial advantages, and its supporting industries, such as paper industry, printing ink, plate-making and machinery manufacturing, also enjoy some degree of competitive advantages. Likewise, the competitive advantages of the automobile industry in the US, Germany and Japan are closely linked to industrial sectors, such as iron and steel, machinery manufacturing and chemical engineering as well as car-related business. Machinery manufacturing in Foshan, China, is a Chinese case in point. It boasts certain comparative advantages, which, in fact, ascribe to the support of such related sectors as aluminum, nonferrous metal and intelligent design. High-tech industries in Shenzhen, China, enjoy a complete range of supporting industries, such as computer and calculator making, for which Shenzhen has, apart from chip production, a comprehensive range of manufacturing factories providing matching products such as computer cases, plug-boards, plate cards and indicators, magnetic heads and hard-disk drives. These factories have a total annual supporting capacity of around 20 million sets. As such, regional government should either foster its own supporting capacity for industries guided by its existing advantage industries, introduce supporting industries in clusters for its dominating industries or heighten its own industrial value chains so as to drive the formation of larger supporting industries.

4.3.3 Competition for talents, science and technology

The primary issue in competition for talents and science and technology is the recognition of the doctrines that human resources are primary resources and that science and technology are primary productive forces. The most fundamental task is to improve local personnel training systems and increase regional investment in personnel training and technological innovation, and the greatest significance resides in creating conditions for talent attraction, introduction, training and employment. The competitiveness of science and technology talents is measured by regional science and technology human resources indexes; the number of people engaged in scientific and technological activities per ten thousand people; the number of scientists and engineers per ten thousand people; the total number of scientific and technological activities per ten thousand people, the number of students in colleges and universities per ten thousand people; annual investment in science and technology talent training index per ten thousand people; total operating expenses of science and technology activities; the percentage of GDP for science and technology expenditure; per capita research funding; the percentage of local fiscal expenditure for financial allocations to local science and technology; per capita government expenditure on education; total local fiscal expenditure on education; numbers of full-time college teachers; and other indicators. Regional government should undertake concerted efforts to improve and enhance related indicators so as to reinforce the overall competitiveness of talents in science and technology.

First of all, what lies at the core of competition for talents and science and technology is highly valuing talents and science and technology and sticking firmly to the doctrines discussed above. Strategies must be formulated and implemented to strengthen the cultivation, introduction and employment of talents; foster a social climate in which knowledge, talents and science and technology are respected; and create a favorable environment conducive to talent cultivation and growth and to technological innovation. The scarcity, uniqueness and non-substitutability of talents give rise to the high-end value of talents. Globally, whichever country attaches importance to talents and science and technology will develop on a track of faster and more sustainable development; the same is true of regions, which is amply demonstrated by Shenzhen, China, the prosperity of which today is attributable not only to China's reform and opening up but also, and more importantly, to its special emphasis on its introduction of talents and its innovation in science and technology.

Second, the most fundamental aspect to competition for talents and science and technology lies in improving the cultivation system of local talents, scaling up the investment in local talents cultivation and increasing the input of innovation in science and technology. Regional government, as a rule, should come up with various ways to intensify investments in education and training, especially in entrepreneurship education, as well as education concerning technological innovation. The proportion of educational training in its fiscal spending should be increased with a view to improving the remuneration of those who are engaged in education and training sectors, bringing forth a talent pool of high quality with a reasonable structure and competitiveness and eventually building up an educational system that integrates general and vocational education, emphasizes degree and non-degree education and incorporates continuing education and lifelong education, thus rendering the popularization of higher education possible in a gradual way. Regional government can employ direct and indirect investments for talent cultivation and technological innovation. Direct investment in technology and education includes financial support for affiliated universities and research institutes, subsidies to encourage individuals and enterprises to engage in education and training activities as well as activities of scientific research by means of project funding, awards for scientific research and fiscal allowances. Indirect investment covers the construction of educational and technological environments, facilities and platforms so that an enabling talent climate can attract and retain those engaged in educational, training and technological activities. Relevant research findings have shown that the greater the improvement for technological research environment within the region, the greater the investment in technological innovation and the more attractive the region becomes to neighboring regions.

Third, the most striking manifestation of competition for talents and science and technology are the conditions created by regional governments to attract talents. The introduction of talents can help solve the problem of inadequate supply of talents in the short run, and local cultivation may lead to talent gaps and failures to meet the need of regional economic and social development. Increasing reduction in the cost of talent flow has made it easier for both talents and technology to become the most active flowing elements in the market. A two-way flowing trend of technological talents is observed between developed economies and less developed economies, and the same takes place between developed regions and less developed regions. What matters in retaining talents is not necessarily whether regional economy is well developed but rather, more essentially, whether there are such needs and policy advantages. As a result, the most noticeable way in which talent competition is initiated is the making of policies towards talents, particularly policies for talent introduction. Regional government will have to compete in policies concerning the provision of financial and material benefits, excellent social services, good child education, financial support for scientific research, preferential income tax reduction or exemption, flexible talent flow, etc.

Finally, what lies at the core of competition for talents and technology are the introduction and cultivation of talents of science and technology. Viewed from the historical and global perspective, talents of science and technology are at the center of competition for talents and technology and are a guarantee for the realization of the primary productive force. They are highly creative and are infused with the spirit of scientific exploration. As the rare resources and valuable wealth in a country or region, they are in a unique position to make contributions to the development of science and technology and the advancement of mankind. The US-based "Manhattan Project", which collected all kinds of technological talents, especially top talents, totaling 530,000 people, enabled the US to become the first country to grasp nuclear technology, which eventually led to victory in the Second World War. Technological talents in China have created numerous scientific miracles in basic science and engineering technology, such as nuclear and hydrogen bombs, satellite launches, manned space flight, a moon probe program, the Beidou navigation satellite, high-temperature superconductivity, nanotechnology and human genome sequencing, as well as super hybrid rice, etc.

Regional government competition for talents and science and technology epitomize competitiveness in science and technology, which is demonstrated by the unit technology-based talents competitiveness; the index of technological talent resources; the number of talents engaged in technological activities per ten thousand persons' the number of scientists and engineers per ten thousand persons; the number of personnel involved in technological projects per ten thousand persons; the number of internal students in colleges and universities per ten thousand persons; the index of yearly input of technological talents per ten thousand persons; the aggregate of expenditures used for technological projects; the share of technological spending in GDP; the expenditure for science and research per capita; the percentage of local financial allocation in technology in local fiscal spending; the per capita fiscal expenditure for education; the total local expense amount for education; and the number of full-time teachers in universities, to name only a few. On top of that, the goal of competitiveness based on talent and technology is realized by improving the above-mentioned indexes in an effort to enhance the overall competitiveness of technology.

4.3.4 *Fiscal and financial competition*

Regional fiscal competition covers fiscal revenue and expenditure competition. Fiscal revenue is mainly achieved through the pursuit of economic growth and the accrual of taxes. Apart from social consumption and transfer expenditure, competition is chiefly realized through government investment, such as investment in infrastructure, science and technology R&D, investment of fiscal policy funds in industries that need urgent development and other fiscal investment expenditure. Fiscal investment expenditure is an important force for driving economic growth. The overall size of fiscal revenues and expenditure is limited; regional government must actively build various platforms for investment and financing – as well as mobilize and attract regional, national and international financial institutions, funds, personnel, information and other financial resources to the greatest possible extent – in order to benefit regional economic development, urban construction, social and livelihood services. Preferential policies and measures adopted by regional governments drive each other into competition for fiscal spending and monetary absorption.

In China, the reform of the tax-sharing system has provided regional governments at all levels with independent interests and made them the entities of interests in terms of market competitiveness, which has turned fiscal and financial competition between regional governments into their major means of competition. Regional fiscal competition consists of competition for fiscal revenues and expenditure. The competition for fiscal revenues refers to the fact that regional government aims to increase income taxes by pursuing the competition of economic growth, which is the most fundamental competition and is intensified through the assessment system for administrative performance on the part of regional governments. The competition of fiscal expenditure means increasing social capital increment by scaling up governmental spending in investment so as to add to the impetus for economic development. For spiral economic growth, there is no essential difference between fiscal revenue and fiscal expenditure. But regarding the impetus for economic growth, fiscal expenditure is the ultimate driving force. Furthermore, judging from the motives of regional government administrative performance, fiscal revenue is in the final analysis for the sake of fiscal expenditure, and fiscal expenditure, especially investment spending, can give full expression to government administrative achievements. Thus, fiscal competition between regional governments is demonstrated in fiscal expenditure. Related research shows that the decentralization of fiscal powers in China, as well as the competition of fiscal expenditure on the basis of the assessment of administrative performance, puts their focuses on the accessibility of basic construction investment, followed by human capital investment and public service.

In addition to fiscal revenue, regional governments can gain financial support for their fiscal expenditure from the financing of financial sectors or investment and financing platforms within regions. Such an approach has won the favor of regional government over recent years. The reason for this is that though investment through financial funding is reckoned as a regular means, there is a huge limitation in this regard; fiscal revenue is restricted by the level of economic development, which causes slow growth and thus results in the restriction of the overall scale. Moreover, fiscal revenue cannot depend on the growth of budgetary revenue. If that happens, business activities of enterprises, as well as disposable incomes and welfares of residents, will be affected considerably, thus incurring objections for enterprises and residents.

Since 2009, a variety of governmental or policy-oriented platforms for investment and financing have been built up by governments at all levels in China, which can, to the greatest extent possible, pool financial resources locally and even nationwide to serve as local investment, thus creating financial competition. Under the condition of the established financial aggregate, regional government must resort to different strategies based on financial competition to attract capital from all channels to flow into financial authorities or platforms in order to access as many financial resources as possible. The building-up of investment and financing platforms serves the purpose of attracting capital, including domestic non-governmental capital and foreign capital as well as national investments and investments from government of all levels. In view of the whole capital market, the amount of capital is always limited, which means that regional government must adopt some preferential policies related to interests, income tax and expenditure and other local and relevant policies to attract the influx of capital in ways that increase the local economic performance in a quick way. Relevant research has pointed out that the transfer price of industrial land agreement in the midst of land competition between regional governments is an important approach to investment attraction. The land preferential price war between regional governments is in itself an investment battle. A deep look shows that it can be regarded as the means of financial competition between regional governments.

4.3.5 Infrastructure competition

Infrastructure competition takes place in the construction of both infrastructure hardware and smart city software. The former includes transportation platforms of highways, ports and aviation; energy supply platforms of electricity, gas and others; information platforms of cable and networks; and science and technology parks, industrial, entrepreneurial and creative parks. The latter includes intelligent city-building platforms of big data, cloud computing and the Internet of things. Infrastructure systems, which can be rated as advanced, adaptive and backward, underpin economic and social development in the region. The moderately advanced infrastructure supply in a region will provide optimal services for urban structure, facility size and spatial layout in market competition so that enterprise costs are reduced, production efficiency enhanced and industrial development facilitated. Whether regional infrastructure is complete directly brings forth differences in regional economy and affects its future.

The competition between regional governments in improving the environment of development, signifying the competition of producing and supplying non-mobile "products", including hard public goods, e.g. infrastructure, and soft public goods, e.g. smart city, targets at the maximization of combined benefits. Not only can this kind of competition make possible the benefit maximization of residents within the jurisdiction and the benefit maximization of the collective, including individual officials and their teams in the region can uphold the overall national interests as well, so as to help to propel the balanced development of regional economy.

The competition of hard environment, broadly speaking, mainly covers the construction of infrastructure and the improvement of the matching environment of industries. The former covers transportation facilities like expressways, seaports and aviation; energy supply facilities like electric power and natural gas; information-based hard platforms like cable; and environmental protection like sewage treatment plants. They are aimed at building a sound supporting system of infrastructure in an effort to create a convenient and efficient environment for investors.

The industrial supporting environment construction covers fostering a good supporting environment of upstream and downstream industries by centering on the promotion of the existing dominant industries and cultivating new industries with further focus on the enhancement of favorable industrial supporting environment, for example, the construction of industrial parks, high-tech business incubator zones and the opening up of economic development zones. The construction of soft infrastructure has turned out to be of greater significance and has become the major area of competition for regional government. The most attractive part is the build-up of big data platforms, cloud computing platforms and smart cities, which is generally implemented through project schemes, a major form of competition between regional governments.

The reason why regional government is committed to the improvement of infrastructure is that infrastructure can play an underpinning and guiding role in economic and social development and can put regional development on a faster track. It is also helpful to ensure the realization of national interests and push forward the coordinated development of regional economy so that the maximization of combined interests can be achieved. The underpinning function can find expression in the capability of the infrastructure system to prop up regional economic and social development. In other words, its supply can satisfy the needs of economic and social development in the region, and the extent of satisfaction can be divided into three basic levels: advanced, adaptive and backward. The advanced level indicates that its supply outstrips the demand of economic and social development and even causes some degree of surplus; the adaptive level indicates that its supply can basically meet the demand of economic and social development without its inadequacy or excessiveness; the backward level indicates that its supply lags behind development requirements and becomes a bottleneck.

Such competition makes it possible for the construction of infrastructure to basically meet the requirements for regional economic and social development. If regional potentials wait to be tapped, its construction may desirably outstrip the level of its economic and social development. However, its supply should not become excessive so as to cause idle capacity, the decrease of marginal benefits of infrastructure supply and the dwindling utilization of resources. If extreme backwardness occurs, its inadequacy will harm the capability of economic and social development and make it difficult to bring it into full play. The theory of the "bucket effect" explains that what decides its level of supply is not the longest board that makes it but the shortest one. Likewise, the major purpose of such competition is just to avoid the presence of any short boards.

The guiding function of infrastructure implies that the infrastructure system of a region, under the influence of market competitive mechanisms and industrial linkage mechanisms, can play guiding and feedback roles through its supply of services in the structure, scale and spatial layout of regional social economic development, for example, the information-based infrastructure, which can make use of information technology to lead reforms in traditional sectors and develop high-tech and modern tertiary industry. A case in point is New York City, which boasts the world's largest financial and information hub and is the key traffic hub in North America, as well as having a strong industrial base, which can all be ascribed to its priority development of infrastructure. Its superior trade port has attracted the industrial agglomeration of processing sectors, which requires advanced logistics distribution as a result of advanced transportation and trade industries. No matter whether it is the industrial agglomeration or logistics industry, it entails the close coordination of the financial and information sectors. Therefore, its function as financial and information hubs begin to be intensified in terms of their underpinning and guiding roles.

In addition, the enhancement of productivity and the improvement of production environment prove to be a huge contribution to regional economic growth. Infrastructure services, such as transportation, water supply, electric power and information, etc., are all intermediate inputs in the course of production, and reduction in such input will improve production efficiency. The improvement of infrastructure services will increase the output rate of other production factors, such as labor force and other kind of capital. The improvement of traffic infrastructure, for example, reduces the duration of commuters and enhances the efficiency of logistics so that the output rate of production factors rises. It follows that whether infrastructure is improved or not is a crucial cause for the disparity in regional economic growth rates and an important motivation for the competition of infrastructure between regional governments.

4.3.6 *Competition in environmental systems*

In addition to infrastructure, environmental systems here mainly cover the construction of ecological environment, humanistic environment, policy environment, social credit system and the like. Regional government competition entails environments for development, including the harmony between investment development and ecological protection; the matching between investment attraction and policy services; the agreement between wealth pursuit and social returns; and the mutual support between legal supervision and social credit. Favorable environment systems are the recipe for success in investment solicitation, project construction and sustainable development; this has been proven by successful experience in China and overseas.

Though the construction of infrastructure is an integral part of environmental system competition, what is emphasized here are regional, human, service and credit environments. The competition of environmental systems mainly encompasses the following aspects.

First, regional governments gain competitive advantages by publicizing their own regional advantages, which are embodied in transportation facilities, geographic location and economic status (especially the advantage of economic resources). For instance, Kunshan in China's Jiangsu Province enjoys proximity to Shanghai, just as the Pearl River Delta does to Hong Kong and Macao, and as Foshan does to Guangzhou. These locational advantages have a great deal to do with regional development in their early days and even in the present stage. In the initial stage of China's reform and opening up, Dongguan of Guangdong Province, China, catered to the needs of industrial transfers of Hong Kong, Macao, Taiwan and foreign countries by making the most of its geographic advantage, low labor force, lower land price and preferential opening policies, thus becoming a processing center of the world's IT sectors in a rapid fashion. Kunshan copied Dongguan, attracting investment from Taiwan and other regions, thus making it another significant IT manufacturing center in China.

Second, regional government tends to obtain competitive advantages by improving service-oriented soft environment. For example, Kunshan implemented special measures to optimize the environment of service and promote the attractiveness of investment by putting forward such notions as "atoning for policy inadequacies through intensifying services" and "nanny-style government service" and "public friendliness towards investment". Compliance with the law and open and transparent administration are considered the basis and prerequisite for the optimization of regional service environments, the core of regional soft power, which can make up for the inadequacies in the hard power of a region. Gutian County in Fujian Province, for example, optimizes the environment of soft power by intensifying government services, which eventually convinced overseas business people to invest extensively in the region. In Beijing, Zhongguancun in Haidian District and Wangjing in Chaoyang District are now both concentrated zones of Internet companies. Their secret is to continuously heighten the level of government services. Their good services and favorable atmosphere of entrepreneurship continue to be great attractions to new Internet companies.

Third, regional government can gain competitive advantages by shaping a good humanistic environment. For example, an obvious difference can be found between the Pearl River Delta and the Yangtze River Delta in terms of the build-up of humanistic environment. The humanistic spirit in the Pearl River Delta can be summed up as "mercantilism, pragmatism and integration". Its young generation does not disguise their aspirations and desire for wealth, as the pursuit of wealth is one of their key goals in life. They prove to be pragmatic, direct and efficient even in cultural pursuits. But people in the Yangtze River region are endowed with deep cultural deposits, with a special focus on education, science and technology and sustainable self-cultivation and family development. It is precisely the differences in their humanistic environment that give different expressions to their historical tracks of economic and social development.

The promotion and creation of a good modern environment turns out to be a primary approach to regional government competition. The humanistic environment, in a sense, has become part of the appraisal of capital cost. The humanistic spirit that enterprises attach great importance to includes the excellence of local human resources in such aspects as modern awareness and product awareness, enterprising folk customs, open-mindedness and moderate public temperament, which can effectively help to reduce risks in legality, economy and operation. The humanistic spirit is an essential element that boosts the competitiveness of a city. The biggest competitiveness of a city lies in giving everyone in the city a sense of belonging rather than a sense of being a "passerby".

The competition of a region or a city goes ultimately to the humanistic environment, depending on whether a favorable humanistic environment can be created for entrepreneurs to start, develop and sustain their businesses. For those companies investing in the Yangtze River Delta, the human spirit is absolutely their priority. When BenQ decided to establish factories in China mainland, a batch of factories funded by Taiwan had already gathered in Shenzhen, Dongguan and other cities in the Pearl River Delta region, which provided it with a strong supporting environment for the IT manufacturing industry. BenQ chose to settle in Suzhou to become the first Taiwan company in Suzhou New District, which is explained by their belief in regional personality, understanding of happiness and hard-working, and other cultural attributes of the region, which have been deeply imprinted in the minds of the people in the region since ancient times and which dovetail with BenQ's corporate culture.

Finally, the competition of social credit systems has been of increasing importance to regional governments. With the development of a regional economy, the build-up of a social credit system has continuously served as a significant means and guarantee of regional competition. A mature social credit system can regulate and standardize regional market order, integrate government administration and social scrutiny and help to enhance regional administrative effectiveness. By accelerating the pace of social credit system build-up, regional government can set up credit system platforms, which undertake credit information collection, management, usage, publicity and release; introduce punitive measures such as the exposure of information concerning dishonesty; and elevate the level of regional governance and regional credit competitive power.

Let us take Zhangjiagang City, Jiangsu Province, China, as an example. In 2012, Zhangjiagang Municipality established a committee for social credit system construction, which was followed by the establishment of the Public Credit Information Center of Zhangjiagang City in 2014, with its main responsibilities being the collection and handling of credit information and its related services. Regarding credit system building, Zhangjiagang City put forth *Provisions for the Build-up of Social Credit in Zhangjiagang City* and *Regulations Regarding Corporate Information Management in Zhangjiagang City* in 2014. The former stipulated the macro-level requirements of the build-up of social credit system in Zhangjiagang City, specified major tasks, objectives and guarantee measures and established a fundamental framework. The latter made relevant stipulations regarding the collection of corporate credit data and the standardization of their collection, release, use and documentation.

In the same year, it initiated the first-phase project featuring "public credit information service platform" and built a passageway for information sharing by coordinating authorities of industry and commerce, state taxation, quality inspection, court and so on, thus forming an information bank of legal persons with information updating mechanisms. The information bank contained a whole set of credit information data of all enterprises. By the end of 2014, more than 700,000 entries from local 40,852 enterprises had been collected. Zhangjiagang City had made some initial attempts at the application of credit information, such as the creation of honest user websites – "Credit Zhangjiagang" and the APP of Credit Consultation as well as promoting corporate credit standards. "Credit Zhangjiagang" was officially put into operation in June 2014, highlighting credit information publicity, inquiries, dishonesty black lists and exposure platforms, as well as credit information assessment.

4.3.7 Competition in policy systems

This involves policies implemented by regional government on both foreign and regional levels and is also true between countries. Policies are public products that are non-exclusive and imitative. Therefore, good competitive policy systems must be (1) realistic, i.e. in line with reality and the requirements for socio-economic development; (2) advanced, in the sense that they are foresighted and innovative; (3) workable, in the sense that they are clear, targeted and enforceable; (4) organized, in the sense that specialized agencies and people perform duties and put them into operation; and (5) effective, which means that there is inspection, monitoring, assessment and evaluation mechanisms, including the involvement of third parties playing their role so as to achieve policy objectives effectively. Whether policy systems are sound or not has great impacts upon regional competition.

Apart from competition in the above-mentioned areas, it is of greater significance for regional government to compete in the policy system. Due to its complexity, diversity and extensive impacts, such competition will affect various aspects of socio-economic development in the region. In this sense, the policy system competition is the most fundamental for regional government, because it may exert extensive influence upon public finance, hard and soft environment, infrastructure, talent development and science and technology. The policy system competition may unfold on two levels: regional governments compete for national preferential policies or pilot trials of antecedent policies, and regional governments may introduce a variety of competitive policies within their own power.

China's institutional transformation and transition are dominated by the national government supply. The national government sets policy bottom lines and thresholds for regional governments. The policy "reservoir" is under the control of the national government, and it is up to the national government when the water in the reservoir is discharged, how and to whom, so experimentation and then promotion have been a major way of making decisions concerning the discharge of the reservoir water. Therefore, striving for pilot trials has become an important part of competition between regional governments, who need to "run to meet higher government officials for policies". Policy experimentation means opportunities of being the first to set up pilot zones for policies, preferential policies granted by the state and minimized risks in policy implementation. The special economic zones, cities under separate state planning, state-level development zones and the current free trade zones are all products of such competition. Without early trials and pilot implementation, there might not be what exist today in different regions of China. As long as a regional government can win over certain preferential and special policies, it will be in a good position to lay a solid foundation for steady regional economic development and the maximization of regional budget revenues.

In addition to the competition of "running for policies", regional governments put forward a variety of policies in line with their own conditions within their own authority. Only when these policies prove to be sophisticated can they be considered competitive and acquire policy dividends, and the policy sophistication is manifested in the form of policy innovation competition in the policy system. In order to obtain potential benefits of policy competition, a region must, to some extent, be predictive, foresighted and ahead of others, just as commodity markets must keep products competitive if they want to gain excess profits. Since policies are public products with non-exclusiveness and emulability, they are easily reproduced, and therefore, the same policy may appear in different regions at the same time; once it is imitated and transcended, the potential benefits of the region will be diminished.

Policy competitiveness depends on whether there is such a policy in the region, whether it is known to the public, whether it is sound and workable, and whether it can achieve its desired effects. Regional governments need to formulate and put into operation such policies as targeting talents, investment and financing, land, personnel training support and other aspects through official channels. They need to make such policies known to the public and let the public publicize, understand and act upon them. They need to promulgate policies that are comprehensive, clear, operable and suited for local socio-economic development. They need to ensure that the policies are implemented through designated agencies and specific personnel and that there are checking, evaluation and supervising mechanisms. And, finally, they need to look into whether the policies have achieved their desired effects, whether they have got positive feedback, whether they play an exemplary role outside the region and whether they bring the aggregation of resources for regional economic and social development.

What is discussed above must be consistent; there should not be contradictions, particularly in terms of policy formulation and implementation. In real life, it is not uncommon that the regional government may put forward quite a number of policies, which do not have their due effects or demonstrate their competitiveness as a result of poor execution. Ningbo City, China, for example, issued between 2010 and 2015 seven official documents regarding talent planning, 13 regarding talent attraction and introduction, ten regarding talent training, two regarding talent selection, eight regarding talent exchange, eight regarding talent rewards, 12 regarding talent appraisal and 14 regarding talent protection. However, very few official documents touched upon talent employment, policy implementation, supervision and others, such as the absence of current policies in constraints and supervision after talent introduction; very few terms dealt with how the introduced talents or technical team serve enterprises, how to fully tap the potentials of these talents to serve enterprises and how to clarify the requirements of the current laws and regulations for work responsibilities. All these partially explain the failures of those talent policies to fully achieve their desired goals and effects and the reasons why they turned out to be not so competitive in Zhejiang Province, China, as expected.

4.3.8   Competition in management efficiency

Regional government management efficiency is an overall indication of its administrative activities, speed, quality and efficiency; this covers macro-efficiency, micro-efficiency, organizational efficiency and individual efficiency. In terms of administrative compliance, regional government bodies should follow the norms of legality, interest and quality, and in terms of administrative efficiency, they should follow the norms of quantity, time, speed and budgeting. Competition in management efficiency is in nature competition of organizational systems, government obligations, service awareness, work skills and technological platforms. Developed regions have been practicing, without precedent, the paralleled and integrated service modes.

Efficiency of regional government administration is an overall reflection of administrative activities, performance, quality and efficacy and a comprehensive evaluation of administrative capacity, executive capabilities and service competence, which reflect both "what to do" and "how to do" on the part of regional government. What regional government does must comply with administrative specifications: legality, i.e. whether administration is in line with the Constitution, laws and regulations, as well as national principles and policies; interest, i.e. whether administrative outcomes are in line with the basic interests of the state and whether they are conducive to regional economic and social development; and quality, i.e. whether administrative processes conform to the prescribed procedures and whether they abide by the budget control process.

"What to do" is the foundation, the bottom line and the touchstone for regional government. "How to do" is concerned with administrative efficiency, against which four standards are proposed for its measurement: quantity, i.e. how much work is done within the unit time; duration, i.e. whether objectives are fulfilled within the prescribed time limit; performance, i.e. whether the completion of tasks is in agreement with the principles of "shortest duration" or "highest speed"; and budget, i.e. whether the costs are reduced and the budget of manpower, materials and financial resources are met, in other ways, whether the budget is strictly controlled and the tasks are completed within a certain budget index. The first three standards are transformable and are in essence the same thing, but they differ in calculation methods and perspectives.

Regional government administrative efficiency may be addressed from the micro and macro perspective and the organizational and individual perspective. The micro perspective refers to the administrative efficiency of a single administrative body or department or individual, while the macro perspective examines from the holistic point of view the regional economic and social development within a certain period, which is measurable by the economic growth or the social development index. The organizational efficiency refers to the timeliness, performance and input–output ratio of specific administrative agencies engaging in administrative activities and public services, which is an overall evaluation indicator of administrative service agencies; individual efficiency refers to the timeliness and performance of a certain administrative person in his performance of duties, which is the evaluation of service efficiency of an administrative individual.

Starting from the above understanding, the competition of regional government administrative efficiency unfolds in the following ways. The first is the overall compliance evaluation of regional government services, which will be deemed uncompetitive if such misconducts happen to its agencies, departments or related personnel as frequent infringements of law, non-compliance with regulations, rules and disciplines and procedures, bribery, rent-seeking through power and so on. The second is the patency of regional administrative service processes and the transparency of administrative information. The fairness and justice of administrative services can be ensured and the services are deemed competitive if processes are easy to follow with clear time indications and task specifications, and there is no prevarication and wrangling between government units, with clear clarification of responsibilities, rights and interests as open and transparent information and appropriate service guides or consultation platforms. The third is the evaluation of the efficiency of regional administrative services, which are deemed competitive if the agencies, departments or individuals, when providing services, are equipped with correct notions, sound service awareness and positive attitudes; are skilled in their work; do not play with double standards; have a strong sense of time; and can concentrate on their work, with clear service objectives in mind.

Therefore, the competition of administrative efficiency is essentially the competition of service awareness, work attitudes, a sense of responsibility, work skills and information technology platforms. Through creating a good service culture, cultivating service awareness, work skills and professional qualifications, and taking advantage of information technology platforms to enhance communication, regional government can enhance service efficiency by providing one-stop services, for the purpose of enhancing administrative efficiency and the competitiveness of investment promotion.

4.4 The core of regional government competition

Innovation entails competition between regional governments, no matter whether it is the competition of finance and economy, talents and science and technology, soft and hard environment and infrastructure or it is the competition in policy systems and administrative efficiency. It is the core of competition. In cases where regional governments have similar financial and policy resources, innovation becomes the major arena for regional government competition. Innovation is the driving force and competitiveness. Continuous innovation is the inexhaustible competitiveness.

Innovation may be interpreted from different angles. Fred Riggs (1981) argued that innovation may be understood from three levels, namely technology, institution and ideological behavior. Cheng Siwei (2005) believed that government innovation includes innovation of technology, administration and institution, which can all essentially be categorized under one heading of "institutional innovation". Liu Jinghua and Jiang Xianhua (2004) classified government administrative innovation on three levels: on the macro level, mainly the innovation in models and notions of government administration; on the mezzo level, mainly the innovation of specific systems of government administration, such as administrative decision-making and supervision, institutional setup, civil services, administrative examination and approval, household registration, social security, performance evaluation and so on; and on the micro level, mainly the innovation of approaches and methods of government administration. The macro-level innovation exerts decisive influence upon on the mezzo and micro levels, and micro- and mezzo level innovation affects and constrains that on the macro-level. The general purpose of innovation is to effectively plan and allocate internal resources and maximize the aggregation of external resources.

In our view, innovation lies at the core of regional government competitiveness, and innovation from the perspective of regional government should cover notional, institutional, organizational and technological, as well as innovation in concept, method, technology, service products and so on in terms of its contents.

4.4.1 Competition in notional innovation

Notional innovation requires conformity to the reality and the discovery and development of new ideas and concepts that are down-to-earth and yet strategically advantageous. Conservative, self-contained and slouch notions will deter us from keeping abreast of the times. Competition requires innovation, which requires, first and foremost, innovation in ideas and conceptualization. The promotion of foresighted concepts, service concepts, competition concepts, responsibility concepts, open concepts and others all need a continuous, long-lasting process.

Regional government needs foresighted concepts. Being foresighted requires shattering the stereotyped ways of thinking, breaking through the status quo and daring to be the first to challenge. It also requires giving full play to the role of regional government in economic orientation, regulation and early warning and in effectively allocating resources and forging the leading edge with resort to market rules and market forces, by means of investment, pricing, taxation and legislation, as well as through innovation in notion, institution, organization and technology with a view to promoting the scientific and sustainable development of regional economy.

Regional government needs service concepts and to transform administrative concepts and management concepts into service concepts to better serve the market, enterprises and society. Service concepts have multiple implications: all regional market participants and general public objects of government service; government service should be oriented towards providing support, monitoring and regulation, development and innovation; service satisfaction is the core standard for the measurement of services; all services should center around their objects and their needs. Government is the provider of public goods and services, and the public, enterprises and institutions within the region are the demanders for public goods and services. A major reason why Israel's innovative competitiveness is second to none in the world is that its governments at all levels positions themselves as service-oriented governments, and civil servants at all levels of government position themselves as service providers.

The Tel Aviv Municipality, from the point of view of entrepreneurs' practical needs, provides all the best possible administrative and basic support services. Entrepreneurial teams work in the CBD zone in the neighborhood of the Rothschild Street for very low rent while enjoying all relevant services and resources. In 2004, China started to carry out its service-oriented government program and specified four functions, namely economic regulation, market supervision, social management and public services, which practice the values of service concepts and push the overall administration level to a new height.

Regional government needs competitive concepts. The market theorists tend to believe that competition takes place only between enterprises and not between governments. However, in reality, competition takes place where resources are limited or scarce and governments have to compete for such resources. Regional governments, especially the leadership team, must be equipped with a sense of competition, a spirit of strong power and the courage for competition. There are scalar economic variations between regional governments in China, ranging from the east coastal region to the central region and to the western region, and the variations result chiefly from differences in competitive concepts and competitiveness, in addition to natural endowments of resources. A gradient of awareness of competition between regional governments is observed starting to wane to varying degrees from the east, to the central and then to the west region.

Regional government needs responsibility concepts, undertakes competition with others responsibly and takes responsibility as its basic starting point to ensure the interests of service objects. It should always put responsibility above rights and interests. The awareness of responsibility requires the identification of responsible persons to be held accountable for any sort of activities and their consequences; the appraisal of responsibilities and their ensuing outcomes; and the mechanisms for supervision of responsibilities, rewards for fulfillment of responsibilities and penalties for failures so that regional government can truly become the subject undertaking responsibilities and their appraisal, supervision and punishment.

Regional government competition requires the concepts of reform and opening up. Foshan City, China, for example, conducted inter-district competition within its jurisdiction over the years in talent introduction, technological innovation, entrepreneurship management, industrial park construction, industrial chain docking and so on. District governments under the Foshan Municipality benefited from such competition and collaboration so as to promote their reform and development and create a good atmosphere for common interests and prosperity.

4.4.2   Competition in institutional innovation

Institutional innovation is the basis and guarantee of regional government innovation and is the concentrated expression of regional government competition. It lands ideas and notions on an operational footing and makes it possible for them to guide practice. Without institutional innovation, there will be no basis for other kinds of innovation to persist and last. For regional government, institutions are provided as public goods, and their innovation should cover public service systems, public security systems, social welfare systems, housing systems, health service systems, social employment systems, education and training systems, income distribution systems, infrastructure construction systems, environmental protection systems and so on. However, when innovation is discussed with focus on the specific systems of regional government–market competition, then what is referred to is the total sum of specific policies, measures and methods based on the specific systems. Compared with the micro-innovation costs of enterprises and individuals in the market, the macro-innovation costs of regional government may be much lower, and the advantages of competition in regional institutional innovation will be definite if the costs become lower with the accrual of benefits.

Since 2000, in China's endeavor to create service-oriented government, the "one-stop service" model launched at the regional government level is representative of operational and competitive system innovation. In October 2000, Nanjing set up the "government supermarket" to provide "one-stop service", the first of its kind in China, followed by Tianjin, which implemented the administrative examination and approval system reform featuring "parallel examination and combined approval, with overtime acquiescence", and by Harbin and Chengdu, which launched the "one-go examination and auditing system" for handling administrative affairs. With the development of mobile Internet, all kinds of "mobile government", such as government APP and WeChat public accounts, mushroomed all over China. All this has made administrative processes easier, more flexible, more convenient and cost-efficient. Institutional innovation has enhanced regional government competitiveness.

Competition in institutional innovation is surging in different regions of the world. Israel can be cited as a successful example. In order to foster and inspire innovation, Israel has formulated a series of laws, regulations and rules and put into operation a series of policies and measures. In 1985, *The Law on Encouragement of Industrial Research and Development* was promulgated, which stipulated the general principle for government encouragement and funding of industrial research and development. According to this law, the Israeli government provides 30 to 66 percent of the funds required for the research and development projects that are approved by the government. This stipulation is specific, clear and highly workable and has contributed immensely to the creation, development, application and popularization of high-tech industries.

In 2002, Israel passed *The Tax Reform Act*, which made significant adjustments to the yield tax on active capital, such as venture capital, securities trading and direct investment, so as to promote the development of high-tech industries. In 2011, Israel promulgated *The Angel Law* to encourage investment of high-tech companies in their early stage. As long as qualified investors invest in high-tech private enterprises, they will get the deduction of the same amount as their investment from their income taxes. Israel also enforced a strict intellectual property protection system, attempting to protect intellectual property rights through *The Property Law, The Trademark Ordinance, The Copyright Law* and others.

In order to promote industry–university–research cooperation, Israel, from the beginning of 1993, implemented the "Magnet Program" to make the industry–university–research combination a sustainable model so as to encourage industrial groups and academic institutions to form partnerships and jointly develop key general technologies. The Israel government conducted assessments of the projects financed by the Magnet Program, and the major indices included economic advantages, export and employment potential, innovative and common technologies, extent of enterprise participation and so on. Each project is undertaken by the R&D consortium of enterprises, scientific research institutions and other members, with a span of three to six years, thus creating incentive and yet binding mechanisms for government, incubators and tenant enterprises and a fast channel for quick knowledge transformation from universities and research institutions into productive forces. It mainly took the following three systems.

First, the Israeli government strengthens its guidance for technological incubators and provides direct or indirect funding for their daily operation. All of them are non-profit organizations with government support of salaries and administrative expenses. The Chief Scientist's Office of the Ministry of Industry and Trade grants 85 percent of the expenses to the incubating enterprises for a period of two years and with the maximum financial funding of US $150,000 per year. It is stipulated that for successful enterprises, 20 percent of their equity goes to the incubator and 3 percent of its market sales is returned to the government incubation fund. By so doing, the Israeli government funds start-up businesses and incubators as well.

Second, measures are taken to control the number of incubation enterprises so as to ensure the quality of incubation. The government of Israel made rigid provisions for each incubator, that is, only eight to 15 start-ups within each incubator, which ensures the possibility of more penetrating incubation of each start-up business within the incubator. After entrepreneurs get into incubators with project-based start-up companies, the government will provide human, financial and material resources for incubators to ensure deep incubation of those start-ups. Incubators start by helping entrepreneurs to set up an entrepreneurial team with full responsibility for financial management, and then provide assistance in developing business plans and R&D plans and finding partners. Start-up enterprises are not allowed to transfer their equities and options within the first two years of their incubation.

Third, a strict examination and assessment mechanism is in place for incubators. At the beginning of each year, the government of Israel signs an annual target agreement with incubators, and at the end of the year, the government provides about US $200,000 to each incubator after their successful assessment. The government avoids signing agreements with the managing entrepreneur of the incubating project so that it entrusts the responsibility of fund management to incubators rather than the entrepreneurs, but it exercises strict control upon the approval of each start-up business budget, work plan, work flow, etc. Incubators are supposed to submit project reports to the government every six months. All this makes sure that incubators take the responsibilities for the spending of government funding.

Fourth, incubators must operate in such ways that the mechanism for effectively integrating industries, universities and research institutions must work properly. Incubators are independent legal entities with government support. Its board members are composed of representatives from government, businesses, research institutes, universities and intermediaries. This composition gives full play to the roles of all relevant parties, and the board of directors of the start-up business consists of the initiator, representatives from incubators and investors, etc.

Israel's policies and institutional innovation have specific targets and clear goals and are highly workable. They have proved to be extremely attractive to innovative entrepreneurs, as well as realizing Israel's dream of creating an "innovative paradise for entrepreneurs".

4.4.3 Competition in organizational innovation

Organizational innovation is the optimization of organizational management of regional government, especially in terms of its structure and mechanism and on both the regional government level and on the level of internal organization. Organizational innovation, as a kind of competition, is the advantage formed through comparison of organizational performance and efficiency between regional governments. Efficiency is the goal government operation strives to achieve from the outset. With the development of the times and technological progress, new forms of organizational management keep emerging for the benefit of better performing government functions and enhancing administrative efficiency. The emergence of networking, for example, aims at providing a wider range of new modes of operation to cater for public goods and public services, the inter-departmental restructuring is introduced to solve problems of inefficient operation as a result of over-departmentalization and functional overlapping, and the matrix structure is designed to remove hurdles and enhance coordination between horizontal departments in the existing administrative system while maintaining corresponding relations between these departments and higher-level departments.

Flattened administration is the result of organizational innovation, in which case levels of regional government administration are reduced, the span of institutional management is moderately expanded, and authorities and responsibilities are relegated to lower levels. A case in point is China's administrative reform of putting some counties under the direct jurisdiction of the provincial government, which was launched under the slogan of "strengthening counties through delegation". Structurally, the three-level administrative system of province–municipality–county is reduced to a two-level system of province–municipality/county. In 1992, the provincial government of Zhejiang, China, experimented by giving greater authority and a greater degree of autonomy to 13 municipal and county-level governments, which released huge momentum for economic development. By 2002, more authorities were delegated to county governments in areas of personnel, finance, planning, project approval and so on. The reform in Zhejiang Province improved county-level government performance, helped mobilize economic and administrative resources and achieved desirable results. Following Zhejiang Province, provinces such as Anhui, Hubei, Henan, Shandong, Jiangsu, Fujian, Hunan and Hebei also launched the organizational innovation of county governments under the direct jurisdiction of the provincial government.

Matrix structural management is another form of organizational innovation, which usually takes the form of functional mergers of departments on the horizontal level and then reduces the number of people. However, such mergers are often plagued by breaking down the corresponding functions of the current administrative system in China. China's linear administrative system features the longitudinal structural correspondence, as there is the Ministry of Culture at the national level, to which the Department of Culture corresponds at the provincial level, and then the Bureau of Culture at the municipal and county levels, and the Station of Culture at the township level. It often turns out to be difficult for reforms of local administrative structures to be carried further without breaking down the vertical correspondence.

Fuyang City in Zhejiang, China adopted a matrix structure in the form of "special committees", which to a certain extent eases the bottleneck problem. It set up 15 special committees, each of which contains a number of functional departments. Its reform followed the principle of "previous practices upwards and reformed practices downwards", which means the original corresponding relations were retained while special committees exercised authorities over subordinate departments under their charge by undertaking functional restructuring so as to remove obstacles across departments. For example, those departments, which now come under the direct charge of the Urban and Rural Co-ordination Committee, were functionally fragmented previously, thus leading to repeated payment and huge waste of funds for financial support to agriculture.

After the establishment of the committee, the agriculture-related funds were all concentrated from previous departments into the committee and were uniformly managed by it. The previous problem of non-cooperation between departments was solved at one go, which considerably improved its administrative efficiency. The inter-departmental restructuring is an example of organizational innovation. Shunde District, Foshan City, adopted the overhaul organizational restructuring, which has become a representative of such reforms. Such reforms aim at streamlining the organization by merging departments into one track, which previously ran on two different tracks, the party and the administrative lines. It followed that district leaders took charge of both party and government work. The new organization had the advantages of easier coordination and relatively centralized administration as a result of "mergers of similar-category items". Since 2008, such streamlined restructuring was gradually implemented from the central to the local level.

A series of organizational innovations have been carried out by the US government around the revitalization of the US manufacturing industry, e.g. the adjustment and concentration of government functions, the setup of new institutions and so on. The innovations have improved organizational management efficiency and contributed to the realization of goals. In 2009, Barack Obama, the then-US president, delivered a speech and proposed to take the revitalization of the US manufacturing industry as a major strategy for long-term US economic development. At the end of the same year, the US government introduced *A Framework for Revitalizing American Manufacturing*, which unfolded from the strategic layout the development path to the specific measures so as to complete the deployment of the manufacturing innovation plan.

In 2011, the US government officially launched the *Advanced Manufacturing Partnership* to speed up the seizure of the advanced manufacturing industry in the twenty-first century. In 2012, the US further launched the *National Strategic Plan for Advanced Manufacturing* to encourage manufacturing enterprises to return to the US. The plan, on the one hand, adjusted the traditional manufacturing structure and enhanced its competitiveness and, on the other hand, facilitated the development of high-tech industries and advanced digital manufacturing technologies, such as advanced platforms for production technology, advanced manufacturing technology and design and data infrastructure, etc.

Israel's administrative system for science and technology is characterized by its looseness and multi-management, and its national decision-making body consists of ministries of science and technology, industry and trade, national defense, agriculture, health, communications, education, environment and infrastructure, together with the Academy of Sciences and Humanities and other institutions. However, the chief scientist responsibility system is implemented for scientific and technological work, and the main government departments have the chief scientist's office. There is also a chief scientist forum, with the Minister of Science and Technology acting as chairman, which concentrates on major issues concerning policies for science and technology, thus avoiding the duplication or omission of science and technology projects and improving the competitiveness of science and technology.

4.4.4 Competition in technological innovation

There are four major aspects to competition in technological innovation for regional government: the technical transformation of regional government and the technical promotion of administrative capacities; the provision of advanced technological environment within the region and the enhancement of regional attractiveness by optimizing its technological environment; regional government's organizing the projects which require higher standards for technological innovation, greater capital flow, more labor and time input, and the projects other innovative bodies are not in a position to undertake within the region; regional government assisting other market participants (enterprises, scientific research institutions or individuals) in pushing forward their technological innovation through increasing financial support.

Electronic administration is a typical example in the technological innovation of regional government. Since the 1990s, regional government in China has constantly improved their management approaches and carried out the electronic transformation. The state has started the construction of e-government projects. China's electronic government construction follows the main thread of "office automation within the organization", "electronic engineering within management departments" and "government online projects". On the basis of office automation, the Chinese government initiated the "Three-Golden Projects" – Golden Bridge (Jinqiao), Golden Customs (Jinguan) and Golden Card (Jinka) in 1993.

The Golden Bridge Project was an information project designed to support national macro-economic control and decision-making and achieve intergovernmental communication by means of special infrastructure network. The Golden Custom Project was an information network system set up to heighten modern management and service level in China's foreign trade and related fields. The Golden Card Project was launched by the national government as a key information infrastructure and an integral part of the electronic administration project to enhance cross-bank bankcard services characterized by government informationalization.

On January 22, 1999, China Telecom and the Economic Information Center of the National Economy and Commerce Commission, along with 40 other information-related ministries, commissions, bureaus and offices under the administration of the State Council, jointly launched the "Government Online Project", together with its host website www.gov.cninfo.net and guide site www.gov.cninfo.net, which were officially open to the public and started to provide information services. Since then, the Government Online Projects at all levels were started in succession and the electronic government construction was in full swing. The introduction of advanced e-government technology into every aspect of public services has greatly improved administrative efficiency and regional competitiveness.

Grid management is a new digital regional administrative model. It divides a region into several grid cells by the grid map technology, and these cells are the smallest administrative and service units. Each grid is equipped with a management supervisor whose duty is to monitor the municipal components or facilities within the grid. For any problems, the supervisor can transfer relevant information through communication technology to the relevant center, which will identify the responsible functional division in the shortest time and have the problem addressed. As the platform center can engage itself with all functional departments, the coordination between functional departments can be accomplished through this platform.

Zhoushan City, Zhejiang Province, has carried this innovation one step forward by offering service content in the grid management in light of the user-oriented philosophy. The city is divided into 2428 grids and a service team of 76 members is designated to each grid. This operation mode is called "grid management and group service". In addition, a comprehensive, integrated and shared information management system has been developed for better operation of the grid. The urban big data center or cloud platform construction is also a manifestation of technological innovation for regional government. In 2014, Foshan City, Guangdong Province, introduced the concept of big data and established a variety of cloud platforms for government administration, such as the social comprehensive governance cloud platform, which provides one-net service and solutions to grassroots governance. Chancheng District government in Foshan divided the whole district into 122 grids and migrated urban administration, public security, safety supervision, judicial and public security departments to the grids. Meanwhile, it established a district- and township-level social comprehensive monitoring center. The grid administrator was responsible for information collection, coordination within communities, dispute mediation, etc. The cloud platform integrated traffic command centers, digital city management and emergency command center, etc. to which residents can report by phone, WeChat, APP or network. In cases where "difficult problems" arise, the district- or township-level command center organizes a joint law enforcement team to address the problems collectively, thus forming new competitiveness for regional government.

The Tel Aviv Municipality in Israel, in order to help the development of incubators, established a database that makes a detailed record of all types of enterprises, including the enterprise size, employee number, location, product market, development stage, scale of production, main financing methods and current problems. By referring to the continuously updated database and by employing professionalized financial analysis tools for optimal financing methods and scales of enterprises, regional government reduces its financial burden and is able to make more effective and reasonable resource allocation. Although most financing is up to the market, the Tel Aviv Municipality hosts a variety of entrepreneurial contests to select the best teams and provide support to them. Once government injects capital into them, the ownership and the right to use the capital will be completely transferred to enterprises and teams. If enterprises fail, the capital does not need to be reimbursed, and if they succeed, the capital should be reimbursed on a yearly basis. Obviously, the construction of big data centers, information centers and coordination centers by regional government can transform the regional technological environment and help regional government to achieve technologically competitive advantages in market competition.

In addition, government involvement in technological innovation is not unusual in different parts of the world. Take the US, for example. In 2012, the Obama administration proposed the construction of the "Innovation Network for National Manufacturing", and up to 45 research centers were established to strengthen the industry–university–research combination between universities and manufacturing enterprises. In 2013, the Executive Office of the President (EOP), the National Science and Technology Council (NSTC) and the Advanced Manufacturing National Program Office jointly promulgated the *Preliminary Design of Innovation Network for National Manufacturing* and invested US \$1 billion in the establishment of manufacturing innovation networks, with concentrated efforts devoted to promoting the innovative development of digital manufacturing, new energy, new materials and other advanced manufacturing industries, and created a number of innovation clusters with advanced manufacturing capacity.

Those efforts included developing lightweight carbon fiber composite materials to improve combustion efficacy, performance and anti-corrosion of the next generation of automobiles, aircraft, trains and ships; ameliorating standards, materials and equipment pertaining to 3D printing technology to achieve low-cost pilot production with digital design; and creating intelligent manufacturing frameworks and methods to allow operators to control the "big data flow" from completely digital factories so as to improve production efficiency, optimize supply chains and enhance the efficiency in using energy, water and materials, etc. In 2012, the US government and the private sector jointly invested US $85 million to set up the National 3D Printer Manufacturing Innovation Institute. The following year, a grant of US $200 million in federal funds was in place for the establishment of the Lightweight and Modern Metals Manufacturing Innovation Institute, the Digital Manufacturing and Design Innovation Institute and the Next Generation Power Electronics National Manufacturing Innovation Institute, followed by a composite materials manufacturing center, which further consolidated competitiveness of technological innovation.

4.5 The impacts of regional government competition on resource allocation

Viewed outwardly, regional competition in projects, industries, matching support, human resources, fiscal and financial resources, infrastructure, environment system and administrative efficiency is the external representation of competition between regional governments, while regional innovation in notion, institution, organization and technology is the core of regional competition and resource allocation; they are two sides of the same coin. Resource allocation, as a basic issue of economics, is an inevitable subject regarding regional government competition. Regional competition results from the disparity in the flow of regional factors, which is caused by imbalanced regional development. In fact, it reflects the regional ability to optimize resource allocation, i.e. resource attraction and market competitiveness. Due to the limitation and scarcity of resources, there is always a trade-off relationship between regions in resource allocation. Regions compete for resource allocation rights as much as possible through competition.

The basic economic goal of regional government competition is to form regional comparative advantages by optimizing resource allocation; the basic idea is that regional governments compete for regional competitiveness and comparative advantages, absorb and gather resources, optimize resource allocation and thus achieve regional sustainable growth. Therefore, regional government competitiveness exerts effective influences upon three types of resource allocation, such that it promotes the optimal allocation of internal resources; emphasizes regional complementariness and collaborative coexistence with resort to inter-regional division of labor; forms cooperation teams to implement optimal allocation of external resources; and builds up its own soft and hard environments with help on innovation in institutions, organizations and technology so as to enhance the optimal allocation of resources by cultivating "internal strength".

Viewed inwardly, regional government competitiveness can exert effective influence upon the allocation of operational, non-operational and quasi-operational resources, such that it may affect the optimal allocation of internal resources and its efficiency within its own jurisdiction; the flow and absorption of scarce resources outside its jurisdiction for the optimized formation of resource allocation and its efficiency within larger areas; and the coordination and matching of both internal and external resources within the region for the formation of new resource allocation optimization and its efficiency.

4.5.1 Influence of regional government competition on the allocation of operational resources: improvement on productive efficiency

Essentially, operational resources are productive resources, enterprise resources and industrial resources. They are resources operated by the market rather than directly by regional government. They fully retain their market purity. Regional governments should adopt measures such as non-interventionism, encouragement and supportive policies, antitrust policies and risk monitoring policies to guarantee the decisive role of the market in their allocation. This "market" is a "market" of enterprises instead of a "market" of regional governments. Therefore, the real effect of regional government competition on the effective allocation of operational resources is improvement upon productive efficiency.

First, it is due to the microcosmic nature of business entities of operational resources. They are enterprises rather than regional governments. Their microcosmic nature resides in their individuality and specificity. Enterprises cannot adjust the allocation of operational resources within a region. Only regional government has the attributes of being macrocosmic and mezzocosmic and can regulate the allocation of operational resources within the region.

Second, it is due to the economical nature of operational resources. Regional government needs to create conditions to guarantee the maximization of economic benefits for enterprises within the region, thus maximizing economic interests.

Third, it is due to the mobility of operational resources. In a sense, operational resources are profit-seeking. Operational resources will flow wherever the greatest benefits can be achieved. What regional government should do is to remove the boundaries so as to realize the free flow of resources. That is the essence of the optimal allocation of operational resources.

As far as operational resources are concerned, regional government should create conditions to protect its micro-subjectivity, operational economics and free mobility, without direct operation or intervention. However, it does not mean that there is nothing regional governments cannot do. In fact, what regional governments should do is generate comparative advantages through competition so as to foster the attractiveness and capacity of operational resources, thus realizing the crossover flows towards themselves. "Crossover" here means breaking regional boundaries and enabling operational resources to flow freely between regions with resort to the free market force. The so-called towards themselves means that regional governments all want the resources to flow into their own regions. Resources flow into their own regions, because the productivity of the region is high, and the marginal productivity of the factors of operational resources is relatively high.

As shown in Figure 4.1, assume that there are two regions: Region 1 and Region 2. The horizontal axis indicates a certain productive factor of operational resources and the vertical axis indicates the marginal productivity. The marginal productivity curve VMP1 of Region 1 is lower than the marginal productivity curve VMP2 of Region 2. The marginal productivity of N11 is W11, that of N12 is W12, that of N21 is W21 and that of N22 is W22. Assuming that N11 equals N21 and N12 equals N22, which are homogeneous productive factors. If this productive factor is only produced in Region 1, when the productive factor needs to change from N11 to N12, it only increases the productivity of S1. However, if the productive factor flows freely, then this productive factor can flow from Region 1 to Region 2 freely. When it changes from N21 to N22, the area is increased by S2. In this case, S2 is larger than S1, which signifies that if the economics of the productive factors needs to be maintained, that is, the productive factors of operational resources can flow freely, the productive factors will flow to areas with high productivity; viewed from the entirety of Region 1 and Region 2, this flow is conducive to expanding the overall production efficiency and improving the overall economic benefits. This is the efficiency of the allocation of operational resources.

Obviously, the realization of this allocation efficiency is based on two conditions: first, there is no intervention. The free flow of operational resources will lead its economic rationality to incline toward the region with high productivity; second, the whole region needs to maintain a high marginal productivity. In the case of regional government competition, the flow of operational resources requires no direct intervention and operation by exerting forces. For the second point, it is imperative to improve regional competitiveness through internal forces. The essence is to improve the overall marginal productivity, find ways to help enterprises carry out technological transformation and enhance the overall productive level of industries, thereby improving the overall marginal productivity.

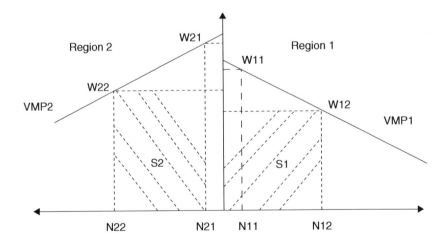

Figure 4.1 Marginal productivity of regional factors and flow effects

4.5.2 Influence of regional government competition on the allocation of "non-operational resources": optimization of development environment

Non-operational resources fall under the general category of all social welfare products and public products within the jurisdiction of regional government. Non-operational resources are managed directly by regional government. Their non-exclusiveness and non-competitiveness exclude them from the category of profit-seeking operational resources, which is the most fundamental difference between them. A major task for regional government is to allocate non-operational resources for the purpose of optimizing regional development environment.

First, it is due to the non-economics of non-operational resource allocation. The goal of regional government's non-operational resource allocation is to maximize economic benefits indirectly by optimizing investment environment, which is reflected in the increase in investment opportunities as a result of business environment improvement.

Second, it is due to the relative stability of non-operational resource allocation. Non-operational resources cannot flow across boundaries or freely at low costs between regions. In this sense, they have the feature of "real estate". Regional government should try to retain their relative stability so as to maintain the steady contribution of non-operational resources to the creation and improvement of favorable environment.

Third, it is due to the macrocosmic nature of entities of non-operational resource allocation. Non-operational resources are non-economic, and their allocation entities can only be regional government. Regional government undertakes their allocation from the quasi-macro perspective with a view to achieving the balance of their allocation and optimizing the macro environment of the entire region.

Fourth, it is due to the exclusiveness and competitiveness of non-operational resource allocation between regions. For example, the Guangzhou Library of China provides free services to residents in Guangzhou, and charges are required only for conditional services to residents outside Guangzhou. Such exclusiveness and competitiveness between regional governments can obtain comparative advantages of the environment.

Regional development environment is a concentrated reflection of all conditions provided by regions to attract investment and is a multi-level and multi-factor dynamically integrated system of both hard and soft aspects. Regional government can adopt two approaches to competition for non-operational resources. It can conduct upward competition for non-operational resources: upward competition for direct non-economic resources, which means obtaining more projects, preferential policies, financial support and transferred payment from higher-level government to improve hard environment of the region. It can also obtain non-operational resources indirectly through self-optimization, which means optimizing regional soft environment through notional modification, cultural reshaping, policy guidance and services so as to attract more operational resources or non-operational resources to converge. Both approaches are conducive to the transformation of a regional development environment. So regional government's allocation of non-operational resources aims at the optimization of development environment.

4.5.3   The impacts of regional government competition on the allocation of quasi-operational resources: promoting comprehensive and sustainable growth

Quasi-operational resources lie in between social welfare products, public products and enterprise resources. For regional government, they are the most competitive and can best inspire the competitive desires of regional government. As they lie in between operational and non-operational resources, they boast the natural flexibility of being operational and non-operational, and being exclusive and non-exclusive under certain conditions. The degree of flexibility can be defined, controlled and manipulated by regional government in the light of its own needs. When regional government feels short of operational resources, quasi-operational resources can be moderately converted into operational resources so as to increase pure private products. When it feels short of non-operational resources, quasi-operational resources can be moderately converted into non-operational resources so as to increase pure public products. Regional government competition for quasi-operational resources focuses on their economic and operational attributes as well as their non-economic and non-operational attributes, but greater emphasis is laid on the flexibility and resilience between the two kinds of attributes. Owing to the relationship between regional government and quasi-operational resources, the competitive functions of regional government to quasi-operational resources are diversified.

First, Regional government competition improves the efficiency of resource allocation. For regional government, resource allocation efficiency means the efficiency of allocating all three types of resources. The allocation efficiency of non-operational resources depends on their stability and that of operational resources their free mobility; that of quasi-operational resources lies in between these two and can be driven by regional government. Quasi-operational resources have a moderate degree of mobility between regions, and this attribute facilitates the allocation of quasi-operational resources between regional governments. When the allocation efficiency of regional non-operational resources is low, it can be compensated by moderately increasing quasi-operational resources. When the allocation efficiency of operational resources is low, it can be compensated by moderately increasing quasi-operational resources.

Second, regional government competition improves productivity. Both quasi-operational resources and operational resources can be allocated under complete competitive conditions as marginal costs are equal to marginal benefits. This mode can generate the greatest productivity and maximize economic benefits. As shown in Figure 4.1, when marginal benefits of Region 2 are high, the same factor increment can yield more benefits than Region 1.

Third, regional government competition can bring forth first-mover advantages. For regional governments, the biggest advantage of quasi-operational resources is their multi-mode utilization. regional governments can develop and utilize them all by itself when financial strength is great, or may jointly develop and utilize them with other micro entities of the market, or may cooperate with other regional governments. For example, BOT and PPP are good business modes for their development. Regional governments with a clearer idea of these resources and more modes of development will form first-mover advantages and improve regional competitiveness.

Fourth, regional government competition promotes sustainable development. Due to government participation and control and the incentives as well as constraints between multiple regional market entities, there will be neither excessive exploitation nor utilization of quasi-operational resources, compared with operational resources, which promote sustainable development. Viewed globally, the allocation of quasi-operational resources is relatively reasonable without overcapacity, because they can take advantage of the double-sided advantages on the part of government and market.

4.5.4 Policy implications of regional government competition to different types of resource management

4.5.4.1 Encourage and support the accelerated development of operational resources

Operational resources represent the direction of pure market economy. Within its jurisdiction, regional government acts more as a supervisor, manager and regulator. It won't participate directly in competition as an entity of micro-economy. Regional government competition takes place through resource flow between regions, and resource convergence and absorption can be obtained through comparative advantages and regional competitiveness, which eventually improve production efficiency.

First, the acceleration of operational resources development gives prominence to maintaining the allocation function of regional market. Regional government should never participate in competition between enterprises and between other micro entities without acting as both athletes and referees. Therefore, rather than intervening too much in market operation, regional government should push regional operational resource projects to the market, society and investors inside and outside the region by means of capitalization.

Second, the acceleration of operational resources development gives prominence to regional macro-control so as to prevent excessive competition and excessive flow. The profit-seeking attribute of operational resources focuses more on individual or corporate benefits, without giving equal consideration to the balance between production and economic benefits within the entire region. The reliance upon government is a sure guarantee for the realization of such balance.

Third, the acceleration of operational resources development gives prominence to the supply-side structural reform of operational resources. Starting from the supply and production sides, regional government should enhance competitiveness to promote economic development by emancipating productivity, continue to focus on the transformation and upgrading of traditional industries as their development direction, innovate and develop new industries and accelerate and support advanced industrial clusters so as to create new economic growth areas.

Fourth, the acceleration of operational resources development gives prominence to notional and institutional innovation. The former is most importantly manifested in market concepts, concepts of corporate autonomy and concepts of government services, and the latter focuses on the creation of legal, competitive, production and market environment for open, fair and just competition.

4.5.4.2   Improve and enhance the allocation function of non-operational resources

Non-operational resources, which are managed by regional government, are the concentrated reflection of its various functions in social undertakings and the main object of regional government competition for the optimization of environment systems. The promotion of the allocation function of non-operational resources can help realize the balance of distribution between regional social welfare products and public products, improve their quality and scale and create a better business environment so as to create more wealth.

First, the improvement of the allocation function of non-operational resources requires that higher-level governments delegate authorities to lower levels under vertical government administration. The subordinate government shouldn't be controlled too strictly but be given full autonomy, self-determination and self-government rights in terms of social welfare and public products allocation within the region. Regional government is economically rational even under tight financial conditions and will maximize the utility of limited financial resources in the allocation of non-operational resources.

Second, the improvement of the allocation function of non-operational resources requires that moderate competition be maintained between regional governments. For non-operational resources, competition is the best way to guarantee allocation effectiveness. Higher-level government should adopt such methods as project competition to promote the competitiveness of subordinate government and the balance of the allocation between social welfare and public products within larger regions. Meanwhile, it should take measures to prevent over-competition, the Matthew effect of the strong becoming too strong, over-concentration at some parts and excessive superiority of social welfare and public products.

4.5.4.3   Innovation and guidance in giving full play to the utility of quasi-operational resources

Quasi-operational resources can oscillate between market commodities and public products, which often fall prey to regional government. Their effective development and utilization can enhance regional development advantages and competitiveness. Their "operational" property may vary from region to region and from time to time. For example, park construction is operational in economically developed regions but non-operational in economically underdeveloped regions. Sewage treatment plants and highways are often operational during the construction fund-withdrawal period and become public products after fund withdrawal. Regional governments should innovate the development, utilization and operational model of quasi-operational resources. Such modes as BOT and PPP are mature models for the development and operation of quasi-operational resources. Regional government should try to study and apply those modes; make innovations in investment and financing platforms and collaborative development platforms; and actively incorporate social capital to jointly develop quasi-operational resources.

4.6 GFL – the key to regional competition

4.6.1 *Notional foresighted leading – the essential competitiveness in the factor-driven stage*

Competition entails innovation, and innovation is competitiveness. Continuous innovation is sustained competitiveness. Regional innovation is the core of regional government competition. Notional foresighted leading is the actual competitiveness in the factor-driven stage of economic growth, which has been amply demonstrated throughout the world. In this stage, regional technology is not as sophisticated, and innovation capabilities, capital accumulation and management experience are limited. The economic growth is mainly realized by simple expansion of inputs of productive factors such as labor, land or other natural resources with focus on competition for resources and in prices. Although government can obtain advantages in regional competition and economic benefits in the short term, such competition is lacking in development potentials in the long term, causing such problems such as excessive exploitation of production factors, lower production efficiency, technological backwardness, resource depletion, brain drain and social conflicts. Ultimately, it may lose the opportunity to cultivate core competencies and sustainable competitiveness and end up deeply trapped in the vicious cycle of resource depletion and economic recession.

Consequently, GFL in development notions, direction and modes becomes decisive in this stage and determines the path and trends of regional development in the future. The height of development notions determines the pattern of the entire regional development. Moreover, once the trend is formed, there will be persistent path-dependency, and it will be costly to break and reconstruct it. The analysis of the advantages and disadvantages of regional competitive factors at this stage requires determining the current foothold and the model framework of the future transformation in a vision for long-term development. Hence, the planning of the factor-driven stage is critical, and the planning needs advanced notions and regional development strategic thinking. Essentially, notional foresighted leading is the real competitiveness in regional competition.

Notional foresighted leading, which is in essence notional innovation, implies the overall grasp of regional factors and their regulation, which shows the broad visions and open-mindedness of regional government and its comprehensive planning of the strategic positioning of future development and development modes, as well as a great challenge. In the factor-driven stage, regional governments should design from the top level long-term development so as to solve problems respecting development modes and motivation; specify the basis and power sources for stable long-term development of the regional economy; make rational allocation of productive factors within the region and coordinate their development; and prevent the imbalance of regional development that may be caused by the driving factors. As the factor-driven economic development model is inclined to plunder resources, regional government should adhere to innovative, coordinated, green, open and shared development in the initial stage so as to avoid the abuse of resources, achieve harmonious coexistence between man and nature and ensure that the economy can go further. Moreover, in the allocation of productive factors, government should have cross-regional visions for global development and for the allocation of regional productive factors; solve linkage problems of internal and external development; and avoid being suppressed at the bottom of the industrial chain as the supplier of production factors. Regional government needs not only to ensure full regional competition but also to achieve win–win cooperation, thereby achieving the stabilized development of global economy through regional and bilateral economic and financial cooperation.

4.6.2 Organizational foresighted leading – the key to competition in the investment-driven stage

Organizational foresighted leading plays a key role in competition in the investment-driven stage, in which period the primary means of regional competition is expanding investment and intensifying its stimulation to economic growth. Driven by investment multiplier effects, investment can enormously expedite economic growth, which has been demonstrated in the Keynesian theory of effective demand. Investment is of great significance for increasing effective demand and boosting GDP. Especially during economic downturns, government can increase investment to reverse the trend of economic downturn and drag economy out. However, problems like quick ups and downs in economy and the lagging-behind of technology and innovation may ensue as a result of "investment hunger" and "investment dependence" after a single short-term stimulus of investment.

Under such circumstances, innovation in organizational administration becomes crucial. This requires the intensification of investment management standards, rapid organizational responsive capabilities, closer relations to market and enterprise services, network and matrix structuring, streamlined administration so as to achieve greater efficiency and flexibility and to improve investment effectiveness. Organizational foresighted leading is crucial to stable and orderly economic development and inter-regional competition in the investment-driven stage. At the investment-driven stage, the major means of regional competition is the expansion of investment and its stimulus of economic growth. The investment is mainly put into infrastructure, real estate and technological renovation. Driven by investment multiplier effects, investment can multiply its effects upon economic growth, which no factor can excel. That is why it has been so attractive to both enterprises and government and has become a regular instrument to drive regional economic growth and gain advantages in competition.

A great deal of research has been conducted concerning the effects of investment on economic growth. The Keynesian theory of effective demand holds that the settlement of economic growth and employment problems needs to be driven by investment, which is the key force for increasing effective demand and expanding GDP. In the economic downturn stage, government may intensify investment to reverse the trend of economic downturn and drag its economy out of the trough. On the basis of the Keynesian economic theory, the Harrod–Domar model for economic growth further suggested that the enormous driving force of investment for economic growth is discernible from the cumulative expansion in cycles of economic boom and the cumulative shrinkage in cycles of economic recession.

Problems may occur in the investment-driven stage, mainly the one-sided pursuit of short-term investment stimulus, which may cause "investment hunger", "investment dependence", quick ups and downs in economy, the lagging-behind of technology and innovation and so on. Without effective organization and leading of investment, problems such as absence of responsibilities for investment, careless decision-making, diversified investments, repeated investments and investment failures will occur. Currently, Japan's economy is in a long-term recession, and the Japanese government continues to employ the easy monetary policy to stimulate business investment and go so far as to lower its interest rates to be negative. Meanwhile, there is continuing growth in financial expenditure by means of investment. However, Japan has not recovered from its economic recession, and one of the explanations is that its organizational solidification is caused by its culture, which constrains its economic dynamics and causes market inactiveness. So, in order to achieve stable economic development in the investment-driven stage, orderly organizational foresighted leading must be put in place.

Organizational foresighted leading focuses on organizational management innovation, which means that regional government must carry out pre-process intervention and planning to prevent blind, repeated and inefficient investment by enterprises, especially real estate enterprises. At the same time, measures must be taken to prevent government from misconduct with their rights which violate market rules, such as excessive financial investment, infrastructure investment, inefficient investment and blind investment. Needless to say, regional government competition should aim to strengthen the standardization and creativity of organizational management; improve its efficiency; strengthen organizational quick response; and get close to the market and to enterprise services. It is also important to downsize bureaucratic organizations and functional departments; develop networking and matrix structure; streamline regional government administrative hierarchy; and moderately expand the span of institutional management so as to improve investment output with greater efficiency and flexibility.

4.6.3   *Technological and institutional foresighted leading – the winning point of competition in the innovation-driven stage*

Technological and institutional foresighted leading is the key to scoring success in regional competition in the innovation-driven stage. Innovation has the most explosive driving force for economic development and pushes socio-economy to transform from quantity- to quality-type, reflecting overall breakthroughs in socio-economic performance and in optimized social allocation. At this stage, technological innovation is the core of all driving forces, and institutional innovation is the fundamental guarantee for continuous technological innovation. Technological innovation gives birth to new formats, new products, new industries and new models. Institutional innovation protects and promotes the integrated innovative development of science and technology, finance and industry, which combine to stimulate innovation-driven sustainability. Technological and institutional foresighted leading becomes an important means of regional competition at this stage.

"Innovation-driven" implies innovation in technology, institution or models to be a breakthrough point for regional economic development. The crux of the innovation-driven stage lies in the breakthrough creation and utilization of all factors in the course of economic growth and in the crystallization of high intelligence achievements. This signifies great leaps forward in promoting the development of the whole of mankind and is the most explosive force in driving economic growth. From the perspective of total factor productivity (TFP), the innovation of technology and business modes is the core driving force in the innovation-driven stage and the engine to effectively meet and even lead social demand. Supply-side reform strives for vigorous development of new technologies through which to meet ever-changing demands for quantity and quality, and to create new demands by means of new business modes when demand growth and economic development become stagnant.

Take US-made iPhones, for example. There did not seem to be any demand for them before their appearance on the market, but their supply on the market created huge demand, as people were surprised to find that numerous applications could run in such little apparatuses. These new demands create the incentives of the market for innovation and the recognition of innovation. In turn, they inspire continuous innovation and the leading of a new round of supply technologies, forming supply-side model innovation and soliciting new demands; this in turn inspires more cyclic demand-side innovations, giving rise to the advancement of such giant companies as Google, Tesla, Facebook, Twitter and a large number of other high-tech entrepreneurial companies.

However, it is hard for the profit motivation of the market and personal wisdom and keenness to trigger off and sustain innovation and to make it long-lasting and penetrating in an aggregative manner. The continuous driving force for innovation and innovation itself requires directional concentration and institutional innovation. The blowout growth of China's new energy vehicle, a good example in this connection, has very much to do with matching supportive government policies. The system foresighted leading formed by system innovation is bound to be connected to technological innovation. The institutional foresighted leading, which stems from institutional innovation, is bound to be integrated with technological innovation. The effective incorporation of technological innovation into policy incentives and leading and the vigorous support of economic development modes – such as the shared economy, the long-tail economy, and the zero cost economy, as well as new-generation information technologies such as big data, cloud computing, mobile Internet, the Internet of things and artificial intelligence – will bring about a comprehensive and in-depth integration of regional government policies with economy, industry and science and technology, and will continue to generate new business modes, new products, new models and new trends for future growth. In the innovation-driven stage, in addition to protecting and encouraging innovation, regional government should endeavor to create a relaxing environment at low costs for innovation and strengthen institutional supply to ensure market access and revitalize market potentials. Meanwhile, institutional foresighted leading must be in place to prevent regional government from infringing upon market rules in competition and to avoid vicious competition between regional governments, thereby facilitating social funding and allocation efficiency.

4.6.4 *The overall foresighted leading – the inevitable choice in the wealth-driven stage*

Under the assumption that regional economic development in the world follows the sequence of factor-driven, investment-driven, innovation-driven and wealth-driven stages, then the wealth-driven stage of economic growth – which is characterized by the full play to individual creativity, comprehensive work–life balance, rapid development of tertiary industries, growing awareness of the importance of resources environment and continuously emerging models of economic and individual development – requires not only innovation in notions, institution, organization and technology but also overall foresighted leading, so as to achieve and guarantee the sustained advantages of regional competition. Therefore, the flexible, quick and diverse development of regional economy in the wealth-driven stage requires the coordination of institutions, policies and measures to match the pulse of the wealth-driven times, orient the values of the wealth-driven stage and maintain the sustainability and vitality of economy. The overall continuous innovation and foresighted leading in the whole process and over the full range of factors is the inevitable option for regional competition at this stage.

5 Effective government and efficient market

Upon its publication, Adam Smith's masterpiece of economic analysis, *The Wealth of Nations*, immediately produced great implications for western economic theories, implications that over time proved profound and far-reaching. As Adam Smith puts it in his book, the perfect marriage between the utility-seeking economic entities and the "invisible hand" generates a wealth-creating force, strong and powerful enough to drive economic development and social evolution and, ultimately, to contribute to the emergence of a new economic modality. As a tool for resource allocation, the price mechanism, once employed, has proven its phenomenal power in improving efficiency, optimizing economic structure and driving the evolution of economic modalities.

In essence, economic development lies in enhancing the efficiency of how scarce resources are allocated, which means reaping the maximum possible amount of economic benefits at the minimum possible cost of resource usage. Economists who have come after Adam Smith, either professedly western economic theorists or believers of Marxist political economy, have acknowledged, almost without exception, the incomparably powerful strengths and efficiency of the market economy in allocating resources. In practice, the economic growth performances (in terms of both growth speed and results) of nations the world over have proved that the market is the most efficient tool for resource allocation. As a result, a consensus has already been reached among economic theorists and over a long process of national policy practice that the market, as a general rule in market economy, is the decisive force for resource allocation and that market economy, by its very nature, is an economy where the market plays a decisive role in allocating resources.

Throughout its history, the world economy has been dominated by two economic systems – one with market economy as its main body and the other with planned economy as its main body. With the development of the world economy, these two systems tend to intermingle so that government and market begin to overlap in function and the modes and consequences of government economic behavior start to exercise increasing impacts upon the volume and structure of the whole economy. As a result, previous economic theories are constantly being shattered. The interdependence and interconnectedness between market and government are clearly discernible through a variety of questions that have arisen in the development of the world economy, including those regarding market inefficiency, the initiative and the competitive nature of government behavior, the multiplicity of key governmental functions and the output rate of margins between market and government. Essentially, the following two critical questions need to be addressed for any given market economy to be effective in the modern era: how do market forces interplay with government policies, and how do we reconcile between them?

Market and planned economic systems are both approaches to the allocation of social resources that aim to resolve by certain means such problems as what to produce, in what amount, in what ways and how to allocate what has been produced over a certain period and under circumstances of resource scarcity. Under planned economy, resources are allocated according to government plans. The central government formulates a wide-ranging program that commands and arranges for all economic activities. Under market economy, the invisible hand of market prices becomes the decisive force that determines what to produce, how much and in what ways.

In reality, pure planned economy and market economy are not common. The planned economic system, which resists market forces, has basically withdrawn from the historical scene in contemporary countries. Plans, however, are retained and commonly employed as regulative means. Under a market economic system, plans are not completely done away with. Countries under that system still make use of macro-level strategies and programs to intervene in resource allocation, but these programs and plans are of a supplementary and guiding nature, relative to the market. Market mechanisms are decisive factors in resource allocation.

5.1   Three types of market

In terms of how full-fledged they are and how much power they wield over economic operation, the market can be categorized into the following three types: weak efficient market, semi-strong market and strong efficient market. Generally speaking, "operational resources" are the focus of market resource allocation. This is because, for one thing, given their totally competitive and exclusive nature, such resources enable a market price mechanism to give full rein to its function, and, for another, where the allocation of "operational resources" is concerned, competitive entities of market are able to reap bounty rewards by abiding by the rules of the market. As a result, high efficiency regarding the allocation of "operational resources" is most likely achievable in a full-fledged market. The allocation of "non-operational resources", which are non-exclusive and non-competitive in nature, goes well beyond the power of the market to affect and control. As such, the allocation of such resources is regarded as falling outside the precincts of the market. There is yet another type of resources – "quasi-operational resources", the allocation of which is, to some extent, subject to the power of the market, except for a market economy that is still in its infancy; in this case there is no clear definition or delimitation of what "quasi-operational resources" are, and there is a lack of competent measures for effectively allocating such resources. In this sense, a market economy can be considered strong or weak according to whether or not it has well-defined entities and well-established measures regarding the allocation of "quasi-operational resources".

In 1970, Eugene F. Fama put forth his efficient-market hypothesis, in which he proposed three types of market efficiency: (1) strong-form efficiency; (2) semi-strong efficiency; and (3) weak-form efficiency. These three types of efficiency are judged according to what information sets are factored in price trends. As Fama suggested, strong-form efficiency assumes that current prices reflect all public and private information in the market or, put another way, current prices are totally and utterly determined by the market. Weak-form efficiency assumes that current prices are determined by many non-market factors. Tucked between strong- and weak-form efficiency is semi-strong efficiency, which assumes that current prices adjust rapidly to the release of all new public information. Let us put aside for the time being the debate over whether it is rational and logical to determine the degree of a market's efficiency on the basis of information sets factored in prices. This author is sold on Fama's idea of categorizing markets into strong-form, weak-form and semi-strong form markets.

This book suggests that the efficiency of a modern market should be defined and assessed according to the degree to which the modern market brings its functions into play. In its original form, a market consists only of a "market element system" and a "market organizational system". With the market developing to higher levels, a "market legal system" and a "market regulatory system" gradually take shape as two new building blocks of the market and become increasingly full-fledged. After the market grows into maturity and evolves into a modern market system, its structure is further cemented with two more building blocks, namely, a "market environment system" and "market infrastructure". Hence, markets can be categorized into weak efficient forms, semi-strong efficient forms and strong efficient forms based on the levels of completeness and maturity regarding the aforementioned six functional systems.

5.1.1 Weak efficient market

5.1.1.1 Signs

A "weak efficient market" refers to one that comprises merely a "market element system" and a "market organizational system", with unclear categorization of resource types. A market of this type often emerges during the infancy of market economy, when the market is still spontaneously exploring which types of resources for which it will be responsible for allocating.

5.1.1.2 Connotation

A "market element system" practically consists of a variety of commodity markets and element markets, including exchangeable commodities and commodity buyers and sellers. Commodities in this regard include tangible material products and intangible services, as well as a diversity of commercialized resource elements, such as capital, technology, information, land, labor force, etc. The most cardinal elements for the operation of commodity and element markets are price, supply and demand and competition.

A "market organizational system" denotes an integral system of interconnected markets that takes shape on the basis of the division of social labor and under the discretion of price mechanisms. Specifically, it is made up of all kinds of market entities and intermediary agencies, including retail markets for commodities and means of production, wholesale markets, cross-border trading organizations, professional labor markets, financial institutions, technology and information exchange agencies, property rights markets and real estate markets. These market entities and agencies are interrelated and mutually restrictive, serving to distribute market elements for production and service activities, improve market operational efficiency and achieve optimal organizational development and consumption utility in a market operational system. Within a market economy that has a "market element system" and a "market organizational system", the invisible hand of the market is able to play a decisive role in allocating resources for economic activities, whether for consumption or for production purposes. Therefore, a market with these two systems can be called an efficient market.

However, a market with and only with these two systems is weak in nature, because in the infancy of market economy – though with its "market element system" and "market organizational system" well-established and the market playing a predominant role in resource allocation – the market has yet to grow to its full-fledged form in order to clearly categorize its resource types. Under such circumstances, given that there is no clear line of demarcation between "operational resources", "non-operational resources" and "quasi-operational resources", serious problems will inevitably crop up to plague the allocation of market resources. Held away by their intrinsic profit-seeking motive, different market actors will scramble for profits wherever profits are obtainable, with a total disregard for the categorization of resources. This problem, compounded with an untenable market structure, asymmetry of information, the absence of regulation and a sound legal system, might give rise to a series of resultant problems, such as the incorporation of some "non-operational resources" – the allocation of which should have been led and undertaken by government – into private domains, collusion between power and money, monopoly for extravagant profits, etc. Problems such as these threaten to jeopardize both market efficiency and social equity.

As there is yet no clear conception of what constitutes "quasi-operational resources" at this stage, problems such as arbitrary intervention and arbitrary abdication are likely to crop up to complicate and disrupt the allocation of such resources. Unclear delimitation of resources means unclear demarcation between the roles of market and government concerning the allocation of resources. Under such circumstances, problems pertaining to the supersession, vacancy and dislocation between market and government will inevitably arise, a situation that speaks volumes of the fact that the market at this stage is still a far cry from a modern market system featuring equity, justice, efficiency and standardization. Once again, all of the above-mentioned analysis points to one conclusion, which is that a market with a market element system and a market organizational system but without regulatory and legal systems is an efficient but weak market.

5.1.1.3 Historical period

Historically, the US market was in its efficient but weak-form between 1776 – when the USA. declared its independence – and 1890, in a period where laissez-faire economics was the dominant economic theory. With the North winning a victory in a bloody civil war against the South, the element system and the organizational system of the US market economy were further developed and perfected. This was an era where fervid objection to government intervention was the prevailing sentiment of the day, and free rein was given to the spontaneous order of the market. This situation did not change until the late 1890s.

5.1.2 Semi-strong efficient market

5.1.2.1 Signs

A market can be called a semi-strong efficient market if it has the following four essential elements: a market element system, a market organizational system, a market legal system and a market regulatory system. A semi-strong efficient market represents an improved version of a weak efficient market, in the sense that both its legal environment and regulatory system are fortified and strengthened, though with its market element system and organizational system remaining the mainstays for market operation and with recognition of the "invisible hand" as the predominant force for resource allocation. In terms of categorization of resource types, the lines of demarcation between "operational resources" and "non-operational resources" have been clearly drawn in a semi-strong efficient market, but there is still neither clear delimitation of "quasi-operational resources" nor visible pathways for enhancing efficiency for the allocation of such resources.

5.1.2.2 Connotation

A semi-strong efficient market refers to one that is building and perfecting its market legal system and regulatory system in an incremental fashion, in addition to having a market element system and a market organizational system. A market legal system denotes an entirety of laws and regulations established and formed in accordance with cardinal market economic theories, which has normative market values, normative market trading behaviors, contract behaviors and property rights behaviors as its objects of regulation. Such a system generally encompasses legal, law enforcement, judiciary and law-related educational institutions. A market regulatory system is built for the overarching objective of creating a fair and viable market ecology that features a level playing field, free flows of commodities and elements, exchanges on an equal footing, honesty and law compliance and transparent and efficient management, as well as a law-based market regulatory environment. To this end, a market regulatory system is normally designed to counter such illicit acts as regional shutdown, industry monopoly, price deception and unfair competition. A market legal system and a regulatory system that are sound and full-fledged are necessary guarantees for the smooth running of a market mechanism.

In a semi-strong efficient market, categorization of resource types is by and large completed, along with clear lines of demarcation between market and government regarding their respective roles for resource allocation – the market dominates the allocation of "operational resources", while government guides the allocation of "non-operational resources". A variety of favorable outcomes can arise from differentiation of resource allocation domains between market and government, i.e. making clear the respective positioning and function of market and government; lessening government intervention in market activities; strengthening the role of government as a guardian of market order; and boosting the efficiency of resource allocation. Nonetheless, given that there is as yet neither clear delimitation of "quasi-operational resources" nor well-devised tools for their allocation, the market at this stage is inescapably plagued by the absence of a well-established and well-regulated operating system for the allocation of "quasi-operational resources", which inevitably means low efficiency for the allocation of such resources. In this sense, a market that fits the aforementioned descriptions can only be said to have developed to its semi-strong efficient form.

5.1.2.3 Historical period

The US market was in a semi-strong efficient form between 1890 and 1990, marked by the establishment and improvement of an antitrust legal and regulatory system, which was the centerpiece of market development efforts. In 1890, the US Congress promulgated the *Sherman Antitrust Act*, which was the US's first federal statute to prohibit trusts and monopoly. In 1914, *the Federal Trade Commission Act* and *the Clayton Antitrust Act* were passed as complements to *the Sherman Antitrust Act*. In accordance with these statutes and regulations, any given enterprise, once adjudicated as guilty of monopoly, would be subject to multiple forms of punishment, including fines, imprisonment, compensation, civil sanction, involuntary dissolution and separation. Once adjudicated as violating antitrust laws, an enterprise would be imposed with fines three times the amount of damage caused. Henceforth, the US's antitrust system and regulatory measures have undergone a century-long process of evolution and perfection, with the country's market legal system and market regulatory system experiencing significant improvements and upgrades along the way. The entire market system exhibited a prominent pattern that featured coexistence between monopoly and competition and between development and supervision. As of the 1990s, the US government, instead of confining its antitrust goals to simply preventing and clamping down on market monopoly and price manipulation, undertook effective measures to combat technical monopoly and Internet oligarchy beyond the realm of IPR protection. These efforts ended up injecting inexhaustible vitality into the US economy, in that they generated economies of scale and provided favorable conditions for the development of innovation-competent SMEs (small and medium-sized enterprises).

5.1.3 Strong efficient market

5.1.3.1 Signs

A strong efficient market refers to one that is in simultaneous possession of a market element system, a market organizational system, a market legal system, a market regulatory system, a market environment system and market infrastructure. A strong efficient market has two more building blocks than its "semi-strong efficient" counterpart, namely, a market environment system and market infrastructure. After a market develops to its strong efficient form, "quasi-operational resources" must have already been clearly defined and delimited and, given that government and market must have arrived at a certain extent of harmony regarding their respective roles in allocating such resources, efficiency for resource allocation will reach a new high in a strong efficient market. This means that the market economy at this point has entered the stage of a modern market system.

5.1.3.2 Connotation

A market environment system encompasses a well-designed real economic foundation, a corporate governance structure and a social credit system. The focus for building a market environment system is to set up a full-fledged market credit system; leverage legal institutions to regulate and restrain trust relations, credit instruments, credit intermediary agencies and pertinent credit elements; and put in place a social credit governance mechanism based on a market credit guarantee mechanism. An increasingly mature market environment system means all-dimensional openness and transparency of information. Under such circumstances, no market entity will be in a position to register exponential growth simply by capitalizing on its information edge or by taking advantage of a certain opportunity. Rather, market entities must battle it out in competition that tests a holistic set of their capabilities in terms of management, product innovation and distribution channel upgrading and regeneration. After market competition enters the stage of "systematic management", market entities are required not only to have distinct edges in certain respects but also to foster systematic management capabilities commensurate with their edges, in a bid to achieve overall improvement in internal management, technical development, marketing, etc. In a mature market environment, how a product is priced is truly reflective of the perfect competitiveness of a market entity.

Market infrastructure is an integrated system encompassing software and hardware facilities. Necessary infrastructural components of a mature market economy include market service networks, supplementary equipment and technologies, market payment and clearance systems of all types and high-tech information systems. The focus for building market infrastructure is to register, settle and take care of infrastructural facilities, achieve sharing of data and information regarding capital market regulation, establish a capital market information system and enhance capacity building for countering cyber attacks, tackling major disasters and addressing technical failure. The establishment and improvement of a market big data information system will propel the information-carrying capacity of market prices to a new level. Taken together, a market element system, market organizational system, market legal system, market regulatory system, market environment system and market infrastructure combine to form a "strong efficient market".

Improving market environment and market infrastructure paves the way for delimiting "quasi-operational resources" and enhancing the means for allocating such resources. A case in point is that in a well-established market environment system, a viable contractual relationship can be formed between government and market to bring about win–win outcomes regarding the allocation of "quasi-operational resources" – where their respective roles overlap or intersect. As far as market infrastructure is concerned, its critical components, such as market clearance systems and risk control systems, can open up a new vista for government–market cooperation in resource allocation. From what is stated above, it can thus be concluded that building and perfecting a modern market system is a process of constantly crystallizing resource categorization as well as resource allocation means. The presence of six market system elements and the clear-cut definition and allocation of "quasi-operational resources" are important indicators of a "strong efficient market".

5.1.3.3 *Historical period*

Asthe Highest among its kind in the world in terms of the level of marketization, the US securities market should be regarded as between a semi-strong efficient market and a strong efficient market. For example, to ensure market fairness, information concerning a potential company takeover is strictly blocked to such a level that the takeover, when it really takes place, sends insignificant or even little shock waves across the market. There is as yet no example of a strong efficient market in absolute terms in real life.

Since the early 1990s, the US market has been moving towards becoming a strong efficient market. The methodology of categorizing markets into "strong efficient forms", "weak efficient forms" and "semi-strong efficient forms" based on the levels of maturity and development of a market's six functional systems – its market element system, market organizational system, market legal system, market regulatory system, market environment system and market infrastructure – is able to shed light on the history of a market economy and its evolutionary process. This methodology is also convenient for clear-cut definition, empirical research and practical assessment when it comes to the study of the market. By shaping a mature modern market system, countries throughout the world will be in a better position to bring out the functions of their market economy for the benefit of economic growth, urban construction and social welfare improvement.

5.2 Three types of government

Government can be categorized into the following three types based on different degrees to which they intervene in the allocation of non-operational resources, operational resources and quasi-operational resources: "weak effective government", "semi-strong effective government" and "strong effective government". A government that focuses solely on non-operational resources can be called a "weak effective government"; a government that not only focuses on non-operational resources but is also able to render assistance and support where the allocation of operational resources is concerned can be deemed a "semi-strong effective government"; and a government can be credited as a "strong effective government" if it is able to directly allocate non-operational resources, supports and assists the allocation of operational resources and offers foresighted guidance on the allocation of quasi-operational resources.

As is resoundingly indicated by the practical experience of governments throughout the world and by China's success story of reform and opening up, governments of most countries would allow market entities to develop, operate and manage part of or a large proportion of "quasi-operational resources", as a precaution against urban resources being left idle and wasted, or for the sake of rectifying low efficiency and disorderliness in urban construction and administration. Under such circumstances, a project's equity nature and equity structure – the carrier of quasi-operational resources – should be designed and constructed in a way that complies with the rules of market-based competition; a project's investment and management mode – the operation of quasi-operational resources – should be determined by the means of market competition. As such, how a country's government performed in propelling economic development can be measured and gauged by how well it fares against governments in other countries or regions in terms of the allocation of the above-mentioned three categories of resources and in terms of the efficacy of policies and measures devised for this purpose.

First, the efficient allocation of non-operational resources through policy guarantee is conducive to maintaining social synergy and stability and optimizing economic environment. Second, the efficient allocation of operational resources with responsive policies can lead to a higher level of equity, fairness and openness in the market and give a tremendous boost to overall social productivity. Third, the efficient allocation of quasi-operational resources by ensuring sufficient competition is a recipe for driving sustainability in all respects of urban construction and socio-economic development. The means and policies for the optimal allocation of resources in these categories converge to form a gigantic framework, in which countries compete fiercely against one another.

5.2.1 Weak effective government

5.2.1.1 Meaning

A government can be called a "weak effective government" if it focuses only on the allocation of "non-operational resources" and on the formulation of corresponding policies. This is because such a government has neither a clear understanding of nor specific measures for the allocation of "operational resources". Such an administrative model is often called "the minarchist government model".

5.2.1.2 Characteristics

A weak effective government holds market mechanism in high esteem, striving to reduce the role of government in resource allocation to the minimal possible size in terms of both thinking and policies. A weak effective government is passive and unmotivated in action when it comes to resource allocation, playing a role only in public domains where "non-operational resources" abound, while adopting a non-interventional approach towards the economic realms. It seeks to guarantee the running of the economy by the smallest possible authority and relies on market forces for the adjustment of economic activities, believing that any given government should refrain from directly intervening in economic adjustment, no matter how big a cost and how much time it might take for the market itself to spontaneously effect such adjustment. In this sense, a weak effective government tends to restrict its power down to the absolute minimal level or assume a role tantamount to that of a night watchman, providing services that are only necessary and fundamental (i.e. the court system, policing, the prison system and national military defense). Moreover, a weak effective government is also characteristic of its advocacy for decentralization and delegation of government power to small jurisdictions (such as cities and towns) rather than concentration of it on large jurisdictions (such as provinces and the central state). Finally, a weak effective government, as a rule, opposes direct government engagement in financial assistance to the needy; it also lashes out at the idea of wealth redistribution and subsidization. In regard to policy arrangement, a weak effective government basically persists in low expenditure, low tax rates and low social welfare, putting a premium on individual free will and the importance of self-management.

5.2.2 *Semi-strong effective government*

5.2.2.1 *Meaning*

A government can be labeled as a "semi-strong effective government" if it lays stress only on the allocation of "non-operational" and "operational" resources. In addition to fulfilling its public duties and responsibilities regarding social security, a "semi-strong effective government" also keeps an eye on how the market is operating or will seek to macro-control, adjust and intervene in the economy by use of effective demand or effective supply policies whenever the market malfunctions, for the sake of preventing severe losses and damages caused by an economic slump. A "semi-strong effective government" might also strive for a dynamic equilibrium between total supply and total demand with a master plan for strategic economic development, which includes the following measures: planning and guiding industrial layout; supporting and adjusting productive and operational activities; tightening up regulation to ensure openness, equity and fairness in market competition; curbing the spike of commodity prices; and controlling unemployment. Nevertheless, a "semi-strong effective government" still fails to have a clear-cut understanding and definition of "quasi-operational resources"; nor does it succeed in fostering responsive policies and measures for the management of such resources.

5.2.2.2 *Characteristics*

A semi-strong effective government fails to clearly define and delimit "quasi-operational resources" but is able to rush in to control and adjust the allocation of "operational resources" whenever the "invisible hand" loses its grip over this matter. Generally speaking, a semi-strong effective government exhibits the following characteristics.

First, it recognizes the idea of the market as the decisive force for resource allocation, but follows closely the way that the market operates, showing no sign of passivity.

Second, it adopts a supportive attitude towards operational resources in critical domains pertaining to the overall economy and people's livelihood and selects supporting or interventional approaches based on the strategic significance of projects and the specific utility of assets.

Third, it promulgates adjustment and instructive policies for economic areas where the market is prone to malfunction.

Fourth, it either gets involved directly in or incentivizes in appropriate ways market resource allocation entities into areas where they otherwise would be unwilling to establish any presence voluntarily.

Fifth, when it comes to adjusting and supporting "operational resources", it shows a certain level of flexibility and temporariness, intervening mainly for the purpose of compensating for the insufficiency of the "invisible hand" in controlling such resources.

5.2.3   *Strong effective government*

5.2.3.1   *Meaning*

A "strong effective government" denotes a government that is already capable of precisely delimiting "quasi-operational resources" and coordinating with the market for the allocation of such resources. A "strong effective government" can tailor its policies and measures towards three different types of resources – namely, "non-operational resources", "operational resources" and "quasi-operational resource" – so as to achieve efficient resource allocation and promote the development of a regional economy towards viability and sustainability. Specifically, it will undertake the following approaches: bringing into full play its role in economic positioning, economic adjustment and early warning; tapping into market rules and mechanisms; leveraging the instruments of investment, consumption, export, pricing, taxation, interest rates, exchange rates, policies and laws; and fostering institutional, organizational, technical and philosophical innovation. As such, a "strong effective government" can be understood as a "foresighted leading" government.

5.2.3.2   *Characteristics*

A "strong effective government" not only attaches importance to the allocation of "non-operational resources" and "operational resources" but also seeks to facilitate the effective allocation of "quasi-operational resources" with well-designed policies. A "strong effective government" will seek in every possible way to achieve efficient allocation of resources in all three categories, such as by bringing into full play its role in economic positioning, economic adjustment and early warning; tapping into market rules and mechanisms by leveraging the instruments of investment, consumption, export, pricing, taxation, interest rates, exchange rates, policies and laws, and by fostering institutional, organizational, technical and philosophical innovation. The efficient allocation of non-operational resources can lead to significant improvements of economic growth environment; the efficient allocation of operational resources is conducive to boosting economic vitality and synergy; the efficient allocation of quasi-operational resources can help create a leading edge and bring about comprehensive and sustainable development. Therefore, fostering a "strong effective government" is the pathway for a country or a region to emerge victorious amid cut-throat competition in the world's grand market system.

(a) A strong government can foster regional competition through regulation and early warning in economic guidance to promote economic development. Within a market economy, a strong government's role should not be confined to administering public affairs and providing public services; rather, it should be extended to coordinate and promote economic development, such as formulating economic norms, maintaining market order, stabilizing macro-economic conditions, providing basic services, nurturing market systems, reallocating income and social wealth, contributing to social equity and justice, etc. A strong government plays a dual role that represents both the micro and macro levels of a market economy – the latter refers to a central government leading and regulating economic development on the macro level.

Enterprises and governments are the dual components of competition in a market economy. On the micro level, enterprises are the sole entity for market competition; on the macro level, in addition to enterprises, strong governments constitute another form of competition entities. Competition on these two levels is the "dual driving force" for rapid and continuing economic development.

(b) A strong government should play its "foresighted leading" role on the basis of market mechanisms and rules.

Within a market economy, the allocation of resources is realized through the functioning of the price mechanism. It must be made clear that emphasizing the role of government does not mean that government has to be involved in everything. Rather, it means that "operational resources" are left to the market to allocate; "non-operational resources" are placed in the hands of government to manage; "quasi-operational resources" are coordinated by market and government, in light of the level of market maturity and the extent of public acceptability. Inappropriate government intervention may hinder the normal development of a market, consequently bringing about the undesirable need for more government intervention. On the contrary, moderate government intervention will contribute to the realization of social goals and facilitate market nurturing. In this sense, government should exercise moderate and appropriate intervention. As indicated by developmental economist William Arthur Lewis (1915–1991), the failure of government may be due to its doing too little or due to its doing too much. It is thus reasonable to conclude that government should properly delimit and undertake its instructive and discretional behaviors for the allocation of three types of resources on the basis of market mechanisms and market rules; through effective foresighted leading in investment, consumption and export; and by employing economic and legal means and various innovative measures.

(c) Foresighted leading by a strong government should be aimed at effectively allocating resources, forging leading edges and achieving sustainable development. Various metaphorical expressions have been used to denote the role of government, from Adam Smith's "night watchman" and John Maynard Keynes's "visible hand" to Friedman's "servant" government, etc. Neither "servant" nor "nanny", however, is enough to cover the full implications behind the role of a strong government. It may be more precise to use the term "leading", which indicates a government's guiding, regulating and early warning function for one thing and, for another, its role in employing such measures as investment, pricing, taxation and law by means of market forces. During the infancy of an economy, it is necessary to "cross the streams by fumbling for the stones", but it becomes a must for government to guide, lead and plan economic development when the economy moves into a higher stage.

5.2.3.3   *Categories of strong GFL*

From the developmental perspective of an economy, institution, organization, technology and notions are all important factors. Accordingly, GFL is classified into institutional, organizational, technological and notional categories.

Institutional foresighted leading means giving full play to the role of government, particularly regional government, in an innovation of systems by creating new and more incentive policies and standards to increase the efficiency of resource allocation and the sustainability of socio-economic development and reform. Its core part is innovation in social, political, economic and administrative systems; in regulations of human conduct and interrelations; and in organizations and relations of its external environment. Its direct consequence is the inspiration of human creativity and enthusiasm, the creation of new knowledge, the fair allocation of social resources and the continuous creation of social wealth, which ultimately promote social progress. Only when there is innovative government can institutional foresighted leading be realized and innovative systems and policies be formulated.

Organizational foresighted leading means the innovation of government, particularly regional government, in such areas as organizational structure, modes and regulations with the aim of strengthening foundations for economic and industrial development and eventually facilitating innovations in policies and technology.

Technological foresighted leading means giving full play to the advantage of government in allocating social resources and enabling government to participate in and lead technological innovations directly or indirectly so as to promote scientific and technological advancement and strengthen the capabilities of cities and businesses to perform scientific and technological innovation. There are two aspects to technological foresighted leading. On the one hand, government should create a favorable environment for enterprises to enhance the capabilities to perform technological innovation, for example the construction of systems for patent application and protection and product standardization. On the other hand, government should implement effective economic measures and policies to encourage businesses to take the initiatives for technological innovation, for example granting funds to support research and development in key technologies, establishing technological funds, recruiting leading experts and so on.

Notional foresighted leading means that in the course of exercising authorities and power, government should conduct foresighted investigation, rational analysis and theoretical thinking concerning newly emerged issues and problems; foresee new social and economic phenomena; and generalize work experience and push it to a theoretical elevation so as to guide innovation and advancement in economic systems and institutional structuring. In the new phase of economic development, only by continuously transforming and upgrading government notions – such as notions of civilian community, restrained government, open government and government efficiency – can government innovate administrative systems, behaviors, methodology and technology and provide right value guidance and boundless innovative incentives.

5.3   Models of government–market combination and their appraisal

According to traditional micro-economics, market price mechanism is the fundamental force propelling economic operation. The fluctuation of prices affects the supply–demand relation on the market. Consumption, production and allocation reach equilibrium under the guidance of the invisible hand of prices and make the best out of resource allocation. In addition, government should not intervene in economic activities. Any government intervention in enterprises and market mechanisms will bring about a loss of efficiency. However, this traditional view proved feeble in the world economic depression of the 1930s, which called forth the era of government intervention in economy. The pattern of market economy under macro-level government intervention became the mainstream, and Keynesian economics and the subsequent neo-classic theories became the mainstream thought of economics.

The analytical paradigm of traditional micro-economics usually assumes the role of government to be an external variable and the market to be the optimal means for resource allocation. Such a value judgment often leads to the conclusion of minimal role of government for achieving maximal economic utility. In reality, however, such an analysis treats government as an external variable, excluding from the very outset the possibility of government and market reaching a certain level of synergy and harmony, which causes total neglect and disregard for the fact that economic development is a dynamic process. In other words, treating the role of government as an internal variable is the way to correctly understanding the relationship between government and market; the efficiency of either government or market in resource allocation is changeable in light of such actual conditions as time, geography and objects. As such, it is imperative to have a dynamic perspective of the effective line of demarcation between government and market in real practice.

In real economic practice, though the majority of countries lay claim to being market economies, huge differences exist among them in terms of economic efficiency and development trends, due to the divergent lines of demarcation they draw between government intervention and market mechanism. Countries like China have attained breakthroughs in traditional macro-economics, especially regarding market entities, competition areas and economic growth rates. It is incumbent upon modern market economic theorists to address questions about economic behaviors and developmental laws – questions that have arisen out of various models of combination between government and market.

5.3.1 The evolution of theories concerning government– market combination modes

The relationship between government and market has always been the centerpiece of debates among economists in the west. At the core of these debates is the issue of to what degree government intervention may affect economic growth, urban construction and social welfare.

An analysis of the government–market relationship must begin with mercantilism, a school of economic thought that gained strength and popularity in the early phase of capitalism from the sixteenth to the eighteenth century. The core belief behind mercantilist propositions was that a nation's power and growth depended primarily on the amount of wealth accumulated through trade surplus, achieved by exporting more than the nation imported. Along this line of argument, mercantilists proposed that government should intervene in economic life by way of prohibiting the outflow of gold and silver and bringing in more of such precious metals. They believed that to acquire more gold and silver, it was best that government regulate and control agriculture, commerce and manufacturing; develop a state monopoly of foreign trade; protect home markets through high tariffs and other trade restrictive measures; and make colonies both a source of raw materials and an export destination for manufacturers of home countries. The mercantilist theory served as a catalyst for the robust development of capitalist economies in their early stages.

The late eighteenth century witnessed the emergence of classical economics, which placed the market at the center of resource distribution. Classical economic theories, as best represented by Adam Smith's economic liberalism and David Ricardo's comparative advantage theory, confined the role of government to the smallest possible scope, sufficient only for the sake of ensuring the effective operation of the market.

In the 1930s, the economic crisis raging in the capitalist world posed challenges to classical economic theories, which culminated in the rise of Keynesian economics. John Maynard Keynes advocated the adoption of expansionary economic policies, arguing that government should promote economic growth by boosting demands. As Keynesian economics followed, not only should governments act to ensure the proper operation of the market, but they should also intervene in economic activities through monetary and fiscal policies, so that an equilibrium could be maintained between supply and demand in the economic system.

In the 1970s and 1980s, economists such as Milton Friedman and Arthur Laffer offered a new recipe for turning the raging economic crisis around, which was centered on unfettering economic activities from direct government intervention. Friedman, Laffer and other like-minded economists proposed to tackle the crisis by improving supplies in the economy.

Throughout the history of the evolution of capitalism, there have been varying descriptions of the relationship between government and the market. Some theories depicted them as contradictory to each other, while others saw them as complementary and coordinated to each other.

Now when we return to the six functional structures of a modern market system and face squarely the issue that confronts government across the globe – the efficient allocation of three categories of resources – we will find that the government–market relationship is by no means a one-to-one relationship between two contradictory forces. The categorization of markets into "weak efficient" forms, "semi-strong efficient" forms and "strong efficient" forms exists within a quantifiable paradigm and reflects a true historical process. The definitions of "weak effective", "semi-strong effective" and "strong effective" governments are reflective of where each country or region stands in the world's real market economy and are conducive to tackling an enormous set of conundrums pertinent to the government–market relationship.

5.3.2 Modes of government–market combination

A review of the history of market economic development reveals that the relationship between government and market has always been one of constant changes. Government and market complemented each other and worked in synergy amid perpetually changing economic circumstances. Theoretically speaking, there are nine models that reflect different forms of combination between government and market (as shown in Figure 5.1).

Model one: a weak effective government and a weak efficient market
Model two: a weak effective government and a semi-strong efficient market
Model three: a weak effective government and a strong efficient market
Model four: a semi-strong effective government and a weak efficient market
Model five: a semi-strong effective government and a semi-strong efficient market
Model six: a semi-strong effective government and a strong efficient market
Model seven: a strong effective government and a weak efficient market
Model eight: a strong effective government and a semi-strong efficient market
Model nine: a strong effective government and a strong efficient market

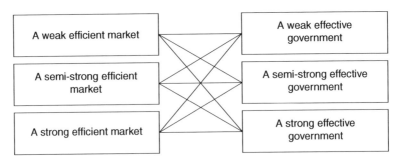

Figure 5.1 Modes of government–market combination

5.3.2.1 Model one: a dual-weak model

This model denotes a combination between a weak efficient market and a weak effective government, which means that neither market nor government is capable of effectively and efficiently allocating resources. Government basically does not play a role in economic management and regulation, and market is underdeveloped in the sense that the functioning of its competition mechanism is often curtailed by an ill-designed legal system and impaired by chaos and disorder. More often than not, many low and medium-income economies fit the descriptions of this model.

The proportion of government spending in total GDP is generally held up as a typical indicator of the role of government in economic activities. According to this indicator, it can be found that in low-income and medium-income countries, government spending takes up less than 20 percent of total GDP, while this percentage is more than an average of 25 percent in high-income countries (as shown in Table 5.1). When examined on a region-by-region basis, the proportion of government spending in total GDP is relatively low in South Asia and Central America, less than 20 percent on average. Despite the fact that it reaches an average of 20 percent in Sub-Saharan countries, a large credit should go to South Africa, whose government spends 34.8 percent of the country's GDP; on the contrary, the proportion in this regard is only 16 percent on average in countries like Kenya, Tanzania and Zambia. In countries with low government spending, it is usually unlikely for government to maintain basic public order, much less develop a national market. Governments in Sub-Saharan Africa, Central America and South Asia are often too handicapped by a shortage of financial resources to adjust and regulate their economies; worse still, with their markets underdeveloped – especially given that some countries in these regions are still subsisting on farming – their market competition mechanisms are often choked and strangled by the absence of a well-established legal framework to effectively keep a proper order. This explains why countries in these regions make up a majority of the low and medium-income ranks in the world.

Table 5.1 Proportion of government spending in GDP on a region-by-region basis (%)

Region/ Year	World average	Europe	Central America	North America	South Asia	Sub-Saharan Africa	Low-income countries	Medium-income countries	High-income countries
2000	25	33.6	19.3	18	15.6	20.9	–	17.1	26.5
2013	28.7	36.6	–	22.7	16.6	20.8	16.8	17.5	28.8

Source: Database of the World Bank, http://data.worldbank.org.cn/indicator/GC.XPN.TOTL.GD.ZS?view= chart&year_low_desc=false.

5.3.2.2   Model two: the laissez-faire model in market economy

The combination between a "semi-strong efficient market" and a "weak effective government" is akin to a laissez-faire model in the development of a market economy, in which information sets determined by and factored in prices are far from complete, but transparency of internal information within enterprises has reached an acceptable level, close to what is hypothesized as "total information" in the theory of classical economics. Under this model of combination, the market plays a somewhat significant role in resource allocation, while government persists in reducing its intervention in economic affairs to a minimum.

This model of combination is, however, practically nowhere to be found in the real economic world, for it requires a legal market system and a market regulatory system, which are unlikely to be put in place and driven forward by a weak effective government. The earliest market economic model of the USA. is the closest thing to this form of combination, which exhibits these features: an absolute dominance of private sectors in the economy, with the public sectors taking up a small proportion; a high concentration of private capital, even to the point of monopoly; a high degree of spontaneous adjustment by the market, coupled with a low level of state intervention; and a high degree of openness in the labor market, with great mobility and intense employment competition. One thing worthy of note is that without necessary regulation and intervention, this model of combination is prone to creating a breeding ground for monopoly and is unable to resolve problems that emerge whenever the market malfunctions.

5.3.2.3   Model three: classical market economic model

Model three, reflective of a combination between "weak effective government" and "strong efficient market", is akin to a classical market economy. This model is characterized by a pursuit of maximum market efficiency, the assumption of the role of government being exogenous and a basic exclusion of government from any economic activity. The working of this combination model is strictly limited by hypotheses, i.e.: Hypothesis of Economic Man, which assumes that every person, by capitalizing on the experience and information sets he or she acquires, will be able to make the best possible economic decisions and perform the best possible economic behaviors; Hypothesis of Perfect Competition, which assumes that perfect competition exists within various markets, to such a point where, once the balance between supply and demand is lost, the levels of prices and salaries will be promptly adjusted accordingly – this form of automatic market adjustment is hypothesized to be able to ensure the running of market economy under an equilibrium of full employment; and Complete Information Hypothesis, which assumes that an economic man is able to achieve optimal results by acquiring "complete information". Idealized hypotheses such as these naturally imply that freedom to choose is the most fundamental principle governing economic activities. With free market competition being held as the one and only path to achieving optimal allocation of resources and full employment under these idealized hypotheses, any government intervention will be deemed as hampering market efficiency. In this sense, government should refrain from intervention in economic activities and, whenever such intervention is truly necessary, the less, the better.

A consensus has been reached in real life about the infeasibility of the theoretical assumption involved in this model of combination, and it is empirically impossible to find any practical example in the real economic world to substantiate the rationality behind it. Put bluntly, therefore, no economic model has yet to emerge to reflect pure classical economic doctrines.

5.3.2.4   Model four: a regulatory model during the infancy of market economy

As a combination of "semi-strong effective government" and "weak efficient market", model four is descriptive of a regulatory model that is often instituted during the infancy of market economy. During the early stage when market economy is relatively weak, the efficiency of the market in allocating resources is somewhat limited as a result of inadequate competition and the inability of price signals to automatically regulate economic activities in a way similar to an invisible hand. Under such circumstances, government is in a position to fulfill its duties and responsibilities pertinent to the allocation of "non-operational resources", by providing basic public goods. In the meantime, the government, though capable of allocating and supporting "operational resources" in some way, is still unable to keep an exact track of the pulse of the market. Thus, a more mature market is needed to resolve problems that keep cropping up. This government regulation model is often adopted during the infancy of a market economy, when the market is weak and the government is growing towards sophistication.

The real-life parallel for this model is the Chinese economy during the early stage of reform and opening up (from 1978 to 1984), in a period when the market was allowed to play its part in certain sectors and regions, though only in a heavily restricted and partial way. At that time, resources were still allocated, by and large, in a planning-based fashion, with regional governments required to formulate plans that not only covered the overall economy but also governed the operation of enterprises down to minute details. Against this backdrop, it was only natural that a market-based competition mechanism did not take shape among enterprises. The Chinese economy in this period was one in which the "invisible hand" of the market was severely hampered, while the government both macro- and micro-managed economic activities, consequently straining the government–enterprise relationship. The government, though having reached its peak in terms of its jurisdictional scope and power, was more of a semi-strong effective government than a strong effective one; despite not being mature enough, it was proactive in finding out where it fit in a changing economic landscape. In short, economic resources of China in this period were allocated in a way that combined a semi-strong effective government with a weak efficient market.

5.3.2.5   Model five: a semi-mature economic model

Model five depicts a combination between "semi-strong effective government" and "semi-strong efficient market". This economic model indicates that the market and the government are well matched in strength, both of which have already developed to a semi-strong form, and yet are still in the process of honing and perfecting their capacity for resource allocation – the market has some untapped potential to be released, while the government is seeking to better position itself in a growing economy. In short, diversified ownership constitutes a predominant feature of most economies in this period, with the balance of power between government and market in constant flux. For one thing, a market-based price determination mechanism has taken shape, but in the absence of full-fledged mechanisms regarding market regulation, legal protection and environment enhancement, prices have yet to factor in all information sets available in the market. For another, unpredictable policy flip-flopping is a commonplace occurrence, mainly because the government, despite having been able to assume its proper role in allocating non-operational resources, is still devoid of mature experience and policy guidelines when it comes to delimiting quasi-operational resources and leading the allocation of operational resources – nevertheless, the government in such an economic model usually has come to recognize the market as a basic regulator of economic activities.

A semi-mature economic model is generally seen in a country that is in its mid-term phase of market economic development. A case in point is China prior to its entry into the World Trade Organization, when the Chinese economy was in its semi-mature form, featuring a combination between a semi-strong efficient market and a semi-strong effective government. On one hand, the Chinese government was beefing up the intensity and mechanisms for planning and guiding industrial layout, supporting and regulating productive operational activities and ensuring openness, equity and fairness in market competition; on the other hand, initiatives were well underway to boost the market's regulatory mechanism, legal protection mechanism and environmental enhancement mechanism.

To cite two more examples: the Russian Federation – which represented countries in transition from a planned to a market-oriented economy – saw the ratio of government spending to GDP rise from 21.2 percent in 2000 to 25.3 percent in 2013. During this period, the Russian government somewhat lowered its intensity for regulating economic activities, which resulted in more and more resources being allocated by the "invisible hand" of the market. However, due to unsteady overall economic growth, the government was being constantly challenged in its ability to manage the economy, thus having to work out a proper relationship with the market. The other example is Brazil, the epitome of countries in Latin America that once persisted in the policy of import substitution industrialization, with "overtaking" as an overarching objective. The overpowering role of the Brazilian government on the country's economic development ended up spurring an industrial boom in the short term, but not without causing some long-term ill-effects, as manifested in the form of a distorted market system, a failure of market mechanisms, a spike of inflation and a disruption of financial order. Against this backdrop, the government spiraled downward in terms of its impact on the economy. To redress its dwindling role in the economy, the Brazilian government resorted to increasing spending, which resulted in the ratio of government spending to GDP slightly edging up from 21.4 percent in 2000 to 24.4 percent in 2013. This meant that the government and the market were in a process of sorting out the scopes and mechanisms of their function.

5.3.2.6   Model six: a regulatory model for the post–market-economy period

Model six describes the combination between "semi-strong effective government" and "semi-strong efficient market", which is an indication that the market has evolved to a highly mature state, so much so that it has primacy in allocating resources in ways that generate tantalizing efficiency and profitability. The government in an economy of this model has an important role to play in allocating non-operational and quasi-operational resources, but with its hands tied by institutional or ideological restrictions, it either fails to clearly delimit operational and quasi-operational resources or takes a somewhat laissez-faire approach to the allocation of these resources, thus showing a lack of good planning, systematicity and foresight for overall economic development.

The current US economy is a real-life mirror image of this model of government–market combination. By tapping into the market's predominant forces in resource allocation, the US government has reaped the bounty of benefits that a highly efficient market can deliver. Although it plays a preeminent role in the allocation of "non-operational resources", the US government, plagued by institutional or ideological impediments, fails to match its deeds to its words and register breakthroughs when it comes to allocating "operational resources" and delimiting or exploiting "quasi-operational resources". As a result, there are weak signs of systematic and foresighted leadership by the US government for overall economic growth and urban improvement. This model of combination between a semi-strong efficient market and a semi-strong effective government is also seen in many other developed economies in the world. To better illustrate this point, let us measure the role of government in economic activities in major developed economies against the ratio of government spending to GDP, as reflected in Table 5.2.

As Table 5.2 shows, the government spending to GDP ratio has exceeded 30 percent in many major developed countries of the west, which is an indication of the high intensity at which governments in these countries have been involved in resource allocation and economic activities. That ratio surpassed 30 percent

Table 5.2 The ratio of fiscal expenditure to GDP in major developed countries (%)

Country	Sweden	Norway	Denmark	Finland	France	Germany	Netherlands	Austria	UK
2000	34.6	32.4	36.8	34.8	44.2	31.3	37.2	45.8	34.7
2013	33.3	34.8	41.9	41.2	48.6	28.7	42.6	46.4	40.8

Country	Canada	USA.	Australia	New Zealand	Israel	South Africa	Japan	South Korea	Singapore
2000	18.8	17.9	24.1	31.6	43.9	27.2	14.2	15.8	15.8
2013	17.2	23.2	26	32.4	37.9	34.8	19.3	18.9	12.6

Source: Database of the World Bank, http://data.worldbank.org.cn/indicator/GC.XPN.TOTL.GD.ZS?view=chart&year_low_desc=false.

in the 2013 estimates in some of the countries listed in Table 5.2, such as in Israel, New Zealand and South Africa, and even rose above 40 percent in the 2000 estimates in countries like Denmark, Finland, France, the Netherlands, Austria, the UK and Israel. That ratio, though kept below 30 percent from 2000 to 2013 in some other developed countries such as the USA., Canada and Australia, was raised above 20 percent by the end of 2013 in the USA. and Australia, which testifies to the growing level of government involvement in resource allocation in these countries. Take the OECD (Organization for Economic Cooperation and Development) as an example. From a historical standpoint, the average ratio of government spending to GDP in OECD countries as a whole stood at 10.7 percent in the late nineteenth century, increased to 18.7 percent in 1920, edged up to 22.8 percent in 1937, skyrocketed to 43.1 percent in 1980 and has remained stable at this level ever since. A review of these countries' actual economic development reveals that the constantly rising level of government engagement in resource allocation has exerted no negative impact whatsoever on their competitiveness; on the contrary, the level of market maturity and competitiveness in these countries has grown higher and higher in tandem with the rise of government intervention. It should be particularly noted that Nordic countries and Israel, though government spending accounts for 40 percent of GDP, are way ahead of other OECD countries in terms of economic openness and labor market vibrancy, and have remained on top of the list of global competitiveness for years. This phenomenon can be explained by the famous Wagner's Law, a law that has predicted the upward sloping trend of the share of government spending in GDP rising continually in tandem with the increase of income per person.

5.3.2.7 *Model seven: a non-existent form of combination*

Model seven depicts a form of combination between strong effective government and weak efficient market, which finds no parallel in real life, because in functional terms, a strong effective government needs a mature market economy in order to play out its role, and should at least be matched with a semi-strong efficient market. Along this line of rationality, a weak efficient market – which means that the market fails to play out its proper function – provides no fertile ground for the formation of a strong effective government. It should be noted that a planned economy does not fall into this model of combination, because there is no such a thing as a market in a planned economy, much less a "weak efficient market". Furthermore, the government in a planned economy adopts, by and large, a repulsive attitude towards the market, thus exercising nothing near effective and foresighted leadership over the market. All told, a government in a planned economy is an "authoritarian government", but by no means a "strong effective government". In this sense, this form of combination is merely an assumption that can be neither logically reasoned in theory nor substantiated by empirical examples.

5.3.2.8   *Model eight: an authoritative government economic model*

This economic model denotes a form of combination between "strong effective government" and "semi-strong efficient market", with "government control" as its core. In an authoritative government economic model, the government capitalizes on its strong "government intensity" and capabilities in a bid to propel economic growth and alleviate various social, political and economic pressures that arise therefrom. An authoritative government economic model can serve as a driver for economic growth and industrialization, mainly due to its ability to guarantee the smooth enforcement of various institutional arrangements through a high degree of "government quality". An authoritative government knows how to bring to bear its tremendous power in mobilizing and allocating resources, but not without grasping and respecting market rules. With vision and foresight for the future of the market, an authoritative government is able to formulate appropriate instructive policies for the development of industries and enterprises, taking into account the overall picture of an economy. In short, the following three words encapsulate the role of an authoritative government in economic activities: proactivity, initiative and power.

Meanwhile, this economic model often comes with a mature and stable market. However, market mechanisms might be hampered in certain areas by overpowering government interventions. Therefore, a market under this economic model, as a general rule, shows a lack of intra-regional competition and is teeming with government–corporation alliances that lay stress on loyalty and coordination among governments, corporations and employees.

Model eight depicts a market economy quite similar to the current Chinese economy. It is usually deemed a government-led economy moving incrementally towards maturity, one that has registered world-acclaimed accomplishments but is still confronted with grave challenges in the form of intensifying market competition and the urgency to foster a better market order, improve market credit systems and upgrade market infrastructure. Other typical examples of this model can be found in east Asia, such as Japan, South Korea and Singapore, whose mature government-led economic systems have yielded universally recognized achievements. This government-led economic model has taken shape and form in these countries for profound historical reasons. As late-bloomers, countries like Singapore and South Korea were once plagued by various challenges, not the least of which were a structurally deformed market, underdeveloped market entities, a lack of mobility for production factors, sluggish economic growth, etc. To accomplish an economic take-off in the earliest possible time, these countries held the role of the state in high esteem from the very beginning, resorting to boosting market efficiency through state intervention in a way that respected the rules of the market. One thing of particular note is that the share of government spending in GDP was anything but high in these countries from 2000 to 2013, all below 20 percent (as shown in Table 5.2). On the surface, the impact of the state on economic growth was unpronounced in these countries; this is because the states in these countries successfully instituted and implemented a development model of government-linked enterprises, which was designed, first and foremost, to incentivize investment from enterprises and individuals for realizing the will of the state. A case in point in this regard is the housing provident fund system in Singapore, which has helped pool and inject needed financial resources into the Singaporean economy through personal mandatory saving schemes and high-yield investment channels. Through systems like this, the Singaporean government has managed to exert powerful influence on the country's economic growth and industrial upgrade. Nevertheless, the existence of government–corporation alliances in abundance tends to breed grounds for collusion between power and money, which is likely to hamper market order and free competition and to induce risks of administrative decision-making faults. This is the new challenge confronting the governments in Japan, Singapore and South Korea.

A review of various economic models, coupled with the aforementioned analysis, reveals that the combination between "weak effective government" and "weak efficient market" is, more often than not, found in countries that are economically backward, and that very few fast-growing countries adopt what neoclassical economists have recognized and advocated, namely, the combination between "weak effective government" and "strong efficient market". What is more commonly seen is the combination between "semi-strong effective government" and "strong efficient market".

5.3.2.9   Model nine: a dual-strong economic model

Model nine is the highest and best possible form of combination between government and market. It depicts what a truly mature market economy looks like and shows the ultimate point of the destination that national and regional economies across the globe should strive to reach through theoretical studies and practical exploration.

5.3.2.9.1   A LOGICAL DEDUCTION FOR THE DUAL-STRONG ECONOMIC MODEL

With GFL practice by regional governments as a point of departure, the dual-strong economic model reveals the dual role of regional governments, discovers enterprises and regional governments as the dual entities for market competition and finally comes to the conclusion of a dual-strong mechanism – consisting of "strong efficient market" and "strong efficient market" – as the indicative feature of a mature market economy.

What is meant by "foresighted leading" is that regional government has an important role to play in economic orientation, adjustment and early warning, and it should bring this role into play in a way that abides by market rules and market mechanisms. Under the foresighted leading theory, regional government should, to the best of its capabilities, develop a leading edge in resource allocation so as to better catalyze the sound and sustainable growth of regional economy. To this end, regional government should guide activities regarding investment, consumption and export; leverage the instruments of prices, taxation, exchange rates, interest rates and legislation; and incentivize organizational, institutional and technological innovation. The reason for regional government being able to exercise foresighted leadership lies in its dual role as a "quasi-state" and a "quasi-enterprise": on the one hand, regional government plays a role tantamount to a "quasi-state", macro-managing and regulating regional economies under its jurisdiction; on the other hand, regional government acts on behalf of the basic interests of the local area, attempting to compete with their counterparts in other regions for the maximization of regional economic profits.

Thus, regional government (as a quasi-enterprise) and enterprises combine to form the "dual entities" in a modern market competition system. The dual-strong mechanism theory for a mature market economy, which focuses on a mechanism comprising a "strong government" and a "strong efficient market", deductively emerges out of the dual-entity theory. As the theory goes, on the premise of giving full play to the decisive role of the market in resource allocation, an "efficient market" and an "effective government" should be developed as the "double wheels" on which an economy runs.

5.3.2.9.2 THE CONNOTATION OF A DUAL-STRONG MECHANISM

Given that regional government plays a dual role and acts as one of the dual entities for market competition, an "effective government" plus an "efficient market" – or, put another way, a "strong government" plus a "strong efficient market" – constitutes the best possible combination for a full-fledged market economic system. For one thing, a "strong efficient market" is able to efficiently allocate resources, while a "strong government" is needed for creating and protecting a good market climate, bringing about new ideas and impetus for development, exploring new vistas for development and building new strengths for development; for another, a "strong government" should not be for the sake of "replacing a strong efficient market", while a "strong efficient market" cannot run smoothly without the underpinning of a "strong government". Only when a "dual-strong mechanism" is put into effect can market failures be redressed and government malfunction be alleviated.

5.3.2.9.3 AN "EFFECTIVE" REGIONAL GOVERNMENT MODEL

To properly exercise foresighted leadership, an "effective" regional government should make clear the purpose, prerequisite and pathway pertinent to GFL: the purpose of GFL is to efficiently allocate resources of all kinds and advance sustainable regional development; the prerequisite to GFL is the market, which means that GFL should be exercised on the basis of the rules and forces of the market. The pathway for effecting GFL is through finance, taxation, legislation and necessary administrative measures.

In the economic realm, government should, first and foremost, exercise foresighted leadership in areas where economic growth, urban construction and resource allocation optimization are concerned, with different approaches and priorities for different stages of development. Take China, for example: in the factor-driven development stage, the Chinese government relied on its control over land supply to drive economic growth; after China entered the investment-driven stage, the government exercised GFL mainly in the provision of public goods, notably infrastructure; currently, as China transits towards innovation-driven development, the government's foresighted leading role is all the more important for scientific innovation, proprietary innovation and synergetic innovation.

The USA. represents another notable example of GFL to boost economic growth. At a glance, the USA. seems to be a market economy with a "weak effective government" and a "strong market", where values of economic liberalism prevail. In actuality, whether the space program enacted during the Cold War era or the "brain project" being implemented right now, the US government has been playing a prominent role in foresightedly leading innovation in science and technology, with R&D investment and government procurement as the two main drivers for this endeavor.

Shunde District of Guangdong Province, China, represents a compelling example of foresighted leading for resource allocation. At the outset of reform and opening up in China, Shunde was neither a special economic zone nor a big city, but rather a county totally dependent on agriculture. As the wind of reform breathed new life into the local economy, the CPC and government leaders of Shunde set forth the development strategy. With inspiration drawn from the ancient Chinese story of five sons successfully passing the imperial examination, the local leaders set priorities in five aspects: following the right paths, fostering excellent leadership, bringing forth talents, realizing good economic returns and enlisting brilliant ideas. As one of the first counties to have focused on developing village and township enterprises, Shunde managed to capitalize on the promise of a burgeoning market economy in China.

In the early 1990s, Shunde once again became a pioneer in China's new reform initiative – this time around, on property rights and ownership. By bringing the development of its secondary industry more in sync with the market economy, Shunde successfully took its private economy to a whole new level. In 2005, one year into this author's tenure as Secretary of the CPC Shunde District Committee, this author took steps to restructure the local economy in an effort to address pronounced problems facing the district, most notably overdependence on three major home appliance manufacturers (Midea, Glanz and Kelon) for economic growth, as well as a severe lack of resilience against risks. A series of reform measures culminated in the formulation and implementation of the "Triple-Three Strategy" for coordinating the development of three major industries in Shunde. The first "three" refers to three major industries; the second "three" means that three key sectors would be singled out in each of the three major industries, sectors that would receive strong government support; the third "three" means that three leading enterprises would be cultivated and developed within each selected sector. Thanks to the success of this strategy, the economy of Shunde managed to weather an array of challenges that came at it in the next several years, the biggest of which was the international financial crisis. As a result, Shunde continues to remain at the forefront of socio-economic development among district-level cities and counties in China.

The key to building an "effective government" is to make good use of finance, taxation, legislation and necessary administrative measures. A look into China's financial structural reform – a crucial part of its supply-side structural reform – can offer some insight and perspectives into the behavioral patterns of an "effective government". For China, an economy that ranked second in the world in total import and export volumes in 2016, drastic fluctuations of exchange rates require it to speed up the pace of exchange rate reform for RMB internationalization. In this connection, China is considering the possibility of establishing an onshore trading center for RMB offshore business, which, once put in place, will be used as a fulcrum for RMB internationalization. This has been an approach taken by major countries in the process of internationalizing their currencies. Two standout examples come to mind. One example is the decision by the Federal Reserve Bank to establish IBFs (International Banking Facilities) in the process of US dollar internationalization, which were designated to undertake offshore US dollar business within the jurisdiction of the USA., such as international lending and deposit activities. This approach ended up being a tremendous boost for US offshore finance. The other example is the step of the Japanese government setting up the Japan Offshore Market (JOM), an institution that has played a critical role in promoting internationalization of the Japanese yen. With full consideration given to its actual conditions, China can establish a pilot onshore trading center for RMB offshore business in either Shanghai Free-Trade Zone or Guangdong Free-Trade Zone, as a springboard for China to leap from a service trade power to a capital power and as a boost for financial structural reform.

5.3.3 Criteria and standards for assessing modes of government–market combination

5.3.3.1 Criteria for assessment

As the optimal form of government–market combination, the dual-strong model does not come into being until both market and government develop to maturity. However, when it comes to practice in real life, one grave mistake has to be avoided, which is mechanically and indiscriminately applying any particular model of government–market combination to a regional economy. This is because the best possible model of government–market combination varies across regions, depending on their differences in economic development stages and levels of maturity regarding government and market. Applying a model of combination that is behind or ahead of a region's development curve will definitely undermine its economy. As a matter of fact, the economic backwardness of a region oftentimes should not be ascribed to its market or government being powerless, but to dislocation and disruption between its market and government, a problem that arises from a misjudgment of the scopes of their respective roles and functions. For this reason, making assessments of the economic efficiency of different combination models is critically important for eschewing exaggeration and restraint of the roles of government and market; doing so can also shed some light on how to properly position and develop the government and market of a regional economy, enabling the regional economy to tap its market potentials; foster better governance; shun problems pertaining to supersession, vacancy and dislocation between government and market; and secure steady and healthy development.

For the sake of tapping the potentials and realizing the sustainability of any given regional economy, a system of criteria and standards for assessing economic benefits of different models of government–market combination must be built and shaped on the basis of five economic parameters – effectiveness, coordination, continuity, creativity and inclusiveness.

5.3.3.1.1 EFFECTIVENESS OF ECONOMIC GROWTH

The effectiveness of economic growth denotes the efficiency and sustainability of economic growth, as well as the employment and price stability generated by economic growth. The growth of an economy cannot be described as effective unless it leads to increased efficiency, stable prices and full employment, because otherwise it will only cause new turbulence and even induce ill-effects that far outweigh the benefits it generates. Assessment indicators of the effectiveness of economic growth include labor productivity, economic growth rate, economic sustainability, employment rate, price fluctuation, etc. Labor productivity, also known as workforce productivity, is the ratio of a region's GDP to the total amount of its workforce. The higher a region's labor productivity is, the higher quality of economic development it has, and vice versa. As compared with conventional assessment indicators, labor productivity can present a clearer picture of whether a region's economic development is quantity-based or quality-based, so that the region's economy can be shifted onto the path of improved worker proficiency. Economic growth that is stable, rational and sustainable is a significant measure of the quality of economic development, as well as a remarkable indicator of a region's development efficiency. A region with high development efficiency necessarily features a continued high growth rate. Increasing economic aggregate in the shortest time possible is a necessary path to social wealth creation. However, if the growth of an economy fails to bring about stable employment or, worse still, leads to severe inflation, then such growth will deal a detrimental blow to long-term economic sustainability. Thus, to make the growth of an economy effective calls for attention to all-rounded development of the whole society.

The effectiveness of economic growth can be judged according to how close real GDP is to potential GDP. Potential GDP is generally defined as the maximum possible level of output that an economy can produce under the condition of available economic resources being used to the fullest possible extent in a specific period of time. Put another way, potential GDP reflects the biggest possible gross domestic product that an economy can produce under the condition of full employment in a specific period of time. The closer the ratio of real output to production capacity is to 100 percent, the more fully the production capacity is being tapped, the higher quality of development the economy has and the lower level of waste and idleness it features. Nevertheless, it should be noted that there still exists some difficulty in measuring potential GDP.

5.3.3.1.2 COORDINATION OF ECONOMIC DEVELOPMENT

As a key indicator of economic development quality, the coordination of economic development mainly describes the level of synergy in industrial structure, urban–rural structure and structure of trade in an economy. Of the three types of structure, industrial structure assumes a dominant position and constitutes a significant component of economic development quality, with its changes bearing critically on economic development. The coordination of economic development can be assessed and measured by industrial structure ratio, urbanization rate and coefficient of openness.

The ratio of the tertiary industry in a region's economy is a crucial indicator of its level of development. As it stands now, this ratio hovers at about 70 percent in most developed economies, and stays at around 50 percent on average in developing economies as a group. Some cities in China have caught up with or even surpassed major cities in developed economies in terms of this ratio. A case in point is Beijing, with its tertiary sector accounting for over 70 percent of its industrial output. However, never before has this ratio reached 50 percent for the whole of China, even at its peak, indicating relatively huge room for improvement. Urbanization rate refers to the percentage of an economy's urban population in its total population, an indicator that helps optimize urban–rural economic structure and facilitate viable economic growth and coordinated social development. Coefficient of openness is reflective of the level of internationalization of a national or regional economy, the competitiveness of its products and services on the international market and its capacity and intensity for soliciting foreign investment. This coefficient is conducive to strengthening the competitiveness and enhancing the external coordination of an economy.

5.3.3.1.3 CONTINUITY OF ECONOMIC DEVELOPMENT

The continuity of economic development defines the capacity of an economy for sustainable development, which is mainly manifested in the carrying capacity of resources and environment for long-term economic development. The continuity of economic development can be measured by the coefficient of resource supply and demand, the energy consumption per unit of output and the variance ratio of environmental quality cost.

The coefficient of resource supply and demand refers to the degree of variation between the availability and demand of resources: if the coefficient is larger than 1, that means the availability of resources is sufficient to meet the demand for resources needed for economic development; if the coefficient is less than 1, that means the availability of resources is below what is needed to ensure economic development. The energy consumption per unit of output refers to the ratio of energy consumption (as measured by tons of coal equivalent) to GDP, an index that is conducive to boosting the efficiency in energy consumption, accelerating technical transformation of traditional industries, forcefully phasing out low-efficient energy sources and alleviating energy shortage in economic development. The variance ratio of environmental quality cost describes the change of environmental quality cost in economic development: if the ratio is on the rise, it signals a deterioration of an economy's sustainability. This ratio can help reduce the damages done to the environment and speed up the recovery of a damaged environment.

5.3.3.1.4 CREATIVITY OF ECONOMIC DEVELOPMENT

The creativity of economic development denotes the impact of technological innovation on economic development. The ratio of R&D spending to GDP is a core indicator of an economy's creativity. If R&D spending accounts for less than 1 percent of GDP, it signals a lack of creativity; only when the ratio stands between 1 percent and 2 percent can it show a certain degree of creativity; if the ratio is higher than 2 percent, it indicates strong capacity for innovation. Other indicators of an economy's creativity include the ratio of high-tech sectors' added value to GDP and the index of patent authorization.

5.3.3.1.5 INCLUSIVENESS OF ECONOMIC DEVELOPMENT

The inclusiveness of economic development describes the impact of economic development on poverty alleviation and improvement of people's livelihood, and can be measured by the growth rate of residents' income, Engel Coefficient and income disparity between urban and rural residents. A market–government combination model can be considered good only if it is conducive to narrowing income gaps and enhancing social fairness, on top of boosting economic growth.

5.3.3.2 *Assessment of the nine models of market–government combination*

Of the nine models of market–government combination, the dual-weak economic model, which is extreme in nature, shows an obvious lack of potential for future development. The two models that encompass either a strong government and a weak market or vice versa only appear in specific stages of history. By no means do they provide the pathway for the future. The models that are both feasible in real life and enlightening for the future are the semi-mature economic model, the regulatory model for the post-market-economy period, the authoritative government economic model and the dual-strong economic model.

The semi-mature economic model is an economic model that indicates both market and government have already developed to a semi-strong form, as best represented by Russia or Latin American countries. The regulatory model for the post-market-economy period denotes the combination of strong efficient market and semi-strong effective government, as best represented by developed countries in North America and the European Union. The authoritative government economic model describes the combination of semi-strong efficient market and strong effective government, as seen in countries like Singapore, South Korea and Japan. The dual-strong economic model specifically refers to the combination of strong efficient market and strong effective government, as is reflected in some regions in China, such as the PRD.

What follows is an assessment of the performances of these four models as measured against various indicators for economic development quality.

5.3.3.3   Economic growth rate

The dual-strong economic model, as best represented by the one adopted in China's PRD, fares much better than the other three models in terms of economic growth rates. Under this model, the PRD has enjoyed steady economic growth on a robust momentum, with tremendous vigor and vitality and with economic activities well under control. In contrast, practically all developed economies, where the regulatory model for the post-market-economy period is enforced, have exhibited negative economic growth and a lack of stamina for the future, with only one exception, namely, Israel, whose economic growth has been sloping downward but at a very gentle gradient. In particular, Sweden, well known for its welfare state, has seen its economic growth turn negative, down by 5.11 percent, indicating an obvious lack of growth impetus. Russia and Brazil, which have followed the semi-mature economic model, have experienced a roller coaster ride of economic development over the past decade, debilitated by fragile economic stability. As for countries where the authoritative government model prevails, Singapore and South Korea have shown a steady pace of growth, but Japan has been plagued by economic fluctuations and a lack of momentum. As is clear from the above analysis and from Table 5.3, the dual-strong economic model presents distinct advantages in terms of growth momentum and stability, followed by the authoritative government economic model and then by the regulatory model for the post-market-economy period. The semi-mature economic model is, distressingly, at the bottom of the pecking order.

Table 5.3 Economic growth rates (%) in countries with different growth models

Year/Model		2005	2006	2007	2008	2009	2010	2011	2012	2013	2014	2015
M1	Brazil	3.2	3.96	6.06	5.09	−0.13	7.54	3.92	1.93	3.02	0.1	−3.85
	Russia	6.38	8.15	8.54	5.25	−7.82	4.5	4.26	3.52	1.28	0.71	−3.73
M2	France	1.61	2.37	2.36	0.2	−2.94	1.97	2.08	0.18	0.64	0.63	1.22
	Germany	0.88	3.88	3.38	0.81	−5.57	3.94	3.72	0.62	0.41	1.58	1.45
	Sweden	2.81	4.95	3.54	−0.72	−5.11	5.69	2.74	0.05	1.23	2.38	3.83
	UK	3	2.66	2.59	−0.47	−4.19	1.54	1.97	1.18	2.16	2.85	2.33
	USA.	3.35	2.67	1.78	−0.29	−2.78	2.53	1.6	2.22	1.49	2.43	2.43
	Israel	4.39	5.63	6.23	3.16	1.23	5.37	5.03	2.86	3.35	2.6	2.49
M3	Japan	1.3	1.69	2.19	−1.04	−5.53	4.71	−0.45	1.74	1.36	−0.03	0.55
	South Korea	3.92	5.18	5.46	2.83	0.71	6.5	3.68	2.29	2.9	3.34	2.61
	Singapore	7.5	–	–	–	–	15.2	6.2	3.4	4.4	2.9	–
M4	The PRD	15.7	16.8	16.3	12.8	9.4	12.2	9.9	8.1	9.3	7.8	–

Source: https://data.oecd.org/ (OECD database),www.adb.org/ (ADB database), www.gdstats. gov.cn/tjnj/2015 (2015 Statistics Yearbook of Guangdong Province).

M1 = the semi-mature economic model; M2 = the regulatory model for the post-market-economy period; M3 = the authoritative government economic model; M4 = the dual-strong economic model

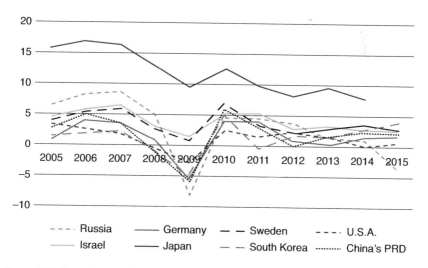

Figure 5.2 Growth rates in countries representative of the four assessed models

5.3.3.4   Unemployment rate

Apparently, judging from the level of unemployment, the authoritative government economic model produces the lowest level of unemployment compared with the other three combination models. Unemployment for China has stayed above 4 percent. Nevertheless, it should be noted that the dual-strong economic model hereby represents only the PRD of China, rather than the whole of China. The PRD has been a region with a high concentration of workforce, which has not only provided enough job opportunities for local population but also attracted a massive number of workers migrating from elsewhere in China. Moreover, despite being just a region of China, the PRD has played a crucial role as a cross-regional labor market for the whole country. Therefore, the PRD, if taken independently, features insignificantly low unemployment. From this perspective, it is fair to say that the dual-strong economic model is the optimal form of combination when it comes to taming unemployment. There is big cause for pessimism regarding unemployment in countries that have instituted either the regulatory model for the post-market-economy period or the semi-mature economic model, as unemployment in these countries has been high for years (as shown in Table 5.4).

Table 5.4 Unemployment (%) under different combination models

Year/Model		2005	2006	2007	2008	2009	2010	2011	2012	2013	2014	2015
M1	Brazil	9.89	10.03	9.35	7.93	8.11	6.76	5.98	5.52	5.4	4.85	–
	Russia	7.56	7.17	6.13	6.36	8.38	7.48	6.5	5.46	5.49	5.16	5.57
M2	France	8.49	8.45	7.66	7.06	8.74	8.87	8.81	9.39	9.89	10.29	10.35
	Germany	11.17	10.25	8.66	7.53	7.74	6.97	5.83	5.38	5.23	4.98	4.62
	Sweden	7.48	7.07	6.16	6.23	8.35	8.61	7.8	7.98	8.05	7.96	7.43
	UK	4.75	5.35	5.26	5.61	7.54	7.79	8.04	7.89	7.53	6.11	5.3
	USA.	5.07	4.62	4.62	5.78	9.27	9.62	8.95	8.07	7.38	6.17	5.29
	Israel	8.99	8.4	7.32	6.1	7.54	6.64	5.6	6.85	6.21	5.91	5.24
M3	Japan	4.42	4.14	3.84	3.99	5.07	5.05	4.58	4.35	4.03	3.59	3.38
	South Korea	3.73	3.47	3.25	3.17	3.65	3.73	3.41	3.23	3.13	3.54	3.64
	Singapore	4.2	–	–	–	–	2.8	2.7	2.6	2.6	2.6	–
M4	China	4.2	4.1	4.0	4.2	4.3	4.1	4.1	4.1	4.1	4.1	–

Source: https://data.oecd.org/ (OECD database), www.adb.org/ (ADB database), http://data. stats.gov.cn/ (China's state-level database).

M1 = the semi-mature economic model; M2 = the regulatory model for the post-market-economy period; M3 = the authoritative government economic model; M4 = the dual-strong economic model

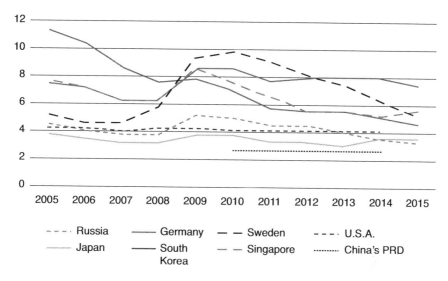

Figure 5.3 Unemployment in countries representative of the four assessed models

5.3.3.5 *Inflation of prices*

Judging from the movement of prices, Japan, South Korea and other countries under the authoritative government model have exhibited the lowest rate of price increase, with a steady trend of price movement. On the flip side, Japan features a certain degree of deflation, which might metastasize into a huge drag on its economy. Countries in western Europe and North America, where the post-market-economy model predominates, have experienced a gentle rise in prices over the past decade, capable of controlling commodity prices in economic development, which indicates a good market climate where there is sufficient economic output to meet market needs. Under the semi-mature economic model, Russia has been plagued by severe inflation, and Brazil has exhibited a steep upward slope of price levels. Commodity prices have been kept within a range of 2–4 percent in the PRD of China, where the dual-strong economic model is being implemented; despite remarkable fluctuations in 2008 and 2009, commodity prices have remained at about 2 percent since 2012, indicating good price stability amid high economic growth (as seen in Table 5.5).

5.3.3.6 *Industrial structure*

Performances in terms of industrial structure speak volumes for how well these four models function in fostering economic synergy, with the ratio of the tertiary

Table 5.5 Inflation of prices (%) under different combination models

Year/Model		2005	2006	2007	2008	2009	2010	2011	2012	2013	2014	2015
M1	Brazil	6.87	4.18	3.64	5.68	4.89	5.04	6.64	5.4	6.2	6.33	9.03
	Russia	12.69	9.67	9.01	14.11	11.65	6.85	8.44	5.07	6.75	7.82	15.53
M2	France	1.75	1.68	1.49	2.81	0.09	1.53	2.11	1.95	0.86	0.51	0.04
	Germany	1.55	1.58	2.3	2.63	0.31	1.1	2.08	2.01	1.5	0.91	0.23
	Sweden	0.45	1.36	2.21	3.44	−0.49	1.16	2.96	0.89	−0.04	−0.18	−0.05
	UK	2.1	2.3	2.3	3.6	2.2	3.3	4.5	2.8	2.6	1.5	0
	USA.	3.39	3.23	2.85	3.84	−0.36	1.64	3.16	2.07	1.46	1.62	0.12
	Israel	1.31	2.12	0.49	4.59	3.32	2.7	3.48	1.69	1.57	0.49	−0.63
M3	Japan	−0.27	0.24	0.06	1.37	−1.35	−0.72	−0.28	−0.03	0.36	2.75	0.79
	South Korea	2.75	2.24	2.54	4.67	2.76	2.94	4.03	2.19	1.3	1.27	0.71
	Poland	2.18	1.28	2.46	4.16	3.8	2.58	4.24	3.56	0.99	0.05	−0.87
M4	PRD	2.3	1.8	3.7	5.6	−2.3	3.1	5.3	2.8	2.5	2.3	–

Source: https://data.oecd.org/ (OECD database),www.adb.org/ (ADB database), www.gdstats. gov.cn/tjnj/2015(2015 Statistics Yearbook of Guangdong Province).

M1 = the semi-mature economic model; M2 = the regulatory model for the post-market-economy period; M3 = the authoritative government economic model; M4 = the dual-strong economic model

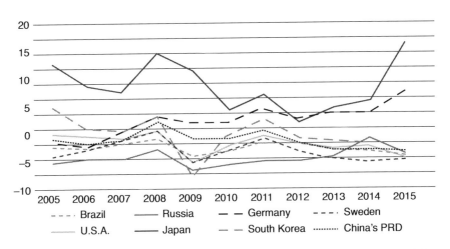

Figure 5.4 Unemployment rates in countries under different combination models

industry in gross domestic product being the key indicator. As is clear from Table 5.6, this ratio has hovered above 70 percent in countries that implement either the post-market-economy model or the authoritative government economic model, indicating an advanced industrial structure and a high level of economic prosperity. In China's PRD, this ratio has remained at about

Table 5.6 The weights of the three industries in GDP under different combination models (%)

		2005	2006	2007	2008	2009	2010	2011	2012	2013	2014
Australia (M1)	Primary industry	2.9	2.7	2.2	2.3	2.3	2.2	2.3	2.3	2.3	2.4
	Secondary industry	24.6	25.7	25.7	25.6	27.0	25.2	26.6	26.5	25.1	25.3
	Tertiary industry	72.5	71.6	72.1	72.1	70.7	72.6	71.2	71.3	72.6	72.3
South Korea (M2)	Primary industry	3.1	3.0	2.7	2.5	2.6	2.5	2.5	2.5	2.3	2.3
	Secondary industry	37.5	36.9	37.0	36.3	36.7	38.3	38.4	38.1	38.4	38.2
	Tertiary industry	59.4	60.2	60.3	61.2	60.7	59.3	59.1	59.5	59.3	59.4
Singapore (M2)	Primary industry	0.1	–	–	–	–	0.0	0.0	0.0	0.0	0.0
	Secondary industry	32.4	–	–	–	–	27.6	26.3	26.4	24.8	24.9
	Tertiary industry	67.6	–	–	–	–	72.3	73.6	73.6	75.1	75.0
PRD (M3)	Primary industry	3.1	2.6	2.4	2.4	2.2	2.1	2.1	2.1	1.9	1.9
	Secondary industry	50.7	51.4	50.5	49.9	47.9	48.4	47.9	46.2	45.2	45.0
	Tertiary industry	46.3	46.1	47.0	47.7	49.9	49.5	50.0	51.8	52.9	53.1

Source: www.adb.org/ (ADB database), ww.gdstats.gov.cn/tjnj/2015 (2015 Statistics Yearbook of Guangdong Province).

M1 = the post-market-economy model; M2 = the authoritative government economic model; M3 = the dual-strong economic model

50 percent and is rising steadily; the secondary industry has seen a drop of its weight in the region's GDP, while the weight of the primary industry has declined to the point of insignificance, just as is the case in developed economies. In terms of development tendency, the PRD is accelerating the pace of industrial transformation and upgrade, with manufacturing being moved to the fringe and towards intelligent application. It will gradually adjust the weight of its secondary and tertiary industries to the level of developed countries.

5.3.3.7 *Share of R&D spending in GDP*

The share of R&D spending in GDP represents the level of creativity in a region's economic development. As is indicated in Table 5.7, Israel ranks top in

Table 5.7 Share of R&D spending in GDP in countries under different combination models (%)

Year/Model		2005	2006	2007	2008	2009	2010	2011	2012	2013	2014
M1	Russia	1.07	1.07	1.12	1.04	1.25	1.13	1.09	1.13	1.13	1.19
M2	Germany	2.42	2.46	2.45	2.60	2.73	2.71	2.80	2.87	2.83	2.90
	Sweden	3.39	3.50	3.26	3.50	3.45	3.22	3.25	3.28	3.31	3.16
	UK	1.63	1.65	1.68	1.69	1.74	1.70	1.69	1.62	1.66	1.70
	USA	2.51	2.55	2.63	2.77	2.82	2.74	2.76	2.70	2.74	
	Israel	4.04	4.13	4.41	4.33	4.12	3.93	4.01	4.13	4.09	4.11
M3	Japan	3.31	3.41	3.46	3.47	3.36	3.25	3.38	3.34	3.48	3.59
	South Korea	2.63	2.83	3.00	3.12	3.29	3.47	3.74	4.03	4.15	4.29
	Singapore	2.16	2.13	2.34	2.62	2.16	2.01	2.15	2.00	2.00	2.20
M4	China	1.32	1.38	1.38	1.46	1.68	1.76	1.79	1.93	2.32	2.37

Source: https://data.oecd.org/ (OECD database), www.adb.org/ (ABD Database), www.gdstats.gov.cn/tjnj/2015 (2015 Statistics Yearbook of Guangdong Province).

M1 = the semi-mature economic model; M2 = the post-market-economy model; M3 = the authoritative government economic model; M4 = the dual-strong economic model

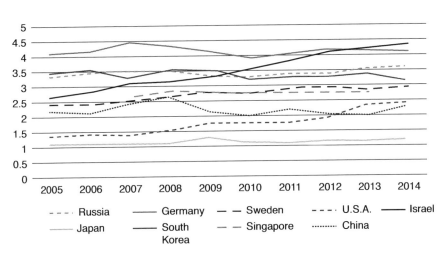

Figure 5.5 Share of R&D spending in GDP in countries under different combination models

this index, spending over 4 percent of its GDP on research and development, followed by the Republic of Korea, which has contributed over 4 percent of its GDP to R&D programs over the past several years. Next in the table are Japan and Sweden, trailed by the USA. and Germany, the latter two spending nearly 3 percent of their GDP on R&D. The share of R&D spending in GDP has also exceeded 2 percent for Singapore, while Russia has always contributed a little more than 1 percent of its GDP to this cause, somewhat behind other countries listed in the table. The PRD has been increasing its spending on R&D over the years, contributing over 2 percent of its GDP to this end in 2013. This trend indicates that the market and the government are on the same page in the matter of R&D. It also reflects the commitment of the PRD to a new growth path driven by R&D and innovation.

5.3.3.8 *Growth of household disposable income*

The PRD has shone brightly in its increase of household disposable income, with growth hovering above 8 percent for the past decade and reaching over 12 percent at its peak (as shown in Table 5.8). In this respect, the PRD has surpassed, by a large margin, other economies under a combination model different from its dual-strong economic model, a fact that testifies to the strength of the dual-strong economic model in driving inclusive economic growth to improve people's livelihood. Russia and Hungary, two economies dominated by the semi-mature economic model, have undergone a roller coaster ride in the growth of household disposable income, even plagued by shrinking household income during the worst of times. Economies dominated by the post-market-economy model and the authoritative government economic model have had their moments of household disposable income growth, though by a very small margin.

Table 5.8 Growth of household disposable income in countries under different combination models (%)

Year/Model		2005	2006	2007	2008	2009	2010	2011	2012	2013	2014	2015
M1	Hungary	4.01	1.6	–4.07	–1.48	–3.66	–2.6	3.31	–3.1	1.64	2.41	–
	Russia	10.92	11.83	12.33	7.23	–1.88	7.01	4.03	4.85	2.43	–	–
M2	France	0.94	2.05	2.82	0.35	1.75	1.44	0.4	–0.32	0.38	1.13	–
	Germany	0.4	0.99	0.4	1.06	–0.09	0.66	1.03	0.62	0.61	1.5	–
	Sweden	1.92	3.41	4.05	1.73	2.53	1.52	3.11	2.76	1.37	1.95	–
	UK	2.2	1.45	2.39	1.1	3.1	0.8	–1.54	2.52	–0.61	0.72	–
	USA.	1.33	3.6	1.83	1.7	–0.08	1.09	2.3	3.07	–1.2	–	–
M3	Japan	–0.27	0.24	0.06	1.37	–1.35	–0.72	–0.28	–0.03	0.36	2.75	0.79
	ROK	2.75	2.24	2.54	4.67	2.76	2.94	4.03	2.19	1.3	1.27	0.71
M4	PRD	8.4	8.4	10.5	11.5	9.3	10.8	12.6	12.4	9.5	8.8	–

Source: https://data.oecd.org/ (OECD database), www.adb.org/ (ADB database), www.gdstats. gov.cn/tjnj/2015(2015 Statistics Yearbook of Guangdong Province).

M1 = the semi-mature economic model; M2 = the regulatory model for the post-market-economy period; M3 = the authoritative government economic model; M4 = the dual-strong economic model

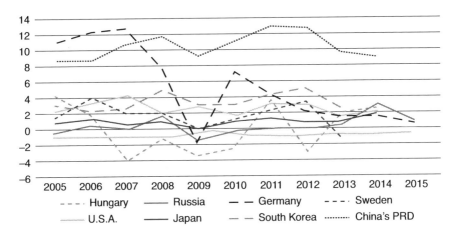

Figure 5.6 Poverty rates in countries representative of the four economic models

5.3.3.9 Poverty rate

As is shown in Table 5.9, countries with a welfare state, most notably Finland, enjoy the lowest poverty rate, at only 0.07 percent as a group. There is little difference in poverty levels among countries under any of the other three models. There is as yet a lack of consensus on the standards for gauging poverty levels in China, and as a result, science-based and world-recognized standards for measuring poverty levels have yet to be produced in China. Given that data on poverty are yet to be included into the country's comprehensive statistical system, it is difficult and even impossible to compare China with other countries in this regard.

5.3.3.10 Gini coefficient

The Gini coefficient is high for China as a whole, an indication of severe wealth polarization amid buoyant economic development. By no means, however, does this give a real and even-handed picture of the income distribution situation in the PRD. As a developed region in China, the PRD has by and large eradicated income disparity through a diversity of channels for employment and a high degree of marketization. Thus, the PRD fares much better than the rest of China in balancing income distribution. Given that the PRD is not a mirror image of the whole of China when it comes to income distribution, the Gini coefficient of China, though over 4 percent, does not speak volumes of the dual-strong economic model being weak in balancing income distribution. Other countries, except Germany and Sweden at below 3 percent, have a Gini coefficient of between 3 percent and 4 percent, an indication that the post–market-economy model and the authoritative government economic model have manifested strong competence in taming wealth polarization (as shown in Table 5.10)

Table 5.9 Poverty levels of countries under different combination models (%)

Year/Model		2005	2006	2007	2008	2009	2010	2011	2012	2013	2014
M1	Poland	0.12	0.11	0.10	0.11	0.11	0.11	0.11	0.10	0.11	–
M2	Finland	0.07	0.07	0.08	0.08	0.07	0.07	0.08	0.07	0.07	0.07
	UK	0.12	0.13	0.13	0.12	0.11	0.11	0.10	0.11	0.10	–
	USA.	–	–	–	–	–	–	–	–	0.17	0.18
	Israel	–	–	–	–	–	–	0.18	0.18	0.19	0.19
M3	South Korea	–	–	–	–	–	–	–	0.15	0.15	0.14

Source: https://data.oecd.org/(OECD database).

M1 = the semi-mature economic model; M2 = the post–market-economy model; M3 = the authoritative government economic model

Table 5.10 Poverty rate in countries under different combination models (%)

		2005	2006	2007	2008	2009	2010	2011	2012	2013	2014
M1	Poland	0.327	0.316	0.316	0.309	0.304	0.306	0.301	0.298	0.3	–
M2	Germany	–	–	–	0.285	–	–	0.291	0.289	0.292	–
	Sweden	–	–	–	–	–	–	0.273	0.274	0.281	–
	UK	0.359	0.364	0.373	0.369	0.374	0.351	0.354	0.351	0.358	–
	USA.	–	–	–	–	–	–	–	–	0.396	0.394
	Israel	–	–	–	–	–	–	0.371	0.371	0.36	0.365
M3	ROK	–	–	–	–	–	–	0.307	0.302	0.302
M4	China	0.485	0.487	0.484	0.491	0.49	0.481	0.477	0.474	0.473	0.462

Source: https://data.oecd.org/ (OECD database), www.adb.org/ (ADB database), http://data.stats.gov.cn/ (China's national database).

M1 = the semi-mature economic model; M2 = the regulatory model for the post-market-economy period; M3 = the authoritative government economic model; M4 = the dual-strong economic model

5.3.3.11 Comprehensive assessment

A comparison of the four combination models – the semi-mature economic model, the post-market-economy model, the authoritative government model and the dual-strong economic model – in their competence for fostering effectiveness, coordination, continuity, creativity and inclusiveness of economic development reveals that the dual-strong economic model is well ahead of the other three models in boosting economic growth, delivering strong performances in curbing inflation and unemployment, and producing good economic development quality. Moreover, as shown in various tables above, an apparent trend shows that this model is vibrantly catching up with the other three from behind in terms of ability to improve the coordination and creativity of economic structure and to make economic growth inclusive and accessible to all people. As such, it can be regarded as the optimal model of combination between government and market. Next in the ranking of viability and effectiveness are the post-market-economy and the authoritative government economic models; as evidenced from their performances in several key areas, these two models are stable and reliable. Due to a lack of stamina and momentum for future development, however, they can only be seen as a suboptimal choice of combination between government and market. As far as the semi-mature model is concerned, although it generates good economic growth in some ways, it also presents a certain level of uncertainty, whether in terms of market function or government regulation. Thus, it can be considered the least viable option, only to be adopted during periods of exploration and transition.

5.3.4 *Different combination models for resource allocation in different economic development stages*

As indicated above, there are basically four stages of economic development, which vary from one another depending on the means by which resources are allocated: the factor-driven stage, the investment-driven stage, the innovation-driven stage and the wealth-driven stage. Priorities for competition measures also vary with regional governments, depending on the stages where the economies under their governance are. Such differences in priorities are mainly mirrored in the arrangements across the notional, institutional, organizational and technological realms. Given that the balance of power between government and market shifts as an economy transits from one economic development stage to another, different government–market combination models should be instituted and enforced for countries and regions in different stages of economic development.

5.3.4.1 *The government–market combination model for the factor-driven stage*

Factor-driven economic growth means that the source of momentum for economic growth stems from the advantages in factors of production that a region has, such as in agricultural products, mineral resources, workforce, etc. A region with such advantages is generally able to register fast economic growth by tapping into its naturally endowed resources. Such resource advantages often lead to the creation of a loosely regulated environment for economic development, which might result in regional government paying no heed to the efficiency of resource allocation and putting premium only on the exploration and allocation of "non-operational resources".

In this stage, regional management is largely restricted to the provision of pure public goods, with a lack of means and capacity for the allocation of "quasi-operational resources". Meanwhile, given the concentration of advantages in factors of production, the market is prone to monopoly, exhibiting a certain level of inadequate competition. From this perspective, the government–market combination model for a region in the factor-driven stage must be the semi-mature economic model, with a semi-strong market and a semi-strong government – the least viable of the four models previously discussed.

Russia is a typical economy in the factor-driven stage, with oil the key factor propelling economic growth. Oil prices of the world took a nosedive in 2008 and have remained low since then, dealing a devastating blow to the Russian economy. Latin America and the Caribbean, which, like Russia, implement the semi-mature economic model, registered a growth rate of merely 1.3 percent as a group in 2015, and are expected to sustain a sluggish 2.3 percent growth rate in 2016. The plunge in oil and commodity prices has prompted a growth forecast downgrade for Sub-Saharan Africa, while casting an ominous shadow over the economic growth prospect of Nigeria and South Africa.

If history is any guide, regional government in the factor-driven stage will have to strive for breakthroughs in the realm of government function and capacity. Specifically, regional government should accelerate the pace of reform towards a market-based economy and beef up its control over economic transformation. The priority of competition orientation for regional government in this stage is to foster notional and institutional innovation.

5.3.4.2 *The government–market combination model for the investment-driven stage*

A region under a factor-driven economic model tends to become dependent on low-cost advantages derived from the abundance of a certain factor of production, while losing sight of the fact that such advantages are, in actuality, tantamount to a drain of resources. To maintain such low-cost advantages, regional government often has no other choice but to allocate a large amount of financial resources as subsidies. Government subsidies on such a large scale not only lead to overconsumption of factors of production but also encourage overdependence on them, thus further weakening the competitiveness of these factors of production. Worse still, government subsidies for production factors are likely to distort investment decisions in both public and private sectors, absorbing fiscal resources that otherwise should be spent on other important matters, including infrastructural development and social services where government spending is badly needed. Dilapidated and unattended infrastructure can end up putting a huge dent in a region's competitiveness and growth potential. In this sense, it is imperative for any region to make the transition from factor-driven growth to investment-driven growth.

An investment-driven growth stage means that government has shifted the way it participates in regional competition, from solely relying on resource-generated low costs to beefing up the intensity of investment in non-operational resources and getting involved in quasi-operational resource investment. This is a stage where government has achieved a quantum leap in its capacity for resource allocation, in the sense that some of the weaknesses previously plaguing economic growth are being remedied and the advantages derived from abundance in production factors are being better tapped and played out. Meanwhile, regional government has developed a deeper understanding of the market, somewhat recognizing the market's primacy in allocating resources. Thus, during the investment-driven stage, a series of beneficial experiments are made regarding the functional scopes of government and market, as well as the form of combination between them, with a view to forging suboptimal combination models better than the semi-mature economic model.

Countries like Ethiopia, Mozambique and Tanzania are well on their way to transitioning from factor-driven growth to investment-driven growth. Between 1995 and 2010, they formulated rational medium-term policies and conducted structural reforms. These policies and measures proved to be crucially effective in enlisting assistance funds that helped to alleviate debts and release the gushing vitality of their resources. Returns from these policies and measures eventually translated into wide fiscal latitude for their governments, allowing them to increase social expenditure and capital investment – especially in infrastructure – for faster economic growth. For example, Ethiopia registered buoyant economic growth by incentivizing investment in the flower sector, aviation and tourism. In the 1990s, Mozambique enlisted a massive amount of foreign and external capital to finance capital-intensive projects regarding the production and transmission of electricity and natural gas – electricity was generated mainly to produce aluminum. Tanzania achieved impressive economic growth and boosted private investment through three rounds of macro-economic and structural reform and, by instituting relevant policies, extended its export scope to cover non-traditional products. These reform measures were rational, well-arranged and inclusive to all social sectors.

Singapore, South Korea and other countries under the authoritative government model have spared no effort to beef up investment in the public and quasi-public sectors. Countries under the post-market-economy model, as best represented by the USA., have attempted to boost economic recovery through quantitative easing and proactive fiscal spending since the outbreak of the financial crisis in 2008. In particular, the USA. has undertaken industrial restructuring through investment in areas that are conducive to increasing productive capital for the future, with an overarching objective of driving up potential output. The growing influx of refugees into Europe has posed a grave challenge to the EU in terms of its labor market's absorption capacity and its political system. What is of critical importance under such circumstances is to implement policies and measures that support the integration of immigrants into the EU's workforce, in the sense that doing so helps tackle social exclusion, eases worry over long-term fiscal burdens from immigration and facilitates the materialization of the long-term economic benefits derived from the inflow of refugees. These problems, however, cannot be well addressed without massive government spending.

A review of reform initiatives and practices by various regional governments reveals that in the investment-driven stage, governments start rendering attention or support to the allocation and development of "quasi-operational resources", coupled with certain actions to explore or innovate the utility of "quasi-operational resources". The priority of competition orientation for regional governments in this stage is to foster institutional and organizational innovation.

5.3.4.3 The government–market combination model for the innovation-driven and wealth-driven stages

Despite its great dependency on investment for economic growth, the USA., under the post-market-economy model, has been plagued by a teetering investment-driven recovery since 2010, mainly due to an ominous shadow surrounding its business prospects. In Europe, where growth is hugely uneven among its economies, financial fragmentation has become increasingly pronounced, continuing to divide the Eurozone. Against this backdrop, lopsided emphasis on economic growth through investment is counterproductive to building core competitiveness in market competition; on the contrary, it will lead to massive capital inflow and currency appreciation, thus creating a huge drag on monetary policies, sending shock waves across the financial system and plunging the European economy into recession. In addition, sluggish economic growth will worsen social pressures arising from stubbornly stagnant wage growth, structural economic changes and hampered welfare programs. Though abdicating it is unrealistic, investment-driven approach is seeing its potential dwindling. As such, regional government is required to develop foresight and insight into questions like this and realize their foresighted leadership through innovation on various levels.

Just take a moment to think about the changes 3D printing, self-driving vehicles and artificial intelligence can bring to the future, and the impact information technology, e-commerce and the sharing economy are having on how people learn, work, shop and travel. Innovation has fundamentally changed the future of the world. Innovation, however, is highly dependent on regional policies – even the slightest bit of government support can give a tremendous boost to innovation and growth. For example, public policies can reduce the cost of private sector R&D by 40 percent, which means that R&D spending in the private sector will increase at the same percentage rate of 40 percent, driving up GDP by 5 percent in the long run. In this sense, innovation-driven and wealth-driven models of government–market combination are able to shift regional government's focus of management towards innovation-centered competition in a holistic range of areas, including in notion, institution, organization and technology.

Research and development constitute the main driver of innovation, and the success of R&D depends on economic incentives and public policies. An IMF (International Monetary Fund) study shows that just a small amount of public support is able to yield returns on R&D investment. For instance, given domestic spillovers, spending 0.4 percent of GDP on R&D as fiscal support is able to boost GDP growth by 5 percent in the long term. The importance of catch-up growth (also known as compensatory growth) for emerging economies like China, South Korea and Singapore cannot be overstated, and the application of foreign technologies is a key to promoting such growth. Globally, an increase of R&D spending can lead to growth of global GDP by about 8 percent in the long run. With international factors taken into account, the cost of fiscal support for R&D will only account for 0.5 percent of global GDP, and the returns yielded by such support will rise proportionally to the rise of fiscal spending, eventually resulting in an 8 percent increase of global GDP. Therefore, innovation by regional government is of critical importance for economic growth. In this connection, the possibility of public–private partnership can be explored to propel innovation-driven growth.

In addition, regional government needs to design and implement a pro-innovation regional system. A case in point is the so-called patent box system instituted and implemented in a small number of countries, which has served to directly incentivize R&D by deducting patent-income tax burdens on companies.

Another thing of note is that when it comes to innovation, regional government should pay special attention to start-up enterprises, which generate a disproportionate share of transformational innovations. In this sense, putting in place efficient processes for the founding, growth and exit of start-up enterprises has a strong bearing on the success of innovation. Government should set up a series of pro-innovation processes to tear down barriers on various levels, such as the issuance of licenses and permits, oversight over the employment market, and financial restrictions and taxation. On top of that, government can render immense support in terms of offsetting taxable losses, streamlining taxation rules and alleviating enterprises' compliance burdens. The government–market combination model in the innovation-driven and wealth-driven stages is a major driver for improving people's lives and achieving long-term prosperity. It is an optimal combination model consisting of strong effective government and a strong efficient market.

A review of the economic development around the world reveals that if the relationship between government and market is defined by the use of oversimplified terms like "strong" and "weak", then more often than not, what we see in real life are combinations either between "strong government" and "strong market" or between "weak government" and "weak market". Never has the combination between "weak government" and "strong market" been observed. Therefore, neither government nor market can be weakened in a modern market economy. The crux of the matter is to rightly position the roles of government and market. A modern market economy cannot function efficiently without an effective government, in the sense that government power is needed for defining and protecting property rights, establishing and maintaining a level playing field, expanding market systems, guaranteeing the enforcement of contracts, curtailing monopoly and curbing malicious competition. The market is remotely likely to function properly in the absence of these conditions. Moreover, an effective government is a stabilizer and a boost for the market to play out its function.

Specifically, an effective government can bring its role into play in a long list of things, from providing public services of all kinds, narrowing down the gaps in income and development and protecting the eco-system to exercising macro-economic regulation and devising medium and long-term plans for development. Government functions in these areas are able to remedy market defects and bring about harmonious development that balances efficiency against equality. Having said that, if government deviates from this direction, overextends its hand at things and even attempts to replace a market-based mechanism with a centrally planned mechanism, then government is definitely going to badly hurt and weaken the market.

5.4   Connotations of and standards for an effective government and an efficient market

No mature theory of modern market economy can come into existence without an adequately developed market economy. The adequate development of market economy in the world today has brought forth a variety of modes of market economy. Whether it is the American or British mode of market economy with regulations, the French mode of market economy with plans, the German mode of social market economy, the northern European mode of welfarism or China's socialist market economic system, they are without exception the result of continuous trials and explorations in the effective pairing of market and government.

Apparently, current theoretical researches and practical explorations should be a clear departure from traditional economics in terms of how to demarcate market competition entities and how to define and position the role of government; this is especially the case considering the fact that competition between governments is on the rise, governments are undertaking planning and foresighted regulation of market and enterprises, government behaviors are going beyond simple macro-level regulation and governments are setting targets beyond securing steady growth of GDP. Against this backdrop, clear answers are urgently needed to such questions as what an effective government is and how to define and devise the standards for an efficient market.

5.4.1   Connotations of and standards for efficient market

5.4.1.1   Market as the decisive force for resource allocation

Adam Smith's *The Wealth of Nations* produced immediate implications for western economic theories, implications that over time proved to be profound and long-lasting. As Adam Smith puts it in his book, the perfect marriage between the utility-seeking economic entities and the "invisible hand" generates a wealth-creating force, strong and powerful enough to drive economic development and social evolution and, ultimately, to contribute to the emergence of a new economic modality. As a tool for resource allocation, the price mechanism, once employed, has proven its phenomenal power in improving efficiency, optimizing economic structure and driving the evolution of economic modalities.

In essence, economic development lies in enhancing the efficiency of scarce resources allocation, which means reaping the maximum possible amount of economic benefits at the minimum possible cost of resource usage. Economists who have come after Adam Smith, either professedly western economic theorists or believers of Marxist political economy, have acknowledged, almost without exception, the incomparably powerful strengths and efficiency of the market economy in allocating resources. In practice, the economic growth performances (in terms of both growth speed and results) of nations the world over have proved that the market is the most efficient tool for resource allocation. As a result, a consensus has already been reached among economic theorists and over a long process of national policy practice, which is that the market, as a general rule in a market economy, is the decisive force for resource allocation and that a market economy, in its nature, is an economy where the market plays a decisive role in allocating resources.

5.4.1.2 *Connotations of and standards for efficient market*

An efficient market is defined as one with fully-fledged basic functions (including a market element system and a market organizational system), a well-established basic order (consisting of a market legal system and a market supervisory system) and a sound and vibrant market climate (encompassing a social credit system and a market infrastructure system). The efficiency of a market is measured and gauged by how well these six functional systems perform and is reflected in how integrated and synergized these three elements are, namely, production competition, market fairness and orderly business operation. The efficiency of an efficient market can be measured and tested against the following three standards – full market competition, orderly law-based supervision and a fully-fledged social credit system.

5.4.1.3 *The indication of strong efficient market*

5.4.1.3.1 IMPROVEMENT OF ECONOMIC BENEFITS: TRADING GAINS AND EFFICIENCY OF PRICE MECHANISMS

In economics, the optimal allocation of resources is described with the use of the term "Pareto optimality" (also known as Pareto efficiency), which defines a state of resource allocation as "Pareto efficient" or "Pareto optimal" when it reaches Pareto optimum (no further Pareto improvements can be made). In general, conditions in the following three aspects have to be met for an allocation to achieve a Pareto efficient outcome: first, optimal conditions for exchange; second, optimal conditions for production; third, optimal conditions for exchange–production ratio. Although it is just a theoretical concept, "Pareto optimality" implies a crucial prerequisite – a market mechanism, free from external interventions; only in the existence of effective price adjustment can such an outcome be realized.

How do price mechanisms contribute to the efficient production and allocation of resources? First, labor division enhances the efficiency of resource production. Market transaction changed the traditional structure of a natural economy, and production activities not purely for the purpose of self-consumption emerged as a consequence. As the sphere of market expanded, labor division was made possible and feasible, which in turn served to push forward the market boundary as it was proven effective in increasing production efficiency and reducing production costs. Thus, it is fair to say that labor division and price mechanisms develop hand in hand through a process of mutual interaction and converge to improve working efficiency and expand market sphere.

Labor division contributes extraordinarily to the improvement of working efficiency. The strengths of the division of labor are well captured and elaborated by Adam Smith in *The Wealth of Nations*. First, the division of labor enables a worker to repetitively complete a single operation and to increase labor skills and working efficiency in consequence of such repetition. In other words, a worker is able to improve his working efficiency through on-the-job learning and specialized laboring, a result most visibly observed and noticed in sectors that have a steep and precipitous learning curve. Second, the division of labor makes it possible to reduce time loss due to the change of work. Third, the division of labor helps to simplify labor and enables workers to focus their attention on a specific target, which is conducive to the creation of new tools and the improvement of equipment. In *The Wealth of Nations*, Smith also cited the example of pin-making to make a convincing case for how the division of labor contributes to increasing productivity. What Smith expounded in his book started a profound transformation of production relations in human history.

Second, price mechanisms help to achieve efficient resource allocation. A price mechanism serves to build up media and bridges that facilitate market transaction, making transaction the most important means for resource allocation. Although the division of labor is able to push forward and extend the production-possibility frontier (PPF) by increasing production efficiency, there is nothing it can do to facilitate the realization of the optimal resource allocation outcome. As subjective assessments on different products may vary from one demand side to another, an act of resource allocation is considered as achieving an efficient outcome only when it is able to distribute a product to whoever needs it the most. It is in this regard that a price mechanism is able to bring its role into full play. As the extent of trading expands, free markets spring up around the globe, in which both the buyer and the seller are able to benefit from free choices.

On the basis of how free exchange served to improve resource allocation, David Ricardo put forth his comparative advantage theory for international trade, emphasizing that international trade was based on relative differences (rather than absolute differences) in production technologies and on the differences in comparative costs arising therefrom. Ricardo thereby argued that both sides with differential production costs would benefit from trading with each other. Ricardo also suggested that each country should, in line with the principle of choosing the lesser of two evils and the better of two goods, focus on producing and exporting that which it has a comparative advantage in producing and import that which it has a comparative disadvantage in producing. The comparative advantage theory for trade, in a more common sense, helps to explain the foundation on which trading activities take place and the gains arising therefrom, and therefore the proposition of the comparative advantage theory marks a giant step for developing the absolute advantage theory for trade.

5.4.1.3.2   OPTIMIZATION OF ECONOMIC STRUCTURE: SIGNIFICANCE
            OF SPONTANEOUS ORDER AND MARKET BEHAVIOR

Although it is true that the division of labor and the allocation of products to those who need them most can increase economic efficiency, such an increase in economic efficiency can be realized either through a price mechanism or through a central-planning mechanism. Under a central-planning mechanism, the division of labor can be realized by means of centrally planned deployment and the allocation of resources can be achieved through central rationing. Nevertheless, a price mechanism has two distinct advantages over a central-planning mechanism, which have been clearly demonstrated and verified in both economic theories and economic practice.

First, supply and demand serves as the optimal information transmission mechanism. Here, mainstream economics assumes that every economic entity is a utility-seeker and a rational subject and that such utility and rationality will automatically and spontaneously adjust to achieve optimal allocation of resources, which Friedrich August Hayek called "spontaneous order". As the extent of the market is vast, information available within the market is as multifarious as it is disorderly, and therefore no one central institution is able to have a total grasp of all minute details of the constantly changing information. As such, a system for labor division and resource allocation that is centered on spontaneous market order is apparently better than one based on central planning.

Second, there should be a democratic order for the distribution of knowledge and free decision-making. Hayek, an eminent economist, pointed out that in contrast to a centrally planned economy, a free market economy is more efficient and better-ordered. Hayek introduced the concept of "local knowledge" to make his case for the "spontaneous order" process. Such local knowledge is possessed and grasped only in the hands of individual actors. The most striking examples are personally favored choices, a type of knowledge that is only controlled by the individual actors who make the choices and thus unavoidably exists outside the awareness of others. Such "favored knowledge" is dispersed and constantly changing, the existence of which cannot be totally understandable or perceivable to any single central authority. With the market bestowing the freedom to choose on every individual actor, these individual actors make their choices spontaneously, which eventually converge to form a catalyst for the spontaneous adjustment of the entire economy.

Hayek believed that the emergence of social order is not a result of rational designing by individual actors or groups, nor is social order controlled by some transcendental power; rather, the emergence of social order is more possibly a result of self-adaptation and self-evolution. The spontaneous order theory provides a set of legitimate grounds for individual freedom and limited government. Given that individual actors enjoy naturally endowed and inalienable freedom in a spontaneous order, a government should not deprive individual actors of such freedom by use of authority and power, much less replace the naturally free order with a humanly designed dictatorial order and substitute a mandatory planned economy for a free market economy. In this connection, the extent and method of government action should be strictly restricted by law, as should the size of government; the power of government should be separated to the point where checks and balances are achieved. Therefore, the spontaneous order theory of the conservatives is one that delves into the relation between individual freedom and limited government.

5.4.1.3.3 EVOLUTION OF ECONOMIC MODALITIES: RATIONAL CHOICE AND
         "SURVIVAL OF THE FITTEST" UNDER MARKET MECHANISMS

Mainstream economics is founded on the assumption of individual behaviors being a result of rational choice. Such an assumption has remained fundamentally unchanged, in spite of its repeated subjection to questioning and criticism by a number of scholars. The case that many economists have made for the rational choice assumption is that a market economy has a powerful function of purification, which is able to improve market environment by pushing irrational individual actors out of the market. Such an attribute of self-improving evolution, as these economists argue, is exactly what has been found lacking in a centrally planned economy.

5.4.1.4 The trial-and-error process on the market

In market transactions, unqualified participants (be they buyers or suppliers) will be phased out through price competition, while individual actors who make rational choices in observance with market rules will be rewarded. It is true that economic paradigms like rational choice and choice maximization are subject to criticism by scholars in both economics (such as Herbert Simon) and psychology (such as Daniel Kahneman), who believe that people have neither the abilities nor the conditions for maximizing their choices. Notwithstanding, even if the prerequisite governing human rational decision-making is stretched to its maximum limit, the decisions made by individual actors, however irrational they may be, will always be rational at the end of the day, as long as the market mechanism functions well. This is because at a microscopic level, decisions made by individual actors will be put to test through trials and errors, and decisions proven "correct" in the process of natural selection will be kept and emulated by other actors. The trial-and-error action is not without its costs, and therefore, when it comes to well-established economic rules and business experience already proven successful, a late-comer (whether an enterprise or a nation) can improve its decision-making by opting for interventional measures.

5.4.1.5   *The role of customs and norms*

Even if all participants in a market transaction are rational actors, they may still find themselves trapped in a dilemma borne out of rational choices; this is called the prisoner's dilemma in game theory terms. The prisoner's dilemma explains why and how two parties in a market transaction end up with reduced mutual benefits when both are in a relentless pursuit of maximizing their individual choices. Table5.2 shows the end results derived from both parties adopting a "tit for tat" strategy. As indicated in the chart, when both parties, guided by the "tit for tat" strategy, make transactions with each other on multiple occasions, a self-healing mechanism emerges. Once adopting the "tit for tat" strategy becomes the predominant norm in a market, favorable behavioral customs and norms, which are tacitly agreed upon by both parties, will occur, resulting in a quantum leap in transaction efficiency.

5.4.1.6   *The role of reputation*

Cooperative behaviors in the market occur as a consequence of two parties repetitively gaming with each other. In a prisoner's dilemma with no repetitive transaction behaviors, participants in the game (which involves multiple participants) can examine and find out which participant(s) is (are) reputable by relying on certain information screening tools. Once a participant in the market is identified to have conducted deceptive behaviors, all of the undeceived participants in the market will downgrade their credibility rating of the deceiving participant and will consequently limit the possibility of making transactions with the deceiving participant. Over time, the participants with low reputation and credibility ratings (due to the fact that they have conducted deceptive behaviors) will be pushed out of the market. In this sense, market reputation is an elimination mechanism that rewards repetitive honest behaviors and punishes deceptive behaviors based on the "tit for tat" customs. Of course, under changed conditions of the game, in a market where full-fledged economic customs and norms are yet to be established and where repetitive transactions rarely occur, behaviors of an opportunistic nature may crop up from time to time. Nevertheless, by no means will such opportunistic behaviors inhibit the market from driving economic development forward as an evolutionary force.

5.4.2 Connotations of and standards for effective government

5.4.2.1 Connotations of effective government

A government cannot be defined as being effective unless it is able to meet all of the following three criteria: first, being capable of efficiently allocating "non-operational resources" with well-designed supplementary policies, in a way that enhances social harmony and stability and optimizes economic environment; second, being able to efficiently allocate "operational resources" with feasible supplementary policies, in a way that guarantees openness, fairness and justice in the market and boosts overall social productivity; and third, being able to efficiently allocate "quasi-operational resources" and engage in market competition, in a way that promotes urban construction and all-round sustainable socio-economic development. The effectiveness of an effective government lies in its competent performances in the allocation of these three categories of resources and in its ability to successfully align policy-making with resource allocation and objective realization.

5.4.2.2 Standards for effective government

STANDARD ONE: A STRONG GOVERNMENT SHOULD RESPECT
MARKET LAWS AND OBSERVE MARKET RULES.

First, it should respect the laws of the market. A strong effective government will bring into full play its role in economic positioning, economic adjustment and early warning; tap into market rules and mechanisms; leverage the instruments of investment, consumption, export, pricing, taxation, interest rates, exchange rates, policies and laws; and foster institutional, organizational, technical and notional innovation. A strong efficient market and a strong effective government are not in a mutually replaceable relation. A strong efficient market and a strong effective government do not mean that the two will struggle for their respective roles and positions in the same realm and dimension. Instead, they have their respective roles to play and they somewhat differ from each other in terms of the scope and level where they play out their roles and the way they function. A strong effective government and a strong efficient market should play out their respective roles, maintain their respective strengths and complement each other in the allocation of three different types of resources.

Second, a strong effective government should observe the rules of the market. A strong government will rely on market economic bases, mechanisms and rules to exercise foresighted leading over economic activities. In other words, a strong effective government will make the most of its visible hand to make up for the blanks and margins left by the invisible hand so as to redress market failures. This function of a strong effective government is mainly reflected in the following aspects: regulating and supporting operational resources to improve productivity; improving and perfecting non-operational resources to boost their optimization and development; and tapping and injecting innovation into quasi-operational resources to synergize regional sustainable development.

STANDARD TWO: A STRONG EFFECTIVE GOVERNMENT SHOULD
SAFEGUARD ECONOMIC ORDER AND STABILIZE ECONOMIC
DEVELOPMENT.

A strong effective government is a guardian of the six element systems that underpin a modern market economy – a market cannot run efficiently without a strong government enforcing laws and exercising regulation through the allocation of non-operational resources; market environment and infrastructure (such as market credit) cannot be perfected without a strong government undertaking to effectively allocate non-operational resources. In this sense, for a strong market to properly bring its role to bear, it is imperative for it to be matched with a government that is strong and effective enough to do whatever the market is unable to do and fails to do well. Thus, a strong government should be one that is able to safeguard economic order and stabilize economic development.

STANDARD THREE: A STRONG GOVERNMENT SHOULD EFFECTIVELY ALLOCATE
RESOURCES AND PROACTIVELY PARTAKE IN MARKET COMPETITION.

Given that regional governments are the subject of mezzo-economic research, competition between regional governments may correct government misconduct and reduce government malfunction. Any given regional government, if it aspires to make itself strong and powerful, will have to depend on competition for the increase of efficiency of resource allocation. Such competition may help avoid such defects as are incurred by government interventionism, e.g. monopoly, bureaucracy, low efficiency and waste. In order to win in such competition, a regional government must regulate and monitor government behaviors through foresighted pre-process regulation so as to prevent possible government failures, reduce government malfunction, keep the cost of remedying economy to the minimum, and enhance its regional competitiveness.

5.4.2.3 *Three conditions for government to be effective*

In reality, a government should, at the very least, fulfill the following three conditions for it to be defined as being effective.

First, be able to keep abreast of the times, which refers to the critical importance of government getting ahead of the technology curve in this specific case. New businesses, new industries, new resources and new instruments, derived from the leaps-and-bounds development of science and technology, are sending shock waves across the existing government managerial apparatus. While being capable of stimulating demand and boosting efficiency in productive and living activities, new technologies also generate an onslaught of new problems (most notably the application of big data) that beset governments in their exercise of administrative authority and power, making it difficult or even impossible for governments to make decisions on a whim. Governments need to constantly renew and regenerate their ideas, policies and measures in a way that reflects the trends of the times if they truly aspire to make a significant difference in economic growth, urban construction and social welfare or in the allocation of non-operational resources, operational resources and quasi-operational resources.

Second, be able to compete in all dimensions, which requires governments to play a foresighted leading role and to compete in all productive factors and in all realms, thoroughly and systematically, by fostering innovation in notion, institution, organization and technology. Competition in this sense spans across social welfare undertakings (for optimizing the distribution of public goods and effectively enhancing socio-economic environment), continues throughout the process of economic growth (by way of leading, supporting, regulating and adjusting market entities and for effectively boosting productivity) and involves all aspects of urban construction (by following the rules of the market and engaging in project development). Competition in this regard is based on the production of goods and entrepreneurial activities, but is by no means confined to the realm of good production in the traditional sense. Rather, it covers all processes required to accomplish the all-dimensional and sustainable development of a nation's economy, including objective designing, policy-making, pathway charting and ultimate outcome delivering.

Third, be able to make government affairs public and transparent, such as in decision-making, policy enforcement, management, administrative services, policy outcomes and key-area information release. Fostering openness and transparency in government affairs enables people from all quarters of the society to fully exercise their rights to know the truths, to participate, to express their views and to supervise the government. It is also conducive to achieving optimal allocation of resources for robust economic growth, fruitful urban construction and better social welfare. A government that is competent, transparent, ruled by law, innovation-focused, service-oriented, clean and honest is what it takes to release the gushing vitality and creativity of the market for the benefits of its people and even the entirety of humanity.

5.4.2.4   *The functional positioning of effective government*

5.4.2.4.1   FUNCTIONAL POSITIONING IN RESOURCE ALLOCATION

First, in the allocation of non-operational resources. In economic terms, public goods are referred to as "non-rivalrous" and "non-excludable" goods. National defense, diplomacy, legislation, judicature, public security, environmental protection, industrial and commercial administration and other public services provided by administrative departments can all be considered non-operational resources, which do not change in availability and quality as a result of their being enjoyed and consumed by more or fewer individuals in a certain period of time. Non-excludability means that any form of non-operational resources cannot be possessed and used by any individual to the exclusion of others and that it is financially costly and practically impossible to exclude any individual from consuming and enjoying the resources. For instance, by reducing air and noise pollution, environmental protection efforts contribute to the increase of public goods in a certain district, such as fresher air and a quieter environment. Technically, it is impossible to exclude a specific individual of that district from enjoying the fresh air and quiet environment. Given that rivalry may lead to a lack of market demand and non-excludability makes it impossible for any form of non-operational resources to be enjoyed exclusively by any specific individual, a market-based economy appears to be powerless in resolving problems pertaining to non-operational resource allocation. It is naturally incumbent upon the government to properly allocate non-operational resources. A government's gross incompetence in the allocation of non-operational resources is likely to cause an insufficiency of merit goods and a rampancy of demerit goods, such as in the form of public pollution.

Second, in the allocation of quasi-operational resources. The allocation of quasi-operational resources is where the resource-allocating roles of market and government intersect. Therefore, a strong effective government should naturally undertake the task of allocating quasi-operational resources under the premise of respecting market laws. Transaction costs can serve as a watershed line between market and government when it comes to the allocation of quasi-operational resources. Market transaction is able to facilitate the effective allocation of resources, but not without generating its cost. The cost that impedes the efficiency of a market transaction is called transaction cost, an economic term coined in 1937 by Ronald Coase, the founder of new institutional economics. Once a powerful individual actor exerts control over quasi-operational resources that have a significant bearing on national economy and people's livelihoods, such as land, roads, mineral resources and energy, then that individual actor is in a position to perform a hold-up behavior against the general public by taking advantage of public dependency on such resources, damaging the price allocative efficiency by doing so. Held sway by rationality, a corporate entity and an individual person are efficiency-geared and result-oriented, and therefore are incapable of fundamentally resolving the hold-up problems caused by exclusive dependency. Based on the above analysis, a state is in a position to play a crucial role in allocating quasi-operational resources.

5.4.2.4.2   FUNCTIONAL POSITIONING IN PROJECT INVESTMENT

In a fully competitive market, as resources are transferred and allocated via the price mechanism, optimal allocation of resources can be achieved without any external intervention. Under such circumstances, it is viable for corporations to make efficient investment decisions based solely on price signals. However, the following factors may reduce the efficiency of market investment, and they include the monopoly factor, the group irrationality factor, the information asymmetry factor and the public good factor. Given the presence of these factors, government investment appears to be extremely necessary.

The first is direct government investment in high-risk sectors. For example, a scientific research project on high and new technology is akin to a complex social undertaking, so technology-intensive, capital-intensive and risk-intensive that it is often beyond the capacity of any enterprise or individual to assume. Therefore, government efforts in investment, management and coordination are needed to advance the industrialization of high and new technologies. Governments across the world make it a government priority to support and develop the high-tech industry and have, by and large, institutionalized and legalized investment in high-tech projects, via the following approaches: formulating policy and institutional incentives for investment and R&D in high technology; encouraging high-caliber personnel mobility and technical exchanges; providing stable distributional markets for the high-tech industry; and reducing social risks pertaining to high-tech R&D. Real practice shows that government investment in high-risk sectors plays a visibly significant part in speeding up the growth of the high-tech industry.

The second is direct government investment in public goods, such as education and national defense. Education and national defense are critically important for the development of any region, but investment in such areas is unlikely to generate profits for private investors. Given the failure of market mechanisms in addressing problems related to public goods, a regional government should undertake direct investment in public goods, including in various kinds of public education institutes, libraries, compulsory educational systems, free training activities and activities designed to popularize and promote knowledge. National defense bears critically on the security of a region but often involves a large pool of technology and an astronomical sum of investment. Thus, national defense is another high-priority area for government direct investment, in addition to education.

The third is direct government investment in the establishment of sound market ecology. For instance, the government is duty-bound to take on problems caused by information asymmetry problems. As a third party with authority, the government is in a position to reduce the level of group irrationality and improve a market's operating efficiency by stringently verifying market information, releasing authoritative information and imposing administrative penalties on opportunists seeking to profit from information asymmetry.

The fourth is direct government investment in social risk protection. On top of investing in high-risk projects in the realm of high and new technology, a government is also duty-bound to offer to its people protection against social uncertainties and risks, because it is virtually impossible to either calculate the probabilities of uncertainties or predict what harm unexpected and uncertain factors might cause to society. It is not financially feasible for corporations to offer protection against uncertain and unforeseeable events; nor is it viable and practical to employ market-based insurance policies as a form of protection against such harm. Under such circumstances, it becomes all the more necessary for the government to provide to the society insurance against uncertain and unexpected factors, such as in the form of relief and assistance efforts against earthquakes, floods and other natural disasters. In this connection, a government can take the initiative to create insurance companies and venture capital institutions for the purpose of lowering social risks. Financial resources needed for investment in this regard can come from both the public and private sectors.

The fifth is government investment and the multiplier effect. By increasing spending for both public consumption and investment, a government is able to redress the lack of effective demand, bring down unemployment and achieve stable economic growth. Government spending can set in motion a chain reaction of multiplication, meaning that a sum of government spending is able to generate a massive income several times larger than the sum of spending itself. This phenomenon is economically called the "multiplier effect". According to the "multiplier effect", when total investment increases, the income generated will be larger than the investment increment value by a factor of K, eventually leading to a growth in national wealth.

5.4.2.4.3   FUNCTIONAL POSITIONING IN MARKET REGULATION

Tax system and supply   Although taxation is a primary source of government fiscal revenue, how a tax system is formulated not only determines how much fiscal revenue government can earn but also has a predominant impact on how efficiently the market is able to operate. Supply-side economics holds excessively high social costs to be the primary cause of economic crises, arguing that to improve the supply side of the economy, it is necessary to reduce the costs borne by corporations and individuals to engage in the market, which, in concrete terms, means that cuts in taxes and fees should be implemented to boost economic growth. In this connection, the formulation of tax systems is a crucial area for regional competition, where the importance for government to play out its role becomes the most pronounced.

The development of a property rights system   As far as a market economy is concerned, defining and protecting property rights constitutes the primary responsibility of government and the prerequisite to building a well-functioning market mechanism. A property rights system consists of a set of rules devised through government authority, which governs how property rights are classified, defined, protected and exercised. In 1960, Ronald Coase emphatically stressed that the responsibility of dealing with property rights–related ambiguities and controversies fell to the government. As far as Ronald Coase saw it, it was incumbent upon the government to unequivocally define property rights by exercising its authority. Coase argued that once property rights were well defined, then the market would be able to reach its optimally efficient state simply through internal trading. Meanwhile, it is also the unshakable responsibility of government to design and safeguard public property rights. Government should serve as an agent for the general public when it comes to public property rights, with its power firmly based on voting and democratic procedures. Thus, a public decision-making information release system and an accountability system are important bricks and mortars for government institutional building.

Currencies and the development of a national credit system   One of the most important aspects of national credit lies in it being able to substitute precious metal as a new medium of exchanges. By endorsing the credibility of its currency by use of its authority, a government can ensure the reliability of its currency for market transactions and, at the same time, lower the transaction costs arising out of distrust between transaction parties, leading to a boost in transaction efficiency. National credit can also be used to raise public funds for the advancement of infrastructural development. For instance, China's national credit has been shaped and formed mainly through the issuance of national bonds, state treasury bonds and special bonds and through bank overdraft or bank lending. It is a type of credit either acquired by the state as a debtor or provided by the state as a creditor. National credit is a special kind of resource, and the government has a special privilege in controlling and allocating it. A good government with accountability shall never abuse its national credit. Instead, a good government will capitalize on its national credit to leverage funds for the following objectives: bolstering public infrastructure development, securing steady economic growth, maintaining social equity, providing to its people more public goods and services and creating a harmonious and peaceful social environment. National credit is usually protected by national laws.

The protection and expansion of international trade   The theory of free trade between sovereign states is based on David Ricardo's theory of comparative advantages, which suggests that the foundation for international trade and specialization is built not just on absolute cost differences but also on comparative advantages between states. However, comparative advantage arises from international trade on an equal footing, which is almost impossible to be realized since trade between states at different developmental stages is not totally equal. In response to an unequal order of international trade, some economically backward states have put forth their versions of economic intervention theories, which are designed to serve their overarching objective of establishing a fully-fledged industry system and boosting the competitiveness of their domestic industries. The following are some of the striking theories on economic intervention.

First, the theory of protecting infant industries arose against the backdrop of unequal trade between leading nations and late-blooming nations. During the first industrial revolution, advanced industrial nations like the UK staunchly advocated free trade, which directly resulted in national industries of some later-blooming nations bearing the brunt of the negative impacts of free trade. At that time, free trade served the interests of early industrialized nations, and therefore if the economically backward nations followed in the footsteps of their richer and more developed counterparts, then they could not but suffer the fate of being reduced to a logging camp or a sheep farm of the UK and a subject of looting. Under such circumstances, Georg Friedrich List argued that as late-blooming nations moved towards becoming developed nations, they should implement protectionist policies to protect their domestic industries, just like the USA. and France had done, and that they could gradually revert to free trade after reaching a certain point of wealth and power.

Second, the strategic trade theory, initially put forth by Paul Krugman, suggests that as returns to scale increase progressively, expanding production scales and achieving economies of scale are necessary steps for domestic industries and enterprises to boost their competitiveness on the international market. As a general rule, it is extremely difficult for an enterprise to expand its production scale solely by relying on its own efforts and strengths. It is even more so for economically backward countries. In this connection, the most effective way to scale production expansion is for the government to protect and support industries with promising development prospects and huge externalities, so that these selected industries can, in a short period of time, expand their production scales, lower production costs, bring trade advantages to the fore and boost competitiveness.

Third, some scholars in the evolutionary economic school put forth some suggestions on how late-blooming countries can upgrade their industries. The key points of their suggestions are as follows: (a) high-quality activities should be learning-centric, meaning that improvements on production sites, product designs and R&D can contribute to boosting the accumulation of knowledge and enhancing the quality of industrial activities; (b) learning should be a process that starts from what is simple and then transitions to what is complex, which means that enterprises of developing countries generally undergo a learning process from being an OEM (original equipment manufacturer) and an ODM (original design manufacturer) to being an OBM (original brand manufacturer); (c) in order to help enterprises break path-dependency, government shall render support to enterprises for their efforts to seek high-quality learning and technological upgrading; and (d) given that learning activities are distributed differently in different industries, some industries are in no need of a large number of learning and upgrading activities, such as the industry of clothing production, while such activities are needed in some other industries, such as in precision instrument manufacturing and in auto manufacturing. Therefore, it is necessary for a government to render support to industries featuring a high concentration of high-quality learning activities.

Fourth, the key points of the theory of the advantages of backwardness are as follows: (a) by leveraging cutting-edge technologies already available, late-developing countries are able to position themselves at a high starting point and avoid the detours made by leading nations; (b) late-developing countries are able to leapfrog technological gaps and bring leading countries' technologies, equipment and capital into their home markets. By so doing, late-developing countries can save time and money that otherwise would be spent on research and development, develop a large pool of local talents and advance towards industrialization from a high starting point. Capital from leading countries can help late-developing countries redress the shortage of capital, which is a commonplace problem plaguing countries in the process of industrialization; (c) late-developing countries are able to learn and draw upon the successful experience of first-mover countries, and at the same time avoid making the same mistakes that first-mover countries have made. In this regard, the advantage of backwardness is most vividly manifested in the availability, diversity and creativeness of models that late-developing countries can pick and choose for achieving industrialization. Put another way, later-developing countries can learn from early developing countries their experience and lessons to avoid making detours, and by taking viable catch-up strategies, they are able to reduce the time length needed for completing primary industrialization and thus leapfrog into a higher stage of industrialization; and (d) relative backwardness can translate into strong social motivations for growth and development.

All in all, there is no need for government involvement if trade is conducted between countries with equal economic power; however, whenever there is trade between a first-mover country and a late-developing country, then the government of the first-mover country might have a motive to strengthen its first-mover advantages, while the government of the late-developing country might have an equally strong motive to harness the advantages of backwardness for leapfrog growth.

5.5 The dual-strong mechanism theory for mature market economies

A mature market economy is distinctively characteristic of the coexistence of a strong market and a strong government. A strong market means that the market has the primacy in determining resource allocation, that all decisions and actions for optimizing regional resource allocation shall be firmly premised on the rules of the market and that no market entity shall be allowed to do anything that might violate the rules of the market. In a nutshell, a strong market is categorically an efficient market. A strong government lays stress on being an effective and competent government within the boundaries of market rules, which is to say that a regional government should actively exercise its foresighted leading role in allocating three types of resources and in fostering innovation in institution, organization, management and technology. in addition, a regional government should become well prepared for undertaking market risks, making up for the deficiencies of the market, providing public goods and capitalizing on its region's advantages of backwardness in international trade, so that a favorable environment is created to ensure the smooth running of the region's market economy and the achievement of leapfrog economic growth. In this sense, in short, a dual-strong mechanism is the organic combination of an efficient market and an effective government.

5.5.1   *The Washington Consensus and the middle-income trap*

In the late 1980s, faced with the world economic depression, real economy grew sluggishly, the momentum for economic growth was becoming insufficient, demand was slumping, the population growth rate was dropping, economic globalization was in turmoil, financial markets were in fluctuation and international trade and investment were in a downturn. In 1989, John Williamson, an economist from the Institute for International Economics, an international economic think tank based in Washington, D.C., first presented the concept and name of the Washington Consensus, a set of ten economic policy prescriptions considered as constituting the "standard" reform package promoted for crisis-wracked developing countries by Washington, D.C.–based institutions, such as the International Monetary Fund, the World Bank and the US Treasury Department. The ten broad sets of relatively specific policy recommendations are as follows: fiscal policy discipline, with avoidance of large fiscal deficits relative to GDP; redirection of public spending from subsidies ("especially indiscriminate subsidies") toward broad-based provision of key pro-growth, pro-poor services like primary education, primary health care and infrastructure investment; tax reform, broadening the tax base and adopting moderate marginal tax rates; interest rates that are market-determined and positive (but moderate) in real terms; competitive exchange rates; trade liberalization: liberalization of imports, with particular emphasis on elimination of quantitative restrictions (licensing, etc.); any trade protection to be provided by low and relatively uniform tariffs; liberalization of inward foreign direct investment; privatization of state enterprises; deregulation: abolition of regulations that impede market entry or restrict competition, except for those justified on safety, environmental and consumer protection grounds, and prudential oversight of financial institutions; and legal security for property rights.

The core value of such policy recommendations is the minimization of government's role in the market, and rapid privatization and liberalization. Theoretically, it advocates the implementation of a completely free market economy model and minimizes the role of government. As long as the market can freely allocate resources, economic growth is achievable. These recommendations involve rapid liberalization of the market and domestic and foreign trade; rapid privatization of state-owned enterprises; and reduction of fiscal deficits and strict restrictions on loaning and currency issuing in order to stabilize macro-economy. The Washington Consensus aims at providing economic reform programs and countermeasures for debt-stricken Latin American countries and a political and economic theoretical basis for the transition of eastern European countries. In spite of their justifiability in stimulating economic development of those countries over certain periods, the ten policy recommendations overlooked the importance of constructing the market system from the above-mentioned six aspects, and more importantly the great value that government attaches to the three categories of resources, thus leading to the combination of "weak effective government" and "weak efficient market"; failure of government in playing a role in regulating economic development; inadequacy in market development; absence of necessary legislation; market chaos; and the frequent failure of the competitive system of the market. Consequently, those policy recommendations did not prove to be sustainable and inevitably ended in predicaments.

The concept of "middle income trap", which was introduced by the World Bank in 2006, specifically refers to the situation in which those middle-income economies, such as the newly emerging market economies – on their way to breaking through the "poverty trap" of per capita GDP of $1000 to develop into high-income countries – will soon enter into the "take-off" stage from US $1000 to US $3000 when their per capita GDP gets close to US $3000, thus causing a concentrated outbreak of the contradictions that have been accumulating in their rapid development. Owing to the fact that the renewal of their own systems and mechanisms has reached a critical stage, the contradictions are difficult to overcome, which causes their economies to be trapped in economic downturn or stagnation, hence the "middle income trap".

At this stage, the costs of resources, raw materials, labor, capital and management remain high, while cutting-edge core technology is hard to obtain, innovation becomes difficult and their industries stay at the low-end of the chain without competitiveness; this results in economic downturn or stagnation, unemployment, social and public service shortages, fragile financial systems, polarization of wealth, corruption, lack of faith, social turmoil and so on. It takes quite some time for these countries to get out of the middle-income stage and into the rank of high-income countries. Interestingly, those Latin American countries which have followed the Washington Consensus in their promoting economic reforms have become examples of the middle-income trap. In 1964, Argentina's per capita GDP exceeded US $1000 and rose to over $8000 in the late 1990s, but it fell back to over 2000 in 2002, though it went back up to $12,873 in 2014. Mexico's per capita GDP reached $1000 in 1973 and $10,718 in 2014, but remained just a little above the middle-income level after more than four decades. Similar examples are found elsewhere in Latin America, where quite a few countries, after two or three decades of repeated efforts, still failed to skip across the threshold of $15,000 for their entry into the rank of developed economies.

Let's take Argentina, for example: its "lesion" analysis reaches the following conclusions. First, there has been a great deal of fluctuation in its economic growth rates. Between 1963 and 2008, it underwent 16 years of negative GDP growth, with an average annual GDP growth rate of only 1.4 percent. In 1963, its per capita GDP was US $842, located at the middle–high income level, but in 2008, it rose to only $8236, remaining at the same income level after 45 years. Second, there has been a severe lack of momentum from innovation in science and technology. The proportion of R&D expenditure to its GDP in 2003 was 0.41 percent, ranking 40th in the world; its R&D personnel accounted for only 1.1 per 1000 people in 2006; in terms of labor quality, its proportion of university graduates and above in its entire labor force was 29.5 percent in 2007. Third, the polarization between the rich and the poor has been serious and social contradictions have been prominent. Argentina's Gini coefficient was about 0.45 in the mid-1980s, close to 0.50 in the late 1990s, and 0.51. in 2007.Its income ratio was 40.9 percent, judging from 10 percent of the highest income class and 10 percent of the lowest income class, which shows that its unfair distribution is not only reflected in property income but also in wage grades. Moreover, urban infrastructure and public services have lagged far behind, social security has deteriorated and social contradictions have been outstanding. Finally, government administration has proved to be ineffective. There has been long-term macro-economic instability, fluctuations in exchange rates, high inflation, commonplace financial deficits, numerous problems with the supply side and weaknesses of legal means and economic instruments in terms of macro-economic management. To address these problems, government has taken stop-gap measures, which eventually resulted in socio-economic imbalance.

The Washington Consensus turned out to be a failed strategy, and its "shock therapy" has proved to be a failed policy. First, an efficient market is one with complete competition, orderly legal supervision and sound social credit. The Washington Consensus focused only on the competition and promotion of the basic functions of the market, i.e. the competition and promotion of the element system and the organization system, but overlooked the improvement of the basic order of the market, i.e. the legal system and the supervision system, as well as the development and improvement of the foundation of the market environment, including social credit systems and market infrastructure. Therefore, the market economy in the Washington Consensus is a free market economy rather than a modern market economy with sound systematic functions.

Second, an effective government is one that complies with market rules, maintains market order and participates in market competition. The Washington Consensus only recognizes the government's protection and provision of non-operational resources, i.e. public goods, and completely ignores the government's planning, guiding and supportive policies as well as policies concerning the adjustment, supervision and management of operational resources, i.e. industrial resources, and enterprise competition. There is entire ignorance of national government's promotion of the construction of quasi-operational resources, i.e. urban resource allocation, and its role in competition. Only those who have obtained policy support for the allocation of three types of resources and achieved tangible results are effective governments in the mature market economy. Therefore, its recommendation for deregulation is essentially anarchism, which appears feeble and lacking in strength in contrast with the theory of modern market economy that advocates the organic combination of effective government and efficient market.

Third, in order to ensure that the real economic growth rate gets close or equal to the potential rate, the primary task for government is to strengthen government capacity building, institutional arrangement and development and transformation of development modes, in addition to improvement upon the modern market system, which all turn out to be lacking in the Washington Consensus. Government capacity building includes compliance with the rules of the market economy and government capabilities for the development of market economy and participation in the market competition. The institutional environment construction includes market legislation, law enforcement, judicature and market legal education; the construction of regulatory bodies, supervision contents and supervision modes according to the requirements of the market economy; and the supervision of institutions, transactions, market, policies and regulations, as well as the amelioration of social and institutional norms for self-implemented reforms and development of administrative organizations. The development models should essentially shift from Adam Smith's theory of market (the invisible hand) coupled with emphasis on supply (commodity, price, supply regulation) and Keynesian theory of government intervention coupled with emphasis on demand (investment, consumption, export, troika's pull) to the theory of modern market economy, i.e. government leading (intervention) coupled with focus on supply (the new structural engine for the supply side), that is, shifting to the model of effective government + efficient market. Government leading should have its part in the market economy on all rounds and in all dimensions.

5.5.2 *The government and the market: a symbiotic and complementary relationship rather than one inversely proportional to the other*

If the share of government spending in GDP is regarded as a striking indicator of the extent to which a government is involved in economic activities, then it is clear that in any country throughout modern history, as per capita income surges, this share rises as well. Such is the famous Wagner's Law, a law that has predicted this upward sloping trend of the share of government spending in GDP rising continually in tandem with the increase of income per person. Take the OECD (Organization for Economic Cooperation and Development) as an example: an organization that consists mainly of developed countries. Among OECD countries, the average share of government spending in GDP stood at 10.7 percent in the late nineteenth century, reached 18.7 percent in the 1920s, inched up to 22.8 percent in 1937, skyrocketed to 43.1 percent in 1980 and has remained flat-lined ever since. The share reaches over 50 percent in Nordic countries such as Sweden, Norway and Denmark. In spite of rising government interventions in OECD countries, their market systems are the strongest across the globe in terms of both development levels and competitiveness. What is particularly noteworthy is that even with government spending accounting for half of the GDP, northern European countries are way ahead of other OECD countries in terms of economic openness and labor market vibrancy. In northern European countries, each with a population of just several million people, there has emerged an array of globally leading multinational corporations that for years have topped the list of global competitiveness, such as Nokia, Erickson and Maersk. Singapore is another striking example in this regard. The share of government spending in GDP is not particularly high in Singapore, mainly due to the forceful implementation of a housing provident fund system, but the Singaporean government has still managed to exert a powerful influence on the country's economic growth and industrial upgrading, largely through fiscal policies and government-linked enterprises. As a result, the economy has undergone a long period of explosive growth, propelling Singapore into the ranks of the world's most competitive countries.

In stark contrast to developed countries, the share of government spending in GDP is usually kept somewhere near or at 20 percent in developing countries. The share is at an even lower level in some Sub-Saharan countries. With this share kept at such a low level, the governments in these countries often find it difficult to maintain public order and develop a national market. If the relationship between government and market is defined by the use of oversimplified terms like "strong" and "weak", then more often than not, what we see in real life are combinations either of strong government and strong market or of weak government and weak market. Never have we observed the combination of weak government and strong market. As such, it is of critical importance that we delve into the complicated relationship between government and market, rather than just scratch its surface.

First of all, there is no government that does not play a role in any modern market economy, and a market economy without a government playing a role definitely goes against modern market economic philosophies. Nevertheless, it does not necessarily mean that an economy with a government playing a role is a modern market economy. The crux of the matter is what kind of a role a government plays and how the government plays its role in the economy. Second, an efficient market cannot function without an effective government, in the sense that government power is needed for defining and protecting property rights, establishing and maintaining a level playing field, expanding market systems, guaranteeing the enforcement of contracts, curtailing monopoly and curbing malicious competition. The market is remotely likely to function properly in the absence of these conditions. Third, an effective government is a stabilizer and a boost for a market to play out its function. Specifically, an effective government can bring its role to play in a long list of things, from providing public services of all kinds, narrowing the gaps in income and development and protecting the eco-system to exercising macro-economic regulation and devising medium and long-term plans for development. Government functions in these areas are able to remedy market defects and bring about harmonious development that balances efficiency against equality. Fourth, despite the above-mentioned functions, if a government deviates from this central task, overextends its hand at things and even attempts to replace a market-based mechanism with a centrally planned mechanism, then the government, though seemingly very strong, is definitely going to badly hurt and weaken the market. In the last analysis, a modern market economy must be built on the basis of a dual-strong mechanism featuring a strong effective government and a strong efficient market. Put another way, there is definitely a strong and righteous government behind a strong and well-functioning market economy.

5.5.3 Demarcation and analysis of strong government and strong market in resource allocation

The government–market relationship is both contradictory and complementary in that on one hand, an overwhelmingly powerful government, such as in a centrally planned economy, will disrupt market fairness and efficiency; on the other hand, the market force, if left unchecked and unregulated, will sometimes cause insufficient supplies of public goods and lead some people to relentlessly pursue short-term benefits, which might eventually result in irrational group mentality and the rampancy of underground shadow marketplaces. Then to what extent can government intervention be deemed as being ideal for economic operation?

5.5.3.1 Government-led resource allocation and price-based resource allocation

It is mainly regarding non-operational resources and quasi-operational resources that a government undertakes its resource allocation tasks. A government allocates non-operational resources by exercising its authority as an agent of public will, which means that a government can assign and distribute resources by issuing executive orders. As to quasi-operational resources, a government often adopts the 3-P mode for allocating them. Under the 3-P mode, the government and the business sector (both non-profit and profit-making) can establish cooperative relationships in a way that enables different parties to bring their respective strengths to bear for achieving win–win outcomes.

The market distributes and allocates operational resources with the use of the price instrument, which means that by emitting and transmitting different price signals, the market constantly assesses the value of resources of all kinds and guides the proper configuration of resources among market entities. Price-based resource allocation is achieved by balancing supply against demand: when the price is high, supply will increase, while demand will decline; when the price is low, supply will decrease, while demand will rise. Ultimately, the price will stabilize at an equilibrium point between supply and demand, enabling resource allocation to be completed. When it comes to "quasi-operational resources", it is true that a government can decide whether to partake in allocating them or not in response to the price signals emitted by the market, for quasi-operational resources are not as strongly excludable and rivalrous in nature as operational resources. However, incentives and instructions from the government in the form of policy support are often needed, given the lack of motivation for market entities to allocate such resources.

When it comes to the demarcation between an effective government and an efficient market in resource allocation, the critical and difficult point mainly lies in the allocation of quasi-operational resources. In other words, quasi-operational resources are often allocated jointly and coordinately by strong government and strong market.

5.5.3.2   *Conditions for the price mechanism to play a strong role*

5.5.3.2.1   RIVALRY AND DEMAND

Economic goods are generally described as being "better-than-nothing" goods, which require rivalry and competition to be obtained. Rivalry in this regard means that whoever is in want of these economic goods is willing to pay for them with money. Meanwhile, given that people's marginal propensity to consume economic goods is declining progressively, the demand curve for economic goods is downward sloping, which means that as the purchased economic goods increase in quantity, people's propensity to consume more will be on constant decline. Nevertheless, it is noteworthy that some economic goods are non-rivalry in nature, such as digital products not subjected to IPR protection, public green space and beaches and certain scientific research products. The aforementioned goods, though often perceived as being better than nothing, are non-rivalry in nature in that whoever wants them is unwilling to pay for them with money. The reasons for this are as follows: first, there is no need to compete for these resources and goods; second, there should not be any competitive activities for these resources and goods, in that once obtained by whoever wants them through competition, then a disruptive blow will be dealt to the fairness and justice of the overall economic system; third, whoever (the demand side) wants these resources has no willingness whatsoever to compete for them, as in the case of infrastructure facilities, because they usually take huge and sustained investment to be built, which cannot be taken care of by the invisible hand of the market.

5.5.3.2.2   EXCLUDABILITY AND SUPPLY

A company is willing to supply what it produces to the market only on the precondition that the gains of doing so outweigh or at least equal the input costs. As the price of its products rises steadily, the company will pocket more and more profits, provided that the input costs remain constant, and therefore, the supply curve is generally sloping upward. However, if individual actors, who have no intention whatsoever to buy the product directly from the company, are able to obtain from other sources, at zero or very low costs, the same product that the company has invested a fortune to produce and supply, then the direct consequence will be that the company becomes unable to obtain any gains from selling the product to compensate for the cost of producing it. Generally speaking, there are three major factors accounting for the non-excludability of a product. The first factor is the impossibility of technically excluding non-payers from using the product. Cases in point include industrial designs, technological processes and some basic research products that are difficult to be patented. The second factor is the excessively high cost of excluding non-payers from using the product, even when it is technically possible to do so. Examples in this regard are a clean environment, fresh air, pleasant music and other resources or goods whose property rights cannot be clearly defined. The third factor is that certain resources or goods should not be used exclusively by a selected few, because their being exclusively possessed by a selected few will induce inequity and unfairness.

5.5.3.2.3   THE "DUAL-STRONG MECHANISM" THEORETICAL ANALYTICAL FRAMEWORK BASED ON RESOURCE ALLOCATION

Resources and goods can be classified into four categories according to their non-excludability and non-rivalry characteristics (as seen in Figure5.7). These four categories are respectively described in four quadrants. Quadrant I refers to resources and goods with excludability and rivalry characteristics. The market dictates how to allocate the resources and goods in this category, whose property rights are clearly defined. The government, as a general rule, does not play a role in allocating resources and goods in this category except during the process of leading foreign enterprises competing against domestic late-developing enterprises or for the sake of protecting its home agriculture. Thus, a "strong market" coupled with a "weak government" is an efficient combination approach to allocating resources and goods in Quadrant I.

In Quadrant II are resources and goods with excludability and non-rivalry characteristics, whose property rights are clearly defined. However, their non-rivalry characteristics can place a great strain on the market in allocating them. The most representative of resources and goods in this category are digital products ubiquitously available on the Internet, including operating systems, apps, digital music pieces and e-books. Given that the demand side is able to obtain such goods and resources at a near zero cost, it is extremely difficult to make people pay for them with currencies. Evidently, it is practically unviable for the price mechanism to independently work out a way of efficiently allocating resources and goods in Quadrant II. The government is able to help the market with the allocation of such resources and goods, mainly in the following three ways. First, the government needs to beef up protection of intellectual property by punishing piracy and infringement. Second, the government can inculcate

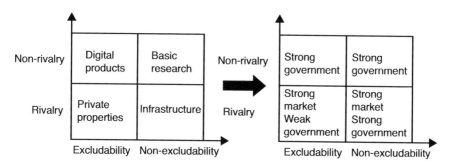

Figure 5.7 Classification of resources and the respective roles of market and government

and raise public awareness of IPR protection through government-sponsored media and other authoritative channels. Third, the government can also directly purchase some intellectual products in order that the income of those involved in the knowledge creation process is well guaranteed.

Quadrant III refers to resources and goods of rivalry but non-excludability characteristics, which the public craves and is willing to pay for with money. Nonetheless, given that it is difficult (unnecessary) to clear define their property rights, how to properly allocate them is still a conundrum too daunting for the invisible hand of the market to crack independently. Resources and goods in this category mainly take the form of infrastructural facilities, such as roads, parks, high-speed rail lines and public transportation means. Given the low efficiency of the market in allocating these resources and goods, it is imperative for the government to directly engage in the allocation and supply of them. Nonetheless, it should be noted that these resources and goods are not created by the government. The government is just the ultimate purchaser of them, while the organization and allocation of these resources and goods is undertaken and completed by the invisible hand of the market under government regulation and supervision. Cases in point in this regard are the launch and solicitation of bids, the recruitment of personnel and the procurement of equipment. In this sense, the combination of a "strong government" and a "strong market" is able to produce synergy powerful enough to compensate for what the market lacks and to enable the government to act as both a supervisor and a coordinator.

Quadrant IV refers to resources or goods that are non-rivalry and non-excludable in nature. The goods fitting into this category are state-funded basic research products, which can neither be turned into private properties to exclude others from using them nor spark market-based competition. As such, strong government support and intervention is imperative for ensuring the sustained supply of resources or goods in this category, while the role of the market mechanism in this regard is only supplementary at best, such as in terms of bringing in R&D personnel through economic instruments. Thus, it is only natural that a "strong government" coupled with a "weak market" is the perfect recipe for allocating resources and goods in this quadrant.

In summary, the government and the market play different roles, depending on the different categories of resources and goods to be allocated. The combination between a "strong government" and a "strong market" has shown remarkable efficiency in allocating certain public goods like digital products and infrastructure facilities.

5.5.4   *The potential economic growth rate and the real economic growth rate*

The potential economic growth rate means the growth rate of the largest volume of products and total labor generated in the modern market system within a country's economy, or the greatest economic growth rate that can be achieved under conditions of the full and optimal collocation of various resources under the modern market system of a country. It can only be derived through the operation of the dual-strong mechanism under the mature market economy. There are two aspects to it. On the one hand, the market must be efficient, which means the perfection of the basic functions of the modern market system (including the market element system and market organizational system), the basic order of the market (including the market legal system and market supervision system) and the basis of market environment (including the social credit system and market infrastructure); on the other hand, the government must be effective, that is to say, the national government can systematically undertake the effective allocation of operational resources, non-operational resources and quasi-operational resources with appropriate policy support and institutional arrangement.

The real or actual economic growth rate refers to the comparison between the gross national product (GNP) at the end of a period and the GNP at the base period. The GNP based on the current price at the end of a period is known as the nominal economic growth rate, while the GNP based on the current basic price (the constant price) at the end of a period is the real economic growth rate, i.e. the speed of real economic growth, which is the dynamic indicator of the economic development of a country over a certain period.

As the degrees of market development and of government effectiveness vary from country to country – combinations of weak effective government and weak efficient market as in some middle-low income countries; semi-strong effective government and strong efficient market as in the USA; strong effective government and semi-strong efficient market as in China, which is still obsessed, to certain extent, with problems regarding market competition, order, credit and infrastructure – there exists some distance between the real economic growth rate and the potential economic growth rate generated from the combination of strong effective government and strong efficient market. The distance indicates the potential of national economic development, and the policy matching or institutional arrangement targeting at such distances are where the innovational vitality resides for national economic development. Mature market economy means the combination of strong effective government and strong efficient market, which is the most sophisticated level of government and market combination, the theoretical goal of the world economic growth rate and the best model governments should explore and pursue for their national development.

In the real economy, the aggregate social supply may surpass the aggregate social demand, or the aggregate social demand may surpass the aggregate social supply. Their root causes, basic solutions and approaches can all be found from the six aspects of modern market systems and the effectiveness of government models for the allocation of the three categories of resources.

5.5.5   *The dual-strong operating mechanism of government and market*

5.5.5.1   *Government and the initial allocation of resources*

Government should not intervene in the allocation of operational resources. However, direct government allocation, intervention and guidance must be undertaken for non-operational and quasi-operational resources. Government investment constitutes the most direct and forceful form of intervention, as in cases where government can attempt to improve supply by way of direct investment when the market fails to independently supply enough products or services to meet social demands, and where government may need to adopt approaches in replacement of the market to price and regulate certain goods and resources when effective allocation of resources cannot be achieved merely through price mechanisms.

5.5.5.2   *The role of government in the reallocation of operational resources*

In addition to being directly involved in the allocation of non-operational and quasi-operational resources, such as through investment and procurement, government can indirectly intervene with the allocation of operational resources, mainly by means of taxation, interest rates and exchange rates.

The lever of taxation is a means by which government indirectly adjusts economic activities. By offering favorable or unfavorable terms to taxpayers through the lever of taxation, a state-level government can direct operational resources to be allocated in a way that complies with the overarching objectives of its macro-economic planning. In terms of interest rate policies, government can leverage the instruments of interest rates in good time to adjust interest rates and interest rate structure, with a view to balancing the supply and demand of social capital and achieving the pre-set objectives for its monetary policies. With respect to exchange rate policies, regional government can endeavor to keep at appropriate levels the rates at which its home currency is exchanged for foreign currencies, through the promulgation of financial laws and regulations and through the implementation of relevant policies and measures. Regional government can devise a series of reward measures for special contributions to incentivize innovation and influence the way "operational resources" are being allocated. Financial assistance, support and rewards in various forms can contribute to boosting scientific and technological capabilities as well as regional economies, with profound and extensive spillover effects.

5.5.5.3   *The dual-strong role of government and market in resource creation*

Government involvement is necessitated by the uneven distribution of knowledge within an industry. Unlike resource allocation, where the emphasis is placed on pricing existing resources, products and services, resource creation puts a premium on producing new resources, new services and new knowledge. When the level of knowledge remains unchanged and highly diffused, resource creation depends more on market entities, and production activities are self-initiated and self-completed under the drive of benefits. Therefore, when knowledge becomes an industry consensus, a strong market can independently complete the work of resource creation without any government involvement. When knowledge is unevenly dispersed within an industry, government involvement becomes a necessity.

Tacit knowledge or tacit technology needs government support and protection to be created. Many studies on corporate competitive advantages consider tacit knowledge, which is inimitable and irreplaceable in nature, to be the source of enterprises' competitive advantages. Such knowledge or technology is difficult to be coded into information or transferred (also known as informationalized knowledge, explicit knowledge is totally transferrable). Whenever new knowledge is created, the market will transform it into information and proliferate it to such an extent and at such a speed that it will quickly become commonplace knowledge within an industry. As a result of the new knowledge becoming commonplace in a short time period, what its creator loses will largely exceed what he or she gains by creating it in the first place. Since whoever imitates and copies the new knowledge can gain a profit tantamount to the industrial average just by imitation, there is neither point nor incentive for creating new knowledge.

Worse still, copying and imitating will, in the long run, lead to the degeneration of both the knowledge system and the innovation capabilities of an industry. For ordinary enterprises, knowledge acts on the production process through the vehicle of applied technologies. Capital and labor are still affected by market-based prices, but technologies, which are infused with tacit knowledge, are hard to be assigned and allocated through the price mechanism. In this sense, instead of bringing about the upgrade of knowledge, the market will only catalyze its degeneration, and therefore, only through government involvement can be new knowledge be truly created to boost the core competitiveness of enterprises and regional economies. For a region to improve its competitiveness, its government needs to help domestic enterprises develop competitive advantages in two ways: rendering support to domestic enterprises in innovation and investing heavily in the protection of know-how. From this standpoint, what government does in this regard runs counter to the forces of the market, and a strong government needs to adopt a strategy focused on knowledge cultivation and innovation.

Conditions for the creation of resources like high and new technology are often provided by governments. The high-tech sectors are both a reflection of the speedy regeneration of knowledge and an embodiment of the sophisticated and tacit nature of knowledge. R&D activities are the centerpiece of industrial activities in the high-tech sectors, where a large number of knowledge-intensive talents conduct cooperation with a high degree of synergy and where innovation and creativity are key to winning competition. Similarly, the high-tech sectors do not just arise naturally out of market competition, just as enterprises in the low-tech sectors are unable to climb up to the top of the technological ladder overnight. How far a country can go in the upgrading of knowledge and technologies is gravely restricted by its educational foundation, culture of creativity, personnel reserves and the technologies already in its possession. All of these factors cannot be cultivated and improved without government investment and support.

5.6   Building up a new engine for global economic development

In 1948, Ragnar Knox likened trade to the engine for nineteenth-century economic growth to justify the rationality of the import-substitution industrialization strategy. During the 2012–2014 financial crisis, the annual growth in global trade was less than 4 percent and was far below the average growth rate of about 7 percent prior to the crisis. Eventually, officials from the World Bank raised the question of how to "restart" the engine of global trade. Many countries, especially those economies that are rich in natural resources such as oil, natural gas, mineral products and agricultural products, utilized such "tangible factors" as land, labor and other resources to the extreme in order to propel their economic growth; this showed the unsustainability of their transformation from the factor-driven to the investment-driven and then to the innovation-driven stage. Under the twenty-first-century modern market system of "effective government" and "efficient market", it will be of primary importance to global economic governance and development to promote and enhance the new supply-side structural engine (not the demand-side "trade engine"), give full play to the role of enterprise competition in the allocation of industrial resources and government competition in the allocation of urban resources and set up the "three engines" of investment, innovation and governance, which incorporate tangible and intangible factors globally.

5.6.1   *Building up a new engine for global investment*

Investment-driven growth depends on the allocation and competition of supply-side products and industrial resources, as well as the supply-side governmental allocation of urban resources and the promotion of infrastructure construction competition. It can deepen national markets, increase capital, create technological innovation and job opportunities and generate long-term sustainability.

First, the supply-side structural reform is facilitated from the angle of industrialization and agricultural modernization. There are three aspects to the promotion of new-type industrialization: (a) to support and guide the restructuring and upgrading of traditional industries. The revitalization of huge inventory assets through the support and guidance of technological transformation undertaken by enterprises and the optimization of the benefits of industrial quality can stimulate demand and promote economic growth; (b) to support and foster the development of newly emerging strategic industries and high-tech industries. Focus should be laid on supporting and nurturing the R&D innovation of core and key technology of enterprises and the transfer and commercialization of research findings so as to cultivate competitive and leading industries and construct complete industrial chains and modernization service networks; and (c) to make efforts in promoting business mergers and takeovers so as to integrate, restructure and enhance the core competitiveness of enterprises by means of market competition, which is one of the major means of realizing the supply-side effective investment and the conversion of old power into new dynamics.

There are five aspects to the acceleration of agricultural modernization: (a) agricultural modernization covers not only the expansion of land management scale but also the modernization of farmers, in which farmers should be guided and nurtured out of ignorance and backwardness and be developed into a new-type that is armed with knowledge, technology and management skills; (b) organizational modes: no matter whether they are large farms or small family businesses, government should support farmer cooperatives or help individual farmers dock with market demands, provide one-stop pre-production, in-production and post-production services and one-stop services in purchasing production materials and the storage, processing, transportation and sales of agricultural products; (c) moderate scale operation; (d) moderate urbanization; and (e) promotion of the professionalization of agricultural technical education. Agricultural modernization can create a stable social environment for industrialization and urbanization, reduce social costs and boom national economy.

Second, the investment in infrastructure is to be intensified: (a) the new-type urbanization is to be promoted. Urban population generally accounts for more than 80 percent in developed countries. With urban and rural integration and the formation of city-centered urban systems, the planning and construction of human-oriented new-type urbanization; the construction of underground facilities for "sponge cities" and "sponge communities"; the integrated construction of water, electricity, roads, and gas in urban and rural areas; the provision of facilities for urban and rural public services such as education, health, culture, sports and so on; and the development of leisure tourism, commerce and logistics, information industry, and transportation will all provide new growth potentials for regional and world economies; and (b) the infrastructure modernization is to be enhanced for energy, transportation, environmental protection, information and irrigation and water conservancy, with a great deal of room for investment and sufficient potentials.

Third, the investment in science and technology projects is to be expanded. For example, the National Networks of Manufacturing Innovation (NNMI) in the US spent $1 billion in the initial stage, with 45 Institutes for Manufacturing Innovation to be set up within ten years. The Knowledge Transfer Partnership (KTP) in the UK and the smart manufacturing based on the Communication

Physics System (CPS) in Germany's Industry 4.0 can integrate innovative resources of personnel, enterprises and institutions; lead industrial research and development; and promote industrial upgrading. The investment in big data, cloud computing, and the Internet of things, and investment in technological development such as nanotechnology, biotechnology, information technology and artificial intelligence, will all give rise new economic growth points.

Fourth, the financial supporting capacity is to be enhanced. It should be emphasized that financial services support entity economy, in addition to the integration of finance, science and technology and industry. The new investment engine will not work without the reform, innovation and development of the financial system.

5.6.2 *Building up a new engine for global innovation*

When switching from their search of how to increase economic growth rates to economic development modes, from giving full play to enterprise competition in industrial resources allocation to national government competition in urban resources allocation, from a single market mechanism playing its role to the combination of effective government and efficient market for the purpose of building up the new investment engine for world economic growth, whether regions, countries or even the world, they will inevitably be faced with such new issues as how to protect fair and equitable principles in the global economic governance system, protect the interests of the developing countries in the global economic order, maintain or expand an open economic system in order to resist protectionism, combat the norms of new economic fields (such as the Internet), and deal with new challenges of global economic development. Therefore, improvement and innovation must be in place to create public mechanisms or provide public goods, i.e. ideological, material, organizational and institutional public goods, which coordinate and govern the global economic order in competition and cooperation.

First, notional innovation is to be promoted for ideological public goods, to which there are three aspects: (a) the market should be an efficient one. Modern market system is composed of six sub-systems. In some countries, overemphasis is laid on competition in market elements and market organization while overlooking the construction of its legal supervision system and the perfection of environmental infrastructure such as the market credit system, which will cause the deviation of the "three fair" market principle; (b) the government should be an effective one. National government should impose planning, guidance, support, regulation, supervision and management on the allocation of operational resources, i.e. industrial resources; provide "basic underpinning, fairness and justice, effective promotion" for non-operational resources, i.e. social public goods; and regulate and participate in the competition of quasi-operational resources allocation; and (c) the mature market economic mode that national government should strive for is the combination of effective government and efficient market. Under the big market economic system, enterprise competition targets industrial resources, and government competition targets urban resources. National government should play an important role in global economic growth.

Second, technological innovation is to be enhanced for material public goods. Currently, the most representative development of science and technology is the integration of informationalization with industrialization, urbanization, agricultural modernization and infrastructure modernization, which can be boiled down to "Internet plus". Therefore, when what a country or a city provides – e.g. public transportation, urban management, education, health, culture, business, government and environmental protection, energy and security configuration – converges with smart intelligence, the public and communities will benefit from the security, efficiency, convenience and greenness and harmony a smart city can provide by combining tangible and intangible factors. This integration will also expedite their transformation in industries, urbanization and internationalization and eventually catalyze the rise of newly emerging countries.

Third, management innovation is to be promoted for organizational public goods. The world is just like a country or a city. Traditionally, urban construction and organizational framework sprawls and road congestion frequently takes place with serious air pollution and low efficiency, even if city traffic is diverted through the first, the second, the third, the fourth and even the fifth ring. The development of modern cities requires grouping layouts which can effectively solve problems that are caused by their traditional sprawling mode of development, just as modern city development requires the reshaping of spatial order and global supply chain development can easily remove boundaries between countries. Like urban configuration, the organizational management of the world economic order must be reformed and innovated from their sprawling modes to grouping layouts. However, it requires corresponding new rules and necessary infrastructure investment so as to form sound layouts and ensure harmonious, coordinated and sustainable development.

Fourth, governance innovation is to be promoted for institutional public goods. National construction requires a trinitarian system of conceptual, urban and rural and land planning, from which is derived its strategic planning, layout positioning, implementation standards, policy evaluation, legal guarantee and so on, thus creating a meticulous and hierarchical implementation mechanism. Global economic governance is conducted by means of regulatory mechanisms such as the United Nations Charter, the United Nations Conference on Trade and Development, the Organization for Economic Cooperation and Development, the World Trade Organization and so on. In order to realize the goals of "letting globalization create more opportunities" and "letting the public share the fruits of economic growth", improvement and innovation must be put in place for economic growth conceptualization and the formulation of regulations and rules; the cooperation of government finance and monetary and structural reform policies; the consistency of economy, labor, employment and social policies; the equal stress on demand management and supply-side reforms; the coordination of short-, mid- and long-term policies; the advancement of economic social development and environmental protection; and joint efforts for global economic governance and sustainable global economic growth.

5.6.3 Building up a new engine for global governance

It requires a perfect governance system for global economy to build the "Four-I" world economy, which is "innovative", "invigorated", "interconnected" and "inclusive". The supply system for international public goods corresponds to non-operational resources in regional economy; the allocation system for international industrial resources corresponds to operational resources; and the allocation system for international urban resources corresponds to quasi-operational resources. They operate in conformity with the existing objective rules.

First, they operate in conformity with the rules for international security order – peace and stability, which has universal recognition. As the basic guideline for the supply system for international public goods, efforts should be made to build a peaceful and stable development environment, strengthen international security and cooperation, safeguard the goals and principles of the UN Charter, maintain the basic norms of international relations and create a peaceful, stable, just and equitable international security order.

Second, they operate in conformity with the rules for international economic competition – fairness and efficiency, which form the basic guidelines for industrial competition in the international industrial resources allocation system. For example, G20 (Hangzhou, China, 2016) formulated the guiding principles for "the trade promotion and investment liberalization", which includes the reduction of tariff and non-tariff trade barriers, the reduction of barriers and restrictions on foreign direct investment, the implementation of trade facilitation measures to reduce border costs, the moderate reduction of post-border restrictions on trade and investment to facilitate wider cross-border coordination and the minimization of discriminatory measures against the third party through multilateral, plurilateral and bilateral agreements to reduce the trade and investment barriers. The governing principle of "promoting competition and improving business environment" embodies the fairness and efficiency of the rules that enterprises all over the world must abide by in their competition, including the strengthening of competition laws and their enforcement; the reduction of administrative and legal barriers to starting up a business and expanding its operation; the promotion of fair market competition; the implementation of efficient insolvency procedures; the reduction of the constrictive rules that impede competition; the reduction of additional regulatory compliance burdens; the effective supervision of regulatory policies; the strengthening of rule of law; the improvement of judicial efficiency; the combat against corruption and so on.

Third, they operate in conformity with the rules for international co-governance – cooperation and win–win, which are the basic guiding principles that intergovernmental competition should follow in the worldwide urban resources allocation system. There are two types of urban resources: tangible factors and intangible factors. Among them, new-type urbanization, smart urban development, investment in infrastructure modernization with energy, transportation, environmental protection, information and water conservancy as the main body will be the new engine for international economic growth and can lead to capital expansion, employment opportunities, technological innovation, market deepening, sustainable economic growth, social benefits, environmental improvement, national strength facilitation and so on. As countries vary in urbanization, policy initiatives and institutional arrangements, their investment-driven growth and competition results differ from each other. However, international governmental competition should be cooperative and sustainable, aiming at common enhancement competition in the global economic governance system and common innovative economic growth mode competition. Its basic principle should be win–win cooperation. Building an innovative, open, interlinked and inclusive world economic system with win–win cooperation as its core will enable us to innovate continuously the economic growth mode and enhance the global economic governance system so as to benefit the whole world.

5.7 A summary of theories on competition between regional governments

Figure 5.8 is a graphic summary of theories on regional government competition. As is shown below, the figure presents a clear overview of theories on regional government competition that are contained in this book, in a way similar to peeling back layer upon layer of an onion, from the core all the way to the periphery.

The role of government is manifested in real life in three aspects: allocating regional resources, administering regional resources and formulating matching policies. Resources pertinent to social welfare are referred to as non-operational resources in a market economy. Policies and principles for the allocation of resources in this category can be encapsulated as providing social security and basic underpinning, ensuring equity and fairness and effective promotion. Resources pertinent to economic growth are referred to as operational resources in a market economy. Policies and principles for the allocation of resources in this category can be summed up as "planning and guiding; supporting and adjusting; regulating and managing".

Resources pertinent to urban construction are referred to as quasi-operational resources in a market economy. Such resources are mainly urban resources, including public service systems (for keeping national economic and social activities running on a day-to-day basis) and software and hardware infrastructure (for providing public services necessary for productive and living activities). Such resources are referred to as quasi-operational resources in that they can be developed and managed by the government – in this case, they are non-operational and not for profit; or, they can be placed into the invisible hand of the market – under such circumstances, they are operational resources and for commercial purposes. Whether they are developed and operated by the

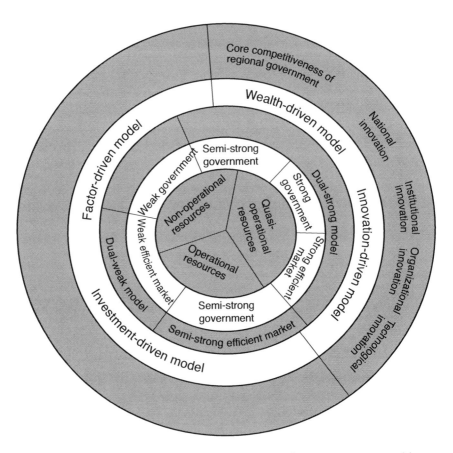

Figure 5.8 A graphic summary of theories on regional government competition

government or by the market can be determined by such factors as the government's fiscal standing, market demands and the level of public acceptability.

Governments and markets can be categorized into three types: weak, semi-strong and strong on the basis of their abilities to define and allocate operational, non-operational and quasi-operational resources. A weak efficient market is one with and only with a market element system and a market organizational system; a semi-strong efficient market is a market with a market element system, a market organizational system, a market legal system and a market regulatory system; and a strong efficient market is a market that consists of a market element system, a market organizational system, a market legal system, a market regulatory system, a market environment system and market infrastructure.

A government can be called a weak effective government if it focuses only on the allocation of non-operational resources and on the formulation of supporting policies, without a clear understanding of or specific measures for the allocation of operational resources. It has yet to clearly define and delimit quasi-operational resources, much less to devise well-directed measures for allocating them. A government can be labeled as a semi-strong effective government if it lays stress only on the allocation of non-operational and operational resources. In addition to fulfilling its public duties and responsibilities regarding social security, a semi-strong effective government also keeps an eye on how the market is operating, or will seek to macro-control, adjust and intervene in the economy by use of effective demands or effective supply of policies whenever the market malfunctions, for the sake of preventing severe losses and damages caused by an economic slump. A semi-strong effective government might also strive for a dynamic equilibrium between total supply and total demand with a master plan for strategic economic development, which includes the following measures: planning and guiding industrial layout; supporting and adjusting productive and operational activities; tightening up regulations to ensure openness, equity and fairness in market competition; curbing the spike of commodity prices; and controlling unemployment. Nevertheless, a semi-strong effective government still fails to have a clear-cut understanding and definition of quasi-operational resources, nor does it succeed in fostering responsive policies and measures for the management of such resources.

A strong effective government denotes a government that not only focuses on the allocation of operational and non-operational resources with policy support but also is capable of precisely delimiting quasi-operational resources and coordinating with the market for the allocation of such resources. A strong effective government can tailor its policies and measures towards the three types of resources, so as to achieve efficient resource allocation and promote the development of regional economy in a way that is viable and sustainable. Specifically, it will undertake the following approaches: bringing into full play its role in economic positioning, economic adjustment and early warning; tapping into market rules and mechanisms; leveraging the instruments of investment, consumption, export, pricing, taxation, interest rates, exchange rates, policies and laws; and fostering notional, institutional, organizational and technological innovation.

As the pinnacle of market economic development, the combination of a strong effective government and a strong efficient market represents the best possible form of government–market relations. This model depicts what a truly mature market economy looks like. A modern market economy cannot run and operate efficiently without the combination of an efficient market and an effective government. The effectiveness of an effective government resides in its capabilities to efficiently allocate non-operational resources with well-designed supplementary policies, in a way that enhances social harmony and stability and optimizes economic environment; to efficiently allocate operational resources with feasible supplementary policies, in a way that guarantees openness, fairness and justice in the market and boosts overall social productivity; and to efficiently allocate quasi-operational resources and engage in market competition, in a way that promotes urban construction and all-round sustainable socio-economic development.

An efficient market implies that the market is one with fully-fledged basic functions, a well-established basic order and a sound and vibrant market climate. The efficiency of an efficient market is reflected in how integrated and synergized production competition, market fairness and orderly business operation are and can be measured and tested against the following three criteria: full market competition, orderly law-based supervision and a fully-fledged social credit system.

In *The Competitive Advantages of Nations*, Porter (1990) points out that a country (or a region) will experience four stages of economic development, which are the factor-driven, the investment-driven, the innovation-driven and the wealth-driven stages. When the market and the government of an economy are yet to go beyond operational resources and non-operational resources in terms of its resource allocation capacity, then the economy is still stuck in the factor-driven and investment-driven stages. It is not until the allocation of quasi-operational resources evolves into the centerpiece of regional competition that innovation and wealth become the main drivers for regional economic development.

As it is among regional governments that regional government competition takes place, such competition should comply with market economic rules, spilling over to projects, policies and affairs in the areas of regional resource allocation, economic development, urban construction, social welfare, etc. Specifically, such competition centers on projects, industrial chain matching, talents and science and technology, fiscal planning and finance, infrastructure, environmental systems and policy systems, as well as management efficiency. In terms of substantive meaning, regional government competition is reflected in how regional governments optimize the allocation of resources through policy-making – what policies to be adopted towards the allocation of operational resources in a way that strengthens corporate vitality; what policies to be implemented for the allocation of non-operational resources in a way that creates a sound and viable environment; and in what way for regional governments to be engaged in the allocation of quasi-operational resources, with what supplementary policies and in compliance with what rules, so as to achieve regional sustainable growth. Innovation is needed to win in regional government competition. As innovation begets competitiveness, continuous innovation means continuous competitiveness; regional innovation is at the core of regional government competitiveness. On the level of innovation, regional government needs to foster innovation in notion, institution, organization and technology. In this connection, GFL becomes the key to success in regional competition and development.

It is imperative to shape and build new drivers (encompassing both tangible and intangible factors) for global investment, innovation and governance by giving full play to the role of competition among enterprises in allocating industrial resources and the role of competition among governments in allocating urban resources. The shaping of these new drivers will surely go a long way towards fostering higher levels of global economic governance and development. Specifically, new drivers for global investment include deeper supply-side structural reform, higher intensity in infrastructural development and higher financial supplementary capabilities; new drivers for global innovation encompass innovation for public goods in notional, material, organizational and institutional dimensions; and new drivers for global governance consist of international security rules for peace and stability, international rules for fair and efficient economic competition and international rules for cooperative and win–win governance.

In a nutshell, the government–market relationship is the Goldbach conjecture in the realm of economics. Massive achievements have been made by synthesizing an effective government and an efficient market, a fact amply testified and proven by an array of success stories in China and abroad. In China, the rise of the PRD is the epitome of the "China Dream" coming true. Shenzhen was an impoverished fishing village to the north of Hong Kong in 1979. In the early 1990s, the PRD embarked on a path to becoming China's biggest labor-intensive manufacturing powerhouse. As it stands now, the PRD, with Guangzhou, Shenzhen, Foshan and Dongguan as its mainstays, is moving at accelerating speed up the industrial value chain. While focusing on building a top-notch national manufacturing innovation center and a national high-tech innovation center, the PRD is on track to becoming a cluster of international megacities. The PRD's obsession with innovation and endeavors towards urbanization are leading China into a whole new model of socio-economic development. Within a short span of 20 years, China's PRD has completed a feat that would otherwise have taken 200 years to accomplish in other regions. Behind this success story of spectacular achievements in economic development, urban construction and social welfare resides a brand new economic philosophy, one that focuses on reshaping an innovation-driven market economy comprising an effective government and an efficient market. Never relenting in its unwavering effort to create synergy between the government and the market, the PRD has been scaling new heights in its economy, urban construction and social welfare undertakings.

The "Singaporean Consensus", which places special focus on all-dimensional social progress, is another example of what can be achieved by synthesizing a competent government and an efficient market. In 1960, Hong Kong's and Singapore's per capita GDP stood at US $405 and $428 respectively. By 1980, they soared to $5,692 and $4,859 and skyrocketed to $38,074 and $54,776 by 2013, which indicates that Singapore's GDP per capita was 1.44 times higher than that of Hong Kong. During this period, Singapore successfully underwent five economic transformations – gravitating away from labor-intensive industries in the 1960s and towards economically intensive industries in the 1970s, shifting towards capital-intensive industries in the 1980s, moving towards technology-intensive industries in the 1990s and focusing on knowledge-intensive industries in the twenty-first century. Behind the push towards these five economic transformations is the visible hand of the Singaporean government. Synthesizing the government with the market and aligning economic policies with social policies is Singapore's recipe for successfully balancing efficiency against equity and development against stability. Such a combination between an effective government and an efficient market has been proven effective for boosting economic growth, upgrading urban facilities and achieving all-dimensional social progress in Singapore. The highly acclaimed "Singaporean Consensus" – an effective government plus an efficient market – has been driving Singapore forward towards all-round and sustainable development.

Bibliography

Bai, Chong-en, Yingjuan Du, Zhigang Tao and Sarah Y. Tong. Local Protectionism and Regional Specialization: Evidence From China's Industries. *Journal of International Economics*, 2004, 2.

Bergstrom, John C. and Alan Randall. *Resource Economics: An Economic Approach to Natural Resource and Environmental Policy*, 4th Edition. UK: Edward Elgar Publishing Ltd., 2016.

Buchanan, James M. *Public Finance in Democratic Process: Fiscal Institutions and the Individual Choice*. Chapel Hill: University of North Carolina Press, 1967.

Bucovetsky, Sam. Inequality in the Local Public Sector. *Journal of Political Economy*, 1982, 90(11), pp. 128–145.

Bucovetsky, Sam. Public Input Competition. *Journal of Public Economics*, 2005, 89(9/10), pp. 1763–1787.

Cai, Fang. How to Change to the Type Driven by Total Factor Productivity. *Social Sciences in China*, 2013, 1.

Chen, Binkai and Yao Yang. The Cursed Virtue: Government Infrastructural Investment and Household Consumption in Chinese Provinces. *Oxford Bulletin of Economics and Statistics*, 2011, 73(6), pp. 856–877.

Chen, Shiyi and Jun Zhang. Has Financial Decentralization Improved the Efficiency of Local Financial Expenditure?. *Social Sciences in China*, 2007, 1.

Chen, Xiushan and Jiu Wen Sun. *Studies of Issues of Chinese Regional Economy*. Beijing: Commercial Press, 2005.

Chen, Yunxian. Operating Cities and Managing Cities as a Resource. *Journal of Foshan College of Science and Technology* (Edition of Social Sciences), 2004, 22(3).

Chen, Yunxian. *Foresighted Leading: Theoretical Thinking and Practice of China's Regional Economic Development*. Berlin: Peking University Press and Springer-Verlag, 2014.

Chen, Yunxian and Wenjing Gu. *Mezzoeconomics*. Beijing: Peking University Press, 2015.

Chen, Yunxian and Jianwei Qiu. *Government Foresighted Leading: Theory and Explorations in the Development of Global Regional Economy*. Oxford: Routledge, 2017.

Cheng, Siwei. Major Measures of Promoting Innovations. *Innovative Science and Technology*, 2005, 10.

Cheung, Steven N.S. *Economic System of China*. Beijing: CITIC Publishing House, 2009.

Coase, Ronald. The Problem of Social Cost. *Journal of Law and Economics*, 1960, 3(10).

Coase, Ronald. *Property Rights and Institutional Change: Collection of Translations From Property Rights School and Neo-Institutional School*. Shanghai: Shanghai Sanlian Bookstore, 1994.

Coase, Ronald, Armen Albert Alchian and Douglass C. North. *Property Rights and Institutional Changes*. Shanghai: Shanghai Joint Publishing Company, 1994.

Coase, Ronald and Claude Menard. *Institution, Contract and Organization*. Translated by Gang Liu. Beijing: Economic Science Press, 2003.

Coase, Ronald, Douglass C. North et al. *Property Rights and Institutional Change*. Shanghai: Shanghai Sanlian Bookstore, 1994.

Coase, Ronald, Douglass C. North et al. *Institution, Contract and Organization: Perspective From the Angle of Neo-Institutional Economics*. Beijing: Economic Science Press, 2003.

Coase, Ronald, Douglass C. North and Oliver Eaton Williamson. *Institutions, Contracts and Organizations: Perspectives From New Institutional Economics*. Translated by Gang Liu and others. Beijing: Economic Science Press, 2003.

Daron, Acemoglu. Institutions and Development: Institutions, Factor Prices, and Taxation: Virtues of Strong States. *American Economic Review: Papers and Proceedings*, 2010, pp. 115–119.

Daron, Acemoglu, Mikhail Golosov and Aleh Tsyvinski. Markets Versus Governments. *Journal of Monetary Economics*, 2008, 55(1), pp. 159–189.

Du, Renhuai. On Government–Market Relations and Their Function Boundary. *Modern Economic Research*, 2006(4).

Du, Xuejun and Zhonghua Huang. Seek Development via Land: Empirical Researches on Land Assignment and Economic Growth. *Land Science of China*, 2015, 7.

Etsuro-Shioji. Public Capital and Economic Growth: A Convergence Approach. *Journal of Economic Growth*, 2001, 6, pp. 205–227.

Fama, E. F. Efficient Capital Market: A Review of Theory and Empirical Work. *Journal of Finance*, 1970, 25(2), pp. 383–417.

Fenge, R., Maximilian von Ehrlich and Matthias Wrede. Public Input Competition and Agglomeration. *Regional Science and Urban Economics*, 2009, 39, pp. 621–631.

Fiva, Jon H. and Jom Rattso. Local Choice of Property Taxation: Evidence from Norway. *Public Choice*, 2007, 132(3–4), pp. 457–470.

Freeman, Christopher. *Technology Policy and Economic Performance: Lessons From Japan*. Translated by Yuxuan Zhang. Nanjing: Southeast University Press, 2008.

Friedman, Milton. *Free to Choose: A Personal Statement*. Translated by Zhang Qi. Beijing: Machinery Industry Press, 2013.

Friedman, Milton and Rose Friedman. *Freedom of Choice*. Beijing: Commercial Press, 1982.

Fu, Yong. Why Is China's Decentralization Different: An Analysis Framework that Takes Into Account Political Incentives and Financial Incentives. *World Economy*, 2008, 11.

Fu, Yong and Yan Zhang. Structural Deviation of Decentralization and Financial Expenditure of Chinese Style: Cost of Competing for Growth. *Management World*, 2007, 3.

Gao, Hongye. *Western Economics*. Beijing: China Renmin University Press, 2011.

Gao, Peiyong. *Public Economics*, 3rd Edition. Beijing: China Renmin University Press, 2012.

National Intelligence Council. *Global Trends 2030: Alternative Worlds*. A Publication of the National Intelligence Council, 2012, 11.

Herrmann-Pillath, Carsten. *Intergovernmental Competition: Analysis Model of Big Power System Transition Theory.* Translated by Ling Chen. Internal Presentation Series of Tianze, 2001, p. 1.

Holtz-Eakin, Douglas, Public-Sector Capital and the Productivity Puzzle. *The Review of Economics and Statistics,* 1994, 76(1), pp. 12–21.

Huang, Rui. *Researches on Regional Economic Development Based on the Competition Between Local Governments.* Xi'an: Xi'an University of Technology, 2011.

Jiang, Zuopei. Change of Economic Development Mode and Execution of Local Governments. *Modern Economic Researches,* 2008, 5.

Kang, Lingxiang. Industrial Transformation & Upgrading Model Based on the Intervention of the Industrial Policies of Local Governments. *Journal of Capital University of Economics and Business,* 2016, 1.

Keen, M. and Marchand, M. Fiscal Competition and the Pattern of Public Spending. *Journal of Public Economics,* 1997, 66, 33–53.

Ke, Wugang and Manfei Shi. *Institutional Economics: Social Order and Public Policy.* Beijing: Commercial Press, 2004.

Keynes, John Maynard. *Monopolistic Theory of Employment, Interest and Money.* Beijing: Commercial Press, 1981.

Krugman, Paul. *Development, Geography and Economic Theory.* Cambridge, MA: The MIT Press, 1995, pp. 7, 28, 24.

Krugman, Paul et al. New Theories of Trade Among Industrial Countries. *American Economic Review,* 1983, 73.

Kuznets, Simon. *Growth of Modern Economy.* Beijing: Beijing Institute of Economics Press, 1991.

Lewis, William Arthur. Economic Development With Limitless Supplies of Labor. *Manchester Journal,* 1954, 5.

Lewis, William Arthur. *The Theory of Economic Growth.* Translated by Liang Xiaoming. Shanghai: Shanghai Sanlian Bookstore, Shanghai People's Publishing House, 1994.

Li, Meng. Effect of the Acts of Local Governments on the Fluctuations of the Chinese Economy. *Economic Researches,* 2010, 4.

Li, Yanjun. Contractual Governance of Public-Private Cooperative Relationship in the Field of Public Services. *Journal of Socialist Theory Guide,* 2010, 1.

Li, Ying. Status quo of the Technology Innovations in China and Analysis of Its Innovation Capability. *Science & Technology for Development,* 2015, 5.

Li, Shi and John Knight. Incentives and Redistribution Effect of the Financial Contracting System of China. *Economic Researches,* 1996, 5.

Lin, Derong. *Terrible Shunde: Chinese Values of a County.* Beijing: Mechanical Industry Press, 2009.

Lin, Derong. *Large Chinese Town of 100 Billion Yuan.* Guangzhou: Guangdong People's Publishing House, 2010.

Lin, Justin. Factor Endowment, Comparative Advantages and Economic Development. *China Reform,* 1998, 8.

Lin, Justin. *New Structural Economics.* Beijing: Peking University Press, 2008.

Lin, Justin. *Economic Development and Transition: Ideas, Strategy and Self-Sustainability.* Beijing: Peking University Press, 2012.

Lin, Yifu. *Rethinking Economic Development: A Framework for New Structural Economics.* Unpublished manuscripts, World Bank, 2009.

Liu, Jinghua and Jiang Xianhua. *Innovation in Government Administration in China.* Beijing: China Social Science Press, 2004, pp. 10–16.

Liu, Jinshi. *Economics Analysis of the Dual Behavior of Local Governments in the Transition of China.* Fudan University, 2007, p. 4.

Liu, Qiang and Chenglin Qin. Competition of Local Governments and Innovation in Regional Institution: Perspective of an Institutional Analysis. *Academic Journal of Zhongzhou,* 2009, 6.

Liu, Qinggang. *Economic Growth, Competition of Local Governments, State Capacity and Structural Imbalance.* Beijing: Peking University Press, 2013, p. 6.

Liu, Shijin. Change of Economic Growth Mode: What Do We Need to Change? *Economic and Management Studies,* 2006, 1.

Liu, Shijin. How to Handle Successfully the Relations Between Government and Market Under the "New Normal". *Qiushi,* 2014, 18.

Liu, Shijin. How to Properly Deal With the Relationship Between Government and Market Under the "New Normal". *Qiushi,* 2014, 18.

Liu, Yaping. *Competition Among Contemporary Chinese Local Governments.* Beijing: Social Sciences Academic Press, 2007.

Lu, Ming, Zhao Chen and Ji Yan. Increase of Returns, Development Strategy and Division of Regional Economy. *Economic Research,* 2004, 1.

Max-Neef, Manfred. Economic Growth and Quality of Life: A Threshold Hypothesis. *Ecological Economics,* 1995, 15(2), pp. 115–118.

Mueller, Dennis. *Theory of Public Choice.* Translated by Chunxue Yang et al. Beijing: China Social Sciences Press, 1999.North, Douglass. *Structure and Change in Economic History* (Chinese version). Shanghai: Shanghai Sanlian Bookstore, Shanghai People's Publishing House, 1991.

North, Douglass. *Institution, Institutional Change and Economic Performance.* Shanghai: Gezhi Press, 2014.

Olson, Mancur. *The Logic of Collective Action: Public Goods and the Theory of Groups.* Revised Edition. Cambridge, MA: Harvard University Press, 1971, 1965.

Osborne, David and Ted Gaebler. *Reinventing Government: How the Entrepreneurial Spirit Is Transforming the Public Sector.* Translated by Dunren Zhou et al. Shanghai: Shanghai Translation Publishing House, 2006.

Ping, Xinqiao. Expansion Trend of the Expenditure Scale of Chinese Local Governments. *Comparative Economic and Social Systems,* 2007, 1.

Porter, Michael E. *Competitive Advantage.* New York: Free Press, 1985.

Porter, Michael E. (ed.). *Competition in Global Industries.* Boston: Harvard Business School Press, 1986.

Porter, Michael E. From Competitive Advantage to Corporate Strategy. *Harvard Business Review,* May/June 1987, pp. 43–59.

Porter, Michael E. *The Competitive Advantage of Nations.* New York: Free Press, 1990.

Porter, Michael E. What Is Strategy. *Harvard Business Review,* November/December 1996.

Porter, Michael E. *On Competition.* Boston: Harvard Business School Press, 1998.

Porter, Michael E. *The Competitive Advantage of Nations.* Translated by Mingxuan Li et al. Beijing: Huaxia Publishing House, 2002.

Qian, Yingyi. Incentives and Constraints. *Comparative Economic and Social Systems,* 1999, 5.

Qian, Yingyi. *Modern Economics and Economic Reform of China.* Beijing: China Renmin University Press, 2003.

Riggs, Fred. *Administrative Ecology.* Taipei: Taiwan Commercial Press Limited, 1981.

Samuelson, Paul A. The Pure Theory of Public Expenditure. The Review of Economics and Statistics, 1954, 36(4), pp. 387–389.

Samuelson, Paul A. and William D. Nordhaus. *Economics*. Columbus: McGraw-Hill Education, 2009.

Schumpeter, Joseph Alois. *The Theory of Economic Development: An Inquiry Into Profits, Capital, Credit, Interest, and the Business Cycle*. New Brunswick, 1983, 1934.

Segerstrom, Paul S. The Long-run Growth Effects of R&D Subsidies. *Journal of Economic Growth*, 2000, 5(3), pp. 277–305.

Sen, Amartya. *Development as Freedom*. New York: Oxford University Press, 1999. Chinese version translated by Ren Ji and Yu Zhen. Beijing: China Renmin University Press, 2002.

Shen, Kunrong and Wenlin Fu. Financial Decentralization System and Regional Economic Growth of China. *Management World*, 2005(1).

Shen, Kunrong and Wenlin Fu. Taxation Competition, Regional Game and Growth Performance. *Economic Research*, 2006, 6.

Solow, Robert M. Technical Change and the Aggregate Production Function. *The Review of Economics and Statistics*, 1957, 39(3), pp. 312–320.

Song, Zheng, Kjetil Storesletten and Fabrizio Zilibotti. Growing Like China. *American Economic Review*, 2011, 101(1), pp. 196–233.

Stiglitz, Joseph E. *Why Does the Government Intervene in the Economy*. Beijing: China Logistics Publishing House, 1998.

Stiglitz, Joseph E. *Economics of the Public Sector*. Beijing: China Renmin University Press, 2005.

Sun, Yuanyuan and Jianqing Zhang. Evolution of Allocation Efficiency of Interprovincial Resources of Chinese Manufacturing Industry: Perspective of Binary Margin. *Economic Research*, 2015, 10.

Thisse, Justman M. and J. F. Ypersele, Taking out the bite of fiscal competition. *Journal of Urban Economics*, 2002, 52, pp. 294–315.

von Hayek, Friedrich August. *The Constitution of Liberty*. Translated by Deng Kailai. Beijing: SDX Joint Publishing Company, 1997a.

von Hayek, Friedrich August. *The Principle of Free Order*. Translated by Zhenglai Deng. Beijing: Sanlian Bookstore, 1997b.

von Hayek, Friedrich August. *The Road to Serfdom*. Translated by Mingyi Wang et al. Beijing: China Social Sciences Press, 1997c.

Wang, Huanxiang. Coordinated Evolution of Government Actions and Market Effectiveness Under the New Normal. *Opening Herald*, 2015, 4.

Wang, Jun. Adaptability Adjustment of Growth Orientation: A Theoretical Explanation of the Behavioral Evolution of Local Governments. *Management World*, 2004, 8.

Wang, Shilei and Jun Zhang. Why Should Chinese Local Officials Improve Infrastructure? A Model of Official Incentive Mechanism. *Economics (Quarterly)*, 2008, (1).

Wilson. J. D., Theories of Tax Competition. *National Tax Journal* 1999, 52, pp. 269–304.

Wilson, John Douglas and David E. Wildasin. Capital Tax Competition: Bane or Boon. *Journal of Public Economics*, 2004, 88(6), pp. 1065–1091.

Wolf, Charles. *Market or Government*. Beijing: China Development Press, 1994.

Wu, Xianhua et al. Calculation of Total Factor Productivity of Major Countries Based on Panel Data. *Practice and Understanding of Mathematics*, 2011, 7.

Xia, Tian. Phase Characteristics of Innovation-Driven Process and Their Enlightenment for the Construction of Innovative Cities. *Science of Science and Management of Science*, 2010, 2.

Xie, Xiaobo. *Competition of Local Governments and Coordinated Development of Regional Economy*. Hangzhou: Zhejiang University, 2006, 2.

Yang, Ruilong. Three-Stage Theory on the Change of the Mode of Institutional Changes in China: Also on the Institutional Innovation Behavior of Local Governments. *Economic Research*, 1998, 1.

Yang, Ruilong and Qijing Yang. Model of Laddered Progressive Institutional Change: More on the Role of Local Governments in the Institutional Change of China. *Economic Research*, 2000, 3.

Yang, Xiutai and Pu Yongjian. *Resource Economics — An Economic Approach to the Optimal Allocation of Resources*. Chongqing University Press, 1993, pp. 2–3.

Yao, Yang and Lei Yang. Consequences of the Imbalance of Institutional Supply and the Financial Decentralization of China. *Strategy & Management*, 2003(3).

Ye, Tuo. *Studies of the Behavior Choice of Chinese Local Governments* [D]. Hangzhou: Zhejiang University of Finance and Economics, 2012.

Zhan, Dongxin and Lilan Ni. Path of Implementing the PPP Mode in Underdeveloped Regions Based on Public Goods Theory. *Fujian Finance*, 2016, 5.

Zhang, Henglong and Xian Chen. Impact of Intergovernmental Transfer Payment on Local Financial Efforts and Financial Equalization. *Economic Science*, 2007, 1.

Zhang, Jun. Economic Development of China: Compete for Growth. *World Economic Papers*, 2005, 4.

Zhang, Jun and Shaohua Shi. Change of Total Factor Productivity of Chinese Economy: 1952–1998 [J]. *World Economic Papers*, 2003, 2.

Zhang, Jun and Li'an Zhou. *Compete for Growth: Political Economics of Chinese Growth*. Shanghai: Shanghai People's Publishing House, 2008.

Zhang, Jun, Gao Yuan, Fu Yong and Zhang Hong. Why Has China Come to Have Good Infrastructure? *Economic Research*, 2007, 3, pp. 4–19

Zhang, Qingyong. Competition of Chinese Local Governments and Selling Prices of Industrial Land. *Studies of Institutional Economics*, 2006, 2.

Zhang, Weiying and Jie Ma. Property Right Foundation of Cutthroat Competition. *Economic Research*, 1999, 6.

Zhang, Weiying and Shuhe Su. Interregional Competition and the Privatization of Chinese State-Owned Enterprises. *Economic Research*, 1998, 12.

Zhang, Xianwei. Overview of Theoretical Researches on Government Behavior in Institutional Change. *Journal of Shenzhen University* (Edition of Humanities & Social Sciences), 2010, 3.

Zhang, Yuyan and Fan He. *Institutional Change Caused by Financial Pressure: From Planned Economy to Market Economy*. Beijing: China Financial & Economic Publishing House, 1998.

Zhou, Li'an. Motivation and Cooperation of Government Officials in Promotion Game: Also on Reasons for Prolonged Existence of Local Protectionism and Repeated Construction in China. *Economic Research*, 2004, 6.

Zhou, Li'an. A Study of the Promotion Tournament Model of Chinese Local Officials J. *Economic Research*, 2007, 7.

Zhou, Qiren. *What Has China Done Right*. Beijing: Peking University Press, 2010.

Zhou, Tianyong. *New Development Economics*. Beijing: Economic Science & Technology Press, 2001.

Zhou, Ye'an. Competition of Local Governments and Economic Growth. *Journal of Renmin University of China*, 2003, 1.

Zhou, Ye'an and Quan Zhang. Marketization, Financial Decentralization and Economic Growth of China. *Journal of Renmin University of China*, 2008, 1.

Zhou, Ye'an and Xiaonan Zhao. Research on the Competition Mode of Local Governments: Analysis of the Theories and Policies for Building the Order of Healthy Competition Between Local Governments. *Management World*, 2002, 12.

Zhu, Jin. "Tragedy of Commons" of Financial Budget: An Explanation of the Increase in the Scale of Financial Expenditure. *Economists*, 2011, 2.

Zhu, Weiping and Lin Chen. Studies of the Connotations and Mode of Industrial Upgrading: With the Industrial Upgrading in Guangdong as an Example. *Modern Finance and Economy*, 2008, 3.

Zhuo, Yue and Daotian Yang. Build a Model Based on Strategy for Evaluating the Performance of the Public Sector. *Journal of Tianjin Administration Institute*, 2007, 11.

Zou, Dongtao and Tao Xi. Economic Analysis of the Subjects of Individual, Enterprise and Government Actions in Institutional Change. *Journal of Peking University* (Edition of Philosophy and Social Sciences), 2002, 2.

Websites

Cihai (online). http://www.cihai123.com/cidian/1062100.html

MBA Think Tank Encyclopedia (online). http://wiki.mbalib.com/wiki/resource

The Science and Engineering Indicators 2016 (National Science Board). https://www.nsf.gov/nsb/sei/infographic1/index.html

Index

Note: Numbers in italics indicate figures and in bold indicate references to tables on the corresponding pages.